ADOBE® INDESIGN® STYLES
MICHAEL MURPHY

How to Create
Better, Faster
Text & Layouts

CS 4

ADOBE
PRESS

Adobe

Adobe InDesign CS4 Styles:
How to Create Better, Faster Text and Layouts

Michael Murphy

Copyright © 2009 by Michael Murphy
This Adobe Press book is published by Peachpit.
For information on Adobe Press books, contact:
Peachpit
1249 Eighth Street
Berkeley, CA 94710
510/524-2178
510/524-2221 (fax)

For the latest on Adobe Press books, go to www.adobepress.com
To report errors, please send a note to errata@peachpit.com
Peachpit is a division of Pearson Education

Project Editor: Susan Rimerman
Developmental Editor: Anne Marie Walker
Production Editor: Cory Borman
Tech Editor: Cathy Palmer
Proofreader: Scout Festa
Indexer: James Minkin
Compositor: Danielle Foster
Cover Design and Illustration: Terri Bogaards

ISBN-13: 978-0-321-60606-8
ISBN-10: 0-321-60606-X

9 8 7 6 5 4 3 2 1

Printed and bound in the United States of America

To my mother and father for their words of wisdom and encouragement.

To my wonderful wife and best friend, Lee Ann, for her words of love and support.

And to Brenna, whose first words I cannot wait to hear.

ACKNOWLEDGMENTS

My name may appear on the cover of this book, but no one person makes an undertaking like this a reality. Scott Citron, my friend and professional inspiration, warned me about the rigors of first-time authorship. Although I didn't listen, I'm grateful for all of his advice. My personal cheerleader and champion, Noha Edell of Adobe Systems, has my deepest gratitude for all the doors she's opened and her unwavering belief in me.

Since I started my podcast, many talented and generous people have provided me with invaluable assistance, including Terri Stone at *InDesign Magazine*, Michael Ninnes at Adobe, Mordy Golding, Ken Chaletzky, and Pam Pfiffner.

Two other colleagues rounded out this book with valuable content. Diane Burns poured her expertise, time, and energy into every word of Chapter 6, and Jim Maivald contributed all of Chapter 10, offering insight into features I'm still learning.

Thanks also to Felecia Stratton and Keith Biondo at *Inbound Logistics* magazine. Without the challenges they've presented me during our 15-year partnership, I would not have learned many of these time-saving techniques, and their flexibility and patience allowed me the time I needed to write this book.

The team at Peachpit Press guided this rookie author through a daunting task. Project editor Susan Rimerman kept me focused and realistic. Anne Marie Walker's editing kept the text concise but concepts intact. Cathy Palmer, who has watched my back from the day we met, did so again as technical editor.

The Fashion Institute of Technology, my alma mater, graciously allowed me to excerpt text from their course catalog as examples in these pages. As a student there, two remarkable people taught me what good design meant long before I ever sat at a computer: Roxanne Panero, who I don't thank often enough, and Marty Bernstein, who I should have thanked more while I had the chance.

—Michael Murphy

Table of Contents

Introduction

I remember the day it happened. I left work early to see a demonstration of the new Adobe Creative Suite at the Apple Store in SoHo. It was the first time Adobe was offering its major print products—Photoshop, Illustrator, Acrobat, and the relative newcomer InDesign—as a package. Yet it was a single feature out of that 90-minute, standing-room-only presentation that was my InDesign epiphany, laying the true path to productivity before me.

I saw it all so clearly. Never again would I manually format a bulleted list or run-in heading, or struggle through large amounts of text applying attribute changes one by one. Text formatting would become an artful balance of design, technology, and efficiency. But more significantly, I would never again deliberately reject what I knew was the right design choice just because it would take too long or require too much work to modify at the last minute. It was all right there in this one new feature: Nested Styles.

Since switching to InDesign, I've been doing the best work of my career. I no longer opt to take the easier design path over the right one because of the limitations of the tools at my disposal. Page layout has become fun again. My editors and clients have also benefited because I can adapt quickly and efficiently to almost any requested changes.

Will InDesign's styles make you a better designer? I can't promise that, but they will help you *work* better, liberating you from cumbersome workarounds and unsatisfying compromises, and allowing you control over your work as never before. And you'll gain the most precious and elusive thing of all: time. Effective use of styles will reward you with time to question your choices and make sweeping improvements instantaneously. You'll have time to consider the big picture and your ultimate goals instead of the annoying details. Perhaps you'll even have time to explore other features—or other applications in the Creative Suite—that will make you *more* productive down the line.

Why Styles Matter

Over the course of the four CS versions of InDesign, styles have evolved and become the core of the application when it comes to automating text, object, and table formatting; speeding up a workflow; building in flexibility; and guaranteeing consistency in a project. Each iteration built on what came before. CS introduced Nested Styles, CS2 incorporated Object Styles, CS3 included Table and Cell Styles, and now CS4 adds GREP styles and Nested Line Styles to the mix.

Styles have also extended beyond mere text formatting, permeating and influencing many other features, some of which rely entirely on styles to work. It's easy to miss those connections as you get caught up in your day-to-day work. But when you step back and look at the big picture, you start to see how adopting a style-based process pays off *everywhere* in InDesign.

Styles matter. They matter because your time matters, your satisfaction with what you do and the tools you use matters, and the quality of your work matters.

About This Book

This book explores every InDesign style type to reveal its full potential. It details, step by step, the creation and implementation of styles, and provides a big-picture perspective for combining styles with other features to increase efficiency, accuracy, and flexibility. Throughout each chapter, you'll pick up many tips and best practices gleaned from real-world experience. Two bonus chapters, "Stroke Styles" and "Project Planning with Styles in Mind" are available for download at www.peachpit.com/indesignstyles after you register your book.

My mission is to put an end to all the arguments I hear from designers at conferences, in classrooms, and among clients I train. This book exists to convince "figure it out as I go" and dialog-phobic designers that they can embrace styles and still work intuitively on the page. It breaks preconceptions and bad habits transferred from less powerful page layout applications that keep new InDesign users from working in far more satisfying and productive ways. It strives to prove to the "I'm too busy" designers that they'll shave hours, if not days, from their workload by adopting these techniques. For those who say they just don't get it, this book is organized to build up from the simplest concepts to the most intricate style-related features.

Where InDesign is concerned, styles truly do equal substance.

CHAPTER 1

The Fundamentals: Paragraph and Character Styles

THE FOUNDATIONS OF almost every topic in this book are related to paragraph and character styles. Not all InDesign styles are text related, but even those that aren't (object styles, table and cell styles) include text style options among their attributes.

Styles are the easiest and fastest way to process and format text in any project. More than 50 distinct kinds of formatting can be applied at the paragraph level. Even if you take advantage of only ten, that's ten separate formatting steps that can be reduced to a single mouse click if they're built into a style. The more complex the paragraph formatting, the more steps a style saves. But the *real* payoff comes when you're deep into a project and must change the look of your body copy, captions, or sidebars—anything on which you've already spent a lot of time. Without styles, you could spend hours manually reformatting your text. With styles, making a few changes to some well-crafted styles could ripple through the entire file and have you back on track in no time.

This book focuses on the relationships between styles. In relationship terms, you could say that character styles have serious dependency issues. They rely a great deal on the paragraph in which they exist. Fewer than half the attributes available for paragraph styles are available for character styles. For those missing attributes, the character style depends on the paragraph style that it resides in. TABLE 1.1 compares the options available to character and paragraph styles.

TABLE 1.1 **Comparison of Available Character and Paragraph Style Attributes**

Attribute	Character Styles	Paragraph Styles
Basic Character Formats	√	√
Advanced Character Formats	√	√
Indents and Spacing		√
Tabs		√
Paragraph Rules		√
Keep Options		√
Hyphenation		√
Justification		√
Drop Caps and Nested Styles		√
GREP Style		√
Bullets and Numbering		√
Character Color	√	√
OpenType Features	√	√
Underline Options	√	√
Strikethrough Options	√	√

As Table 1.1 shows, no attributes are *unique* to character styles. All options available for character styles are available for paragraph styles as well.

Yet, even with all of their additional options, paragraph styles have a very significant limitation: they affect the *entire* paragraph. From the first character in the paragraph to the last, they are absolute and unwavering. But how much of your text is completely uniform from the beginning of a paragraph to the end? What about bullets, run-in headings, or just simple bold and italics? If you include attributes for those formatting needs in a paragraph style, the whole paragraph takes on that appearance. For this reason, paragraph styles depend on character styles for any *variation* in formatting. For all of its other limitations, it's the character style that enables exceptions to paragraph styles. With just these two basic style types, relationships start to form.

Character Style Attributes

This book assumes that you're familiar with InDesign's basic features and the conventions of typography and page layout used by the application. Rather than rehashing concepts like how to select a typeface, this chapter focuses on attributes that significantly impact how styles work, which will help you toward a more efficient and strategic style-based workflow.

Even though all character style attributes can also be assigned to a paragraph style, some attributes really have no business in a paragraph style and are far better suited to character styles. For example, underlining is an unlikely paragraph-level attribute, but it's ideal for a character style that will be applied selectively to certain text.

BASIC CHARACTER FORMATS

Let's take a look at these character style-friendly attributes in the order in which you'll find them in the Character Style Options dialog. This list isn't *every* option available, just those that make more sense for a character style than a paragraph style.

Leading. Leading is, in the strictest sense, a paragraph-level attribute, but both paragraph and character styles include leading options. A character style *can* use different leading than the paragraph in which it's used, but how that leading affects the paragraph as a whole depends on whether the Apply Leading to Entire Paragraphs preference (Preferences > Type) is turned on or off (the default setting).

With the default setting, leading *increases* made to a small portion of text within a paragraph will only affect the leading of the lines on which that change occurs. Leading *decreases* will not make any change to either the line or the paragraph unless that reduced leading happens to encompass the entire line on which it occurs. If Apply Leading to Entire Paragraphs is turned on (which is recommended), a local leading increase will change the leading for the entire paragraph. Leading decreases applied as local overrides will reduce the leading of the entire paragraph, but leading decreases built into character styles will not unless that character style is applied to an entire line. Even then, the overall paragraph remains unaffected. Only the line to which the character style is applied is affected regardless of the Apply Leading to Entire Paragraphs preference.

Tracking. Tracking is an overall tightening or loosening of all text to which it's applied, including word spacing. As such, it is a far less desirable means of controlling spacing in an entire paragraph than InDesign's justification options, which handle word and letter spacing independently. For that reason, tracking should *never* be a built-in attribute of a paragraph style.

NOTE
Mention of the Paragraph Style dialog or Character Style dialog in this book refers to both the New Paragraph Style *and* Paragraph Style Options dialogs, or to the New Character Style and Character Style Options dialogs, respectively. Although the headings at the top change if you're creating a new style or modifying an existing one, the options are identical in both instances.

Character styles, on the other hand, lack *any* justification options. They inherit everything from the paragraph. Because of this limitation, tracking is the only way to build word and letter spacing changes into a character style. If a nested or locally applied character style looks too loose or too tight, build the appropriate positive or negative tracking into the character style to achieve optimal spacing.

Case. The Normal and All Caps options are self-explanatory. Small Caps is smart enough to recognize the presence of "true" small caps in an OpenType font and apply them properly. For fonts that lack true small caps, InDesign uses scaling (also known as "fake" small caps) to approximate their appearance. There is no Small Caps check box under the OpenType options, so this pull-down menu serves double duty for OpenType and non-OpenType fonts. This dual functionality makes the Small Caps option very versatile in a character style, because it will support both real and fake small caps, depending on what the typeface includes.

All OpenType Small Caps. This option is (sort of) the opposite of All Caps. In OpenType fonts with *true* small caps, everything is displayed in its lowercase form but uses small caps (in other words, even uppercase letters are shown as "lowercase" small caps). In non-OpenType fonts or OpenType fonts without true small caps, this setting does nothing.

TIP

InDesign doesn't *automatically* detect and apply "true" superscript or subscript characters in an OpenType font the way it does with small caps. To take advantage of those options in an OpenType font, you must specifically activate them from the OpenType area of the dialog. Interestingly, if either of these two OpenType options is turned on for a *non*-OpenType font, the *simulated* position adjustments are automatically applied instead.

Position. It's quite unlikely that the position attribute for a paragraph style would ever be set to anything but Normal. All other position settings— Superscript or Subscript, OpenType Superior/Superscript or OpenType Inferior/Subscript, and OpenType Numerator or OpenType Denominator—are far more useful in character styles to format isolated changes in number position for items like footnote references ([1]), chemical or mathematical expressions (CO_2), or fractions (¾).

No Break. The No Break option prevents the letters to which it's applied from ever being separated when text wraps at the end of a line. As such, this is a disastrous attribute for a paragraph style. If No Break is switched on for a paragraph, that *entire* paragraph would be perpetually overset. It could never display properly unless it was in a frame wide enough to contain the entire paragraph on a single line. However, as a character style attribute, No Break is ideal for keeping specific words from hyphenating or phrases from breaking when text wraps.

ADVANCED CHARACTER FORMATS

The so-called advanced character formats include three options that distort type (horizontal scale, vertical, scale and skew) and should rarely if ever be used, and a useful option—baseline shift—that is more of an attribute to apply by exception rather than include in a style. But there's one very different option in this group of settings that lends itself well to a character style.

Language. The Language option specifies the dictionary against which InDesign performs spell check operations. For paragraph styles, this should be set to the language used throughout your text. However, changing the language of a character style can be *very* useful. For example, in a U.S. English document that contains a few French phrases, you can create a character style for which the language is set to French (FIGURES 1.1 to 1.3). Once that character style is applied to the French phrases, they won't show up as spelling errors and, better yet, spell check will offer language-appropriate corrections if any of the French is misspelled.

TIP
If you use a character style for URLs and they continually show up as spelling errors, consider switching the URL style's language to No Language. Any text using No Language is ignored by the spell check. It also prevents any hyphenation from taking place. The downside of course is that the responsibility rests entirely on you and your proofreader to find URLs that may actually be misspelled.

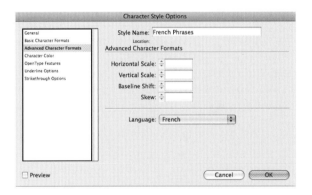

FIGURE 1.1 French as the designated language for a character style.

"This charming little bistro has a certain *je ne sais quoi* that's sure to be a hit with diners looking for a taste of Paris not only in the food, but the atmosphere as well. A perfect location for a romantic *tête à tête*."
—*The Budget Gourmet*, 9/26/2008

FIGURE 1.2 French phrases in text with that character style applied.

FIGURE 1.3 Spell check finds no errors in the paragraph because the English:USA dictionary is used to check the paragraph, but the French dictionary is referenced for the phrases using the character style.

OPENTYPE FEATURES

Many OpenType features could find their way into a character style for specific purposes, but most pose no specific problem if they apply to the entire paragraph. But there are a handful of OpenType features that are best reserved for character styles.

Swash Alternates. Swash Alternates are typically supported only in the italic versions of serif OpenType fonts (for example, in serif faces like Minion Pro Italic or Adobe Caslon Pro Italic). When the Swash Alternates option is turned on, swash characters are automatically substituted for the initial capitals in words and for select lowercase characters (FIGURE 1.4).

A Swash Alternates character style can come in handy if you want to apply the swash attribute to a drop cap (see Chapter 7, "Drop Caps, Bullets, and Numbering") or designate only the first character in a paragraph to use this attribute in either a nested style (Chapter 2, "Nesting and Sequencing Styles") or a GREP style (Chapter 3, "Automatic Styling with GREP"). In any of these cases, that character style would use *both* the Italic font style and have the OpenType Swash Alternates attributes turned on.

FIGURE 1.4 Swash Alternates applied to Adobe Garamond Pro Italic.

Ordinals. In numeric rankings—1st, 2nd, 3rd—ordinals are the letters following the number at a raised position. Like true small caps and fractions, OpenType ordinals are designed to match the appearance and weight of the other glyphs in the same font. Be careful when turning on Ordinals in a paragraph style, because ordinals get applied to *any* character that qualifies as an ordinal (FIGURE 1.5) whether or not it follows a number. It's best to limit this attribute to a character style.

abcdefghijklmnopqrstuv

FIGURE 1.5 Although Ordinals are turned on for this entire line, only certain characters in the typeface qualify as ordinals. The others remain unchanged.

Fractions. OpenType's support for real fractions eliminates tedious and unsatisfying workarounds for "faking" fractions. OpenType fractions are designed to match the weight and appearance of the rest of the font (FIGURE 1.6). Fractions are yet another OpenType feature best reserved for character styles that, when combined with a well-formed GREP style, can be switched on automatically.

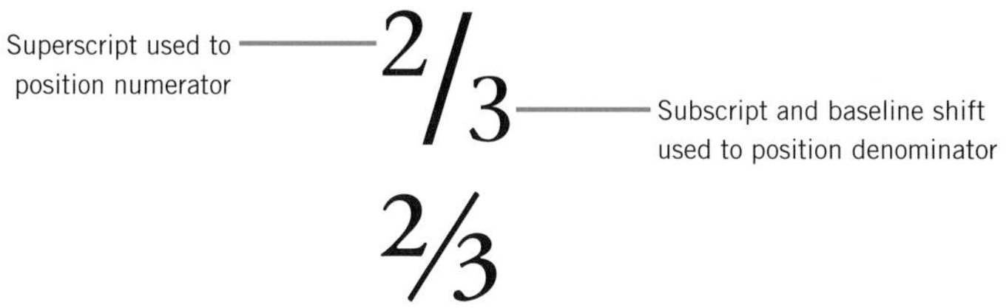

Superscript used to position numerator ———— 2/3 ———— Subscript and baseline shift used to position denominator

2/3

FIGURE 1.6 A faked fraction in a PostScript font (top) versus a real fraction in an OpenType font (bottom).

Discretionary Ligatures. Discretionary ligatures are exclusive to OpenType fonts and are specifically separate from standard ligatures because they may be too elaborate for general use or flat out inappropriate for your needs (FIGURE 1.7), so be selective about activating this option. In a paragraph style, every possible letter pair that *can* take advantage of discretionary ligatures will do so. Your best bet is to create a character style for this particular typographic flourish and apply it manually, as the name suggests, with discretion.

acting
casting
thespian

FIGURE 1.7 Discretionary ligatures in Minion Pro.

UNDERLINE AND STRIKETHROUGH OPTIONS

Underlining is an unlikely attribute to use at the paragraph level (unless of course you actually *want* an entire paragraph underlined). It is more typically attached to a character style. The same goes for strikethroughs. Underlines and strikethroughs in InDesign can be customized almost as much as paragraph rules. They can't include indents or be set to span the width of a column, but nearly all other paragraph rule attributes are available for underlines and strikethroughs.

The weight, type, color, and tint options for underlines and strikethroughs are *exactly* the same, but the position is different: Strikethrough lines start midway through the text, not at the baseline as underlines do.

InDesign's defaults don't make for very elegant underlines (FIGURE 1.8). When underlining is turned on, I highly recommend customizing the following options when underlining text and then preserving that customization in a character style.

Default Underline
Custom Underline
Custom Underline

~~Default Strikethrough~~
~~Custom Strikethrough~~

FIGURE 1.8 InDesign's default underlines and strikethroughs versus underlines and strikethroughs customized in the Underline Options and Strikethrough Options, respectively.

Weight. InDesign uses a default line weight when you click the Underline icon in the Control panel or press Shift-Command-U/Shift-Ctrl-U to add an underline. The default weight is proportional to the size of the typeface (a 0.6 pt underline for 12 pt text and a 1 pt underline for 20 pt text, for example), but *any* weight can be assigned to an underline.

Offset. The default Offset value positions an underline a certain distance from the baseline, relative to the size of the text to which it's applied. This option is entirely customizable to achieve the best-looking position. Increasing the Offset value moves the underline down, away from the baseline; decreasing it brings the underline closer to the baseline; and negative values move the underline up *into* the text. Underlines are always drawn *behind* text and cannot be positioned on top of it. To achieve that look, use strikethrough instead.

For strikethroughs, positive Offset values move the line up into the text, lower values move them down closer to the baseline, and negative values position them below the baseline.

NOTE
To access bonus chapters for this book go to www.peachpit.com/ indesignstyles. You will need to register your book before you can access the content.

Type. Any of InDesign's built-in stroke styles—solid, dashed, dotted, and so on— can be used for an underline just as they can for paragraph rules. Any custom stroke styles you create (see bonus online chapter, "Stroke Styles") are also available from this pull-down menu.

Color and Tint. Underlines default to the color of the text to which they're applied. You can change the underline color to any *existing* swatch in your document.

Gap Color and Tint. For stroke types *other than* Solid, the gap between dots, dashes, or stripes can be filled with another color or no color. The default is None. You can change the gap color to any *existing* swatch in your document.

Overprint Stroke and Overprint Gap. Each color for an underline can be set to over-print any background color on the page. Strikethroughs, which draw on top of text, also overprint the text.

Paragraph Style Attributes

Paragraph-level settings not only determine what your text looks like, but where that text appears (Keep Options) and what style should be applied to subsequent paragraphs (Next Style). Only paragraphs can be associated with running lists (Numbered Lists), incorporate character styles (Drop Caps, Nested Styles, and Nested Line Styles), and dynamically format text that matches specific patterns (GREP styles). In later chapters you'll also see how paragraph styles can generate text that's used by *other* InDesign features (Tables of Contents, Text Variables, and Conditional Text).

Fake Highlighting with a Custom Underline Character Style

To mimic the appearance of yellow text highlighting, create a character style with underlining turned on and use a weight setting slightly larger than the point size of your text so the highlight will extend just above the ascenders and uppercase letters, and just below the descenders. Set the underline color to yellow (or pink, or blue, whichever you prefer) and adjust its offset so that it's positioned *behind* the text instead of below it (**FIGURE 1.9**).

Since underlines are drawn from the baseline in both directions (in other words, a 10 point underline without any offset draws 5 points of its weight above the baseline and 5 points below it), it can be a bit tricky to figure the right line weight and offset. Here are the general rules for quickly setting up a fake highlighting underline:

- Make your underline weight 4 points greater than the point size of your typeface (a 14 point underline for 10 point text, for instance).

- Make your offset a negative value that's 25 percent of the line weight (a -3.5 point offset for a 14 point underline, for example).

In most cases, these guidelines will put your highlight underline within a fraction of a point of its ideal position. Every typeface is slightly different, so there's no perfect setting for all fonts, but this ballpark formula should get you very close (**FIGURE 1.10**).

A variation on this technique can simulate "redacted" text by using a strikethrough and setting the color of the strikethrough to the same color as the text. This is good to know if you ever have to set type for a book with content that's been deemed a potential threat to national security.

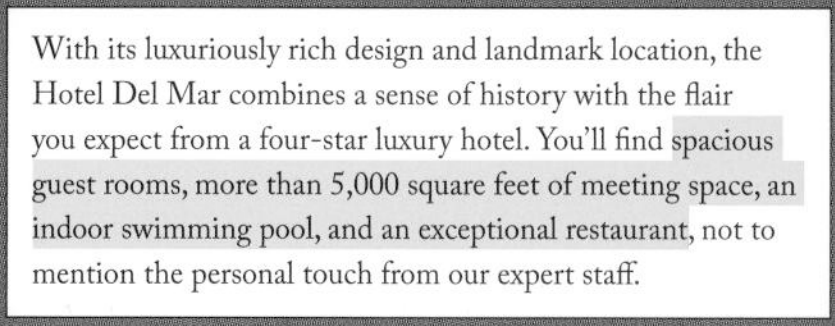

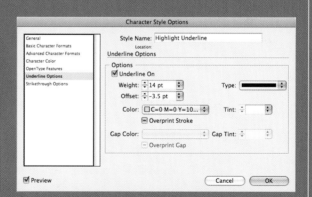

With its luxuriously rich design and landmark location, the Hotel Del Mar combines a sense of history with the flair you expect from a four-star luxury hotel. You'll find spacious guest rooms, more than 5,000 square feet of meeting space, an indoor swimming pool, and an exceptional restaurant, not to mention the personal touch from our expert staff.

FIGURE 1.9 A highlight character style applied to a portion of a paragraph.

FIGURE 1.10 Custom underline settings for a fake highlighting effect.

Assuming that paragraph-based principles like how to set a tab are well within your grasp already, I'll concentrate on the most strategic and useful paragraph-level settings a style can include.

GENERAL OPTIONS

With only one exception (Next Style), the General options for paragraph and character styles are identical (**FIGURE 1.11**).

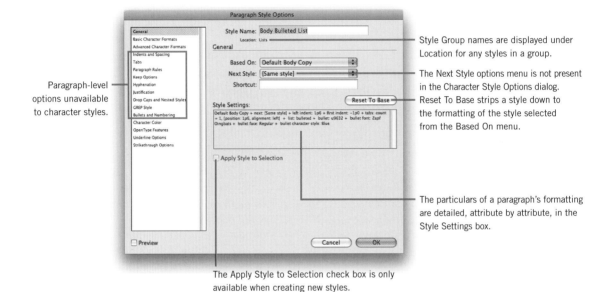

Paragraph-level options unavailable to character styles.

Style Group names are displayed under Location for any styles in a group.

The Next Style options menu is not present in the Character Style Options dialog. Reset To Base strips a style down to the formatting of the style selected from the Based On menu.

The particulars of a paragraph's formatting are detailed, attribute by attribute, in the Style Settings box.

The Apply Style to Selection check box is only available when creating new styles.

FIGURE 1.11 The General options area of the Paragraph Style Options dialog.

Style Name. Keep style names as logical and descriptive as possible. As you add more and more styles, clear naming conventions will help you quickly determine which styles are which. If you'll ultimately need to export your text for the Web, consider naming your styles consistently with the naming conventions used for your Web pages to take advantage of style mapping in the export process (see Chapter 10, "Styles, CSS, and XML").

Location. If a style is part of a Style Group (a folder-based method of organizing similar styles in the Paragraph Styles and Character Styles panels), the group name is displayed here (see Chapter 11, "Style Management").

Based On. Any paragraph style can be based on any other paragraph style, and any character style can be based on any other character style. This is especially useful for variations on overall formatting (such as bulleted lists based on a main body copy style) where only a few attributes of the new style are different from the existing style (see Chapter 2).

Next Style. This is the one General option unavailable to character styles. Only a paragraph style can include instructions as to what style should be used for the paragraph that follows it either as you type or when you apply styles in sequence to multiple paragraphs (see Chapter 2).

Shortcut. A limited number of keyboard shortcuts can be assigned to paragraph and character styles to speed up their application in a layout. Only numeric keypad characters, together with the Shift, Option, and Command keys (Mac) or Shift, Alt, and Ctrl keys (Windows) in any combination, can be assigned as style shortcuts.

Reset To Base. This button strips out all differences between the current style and the style on which it is based (see Chapter 2). The result is a style that is *still* based on another style, but both are identical in every way.

Style Settings. This info box reports back all attributes of a style beyond the parameters of the style on which it's based. Put more simply, a style based on [No Paragraph Style] that has its font family changed to Adobe Garamond Pro will be described in this box as [No Paragraph Style] + next [Same style] + Adobe Garamond Pro. As more unique attributes are added to the style, each will be tacked onto this base description with plus signs.

Apply Style to Selection. This check box eliminates a common mistake I've made more times than I care to remember. When I select text to act as the source for a new style, I diligently create and name the style, but all too often forget to *apply* it to the selected text after closing the dialog. Selecting this box—which is only available when creating new styles—solves that problem.

Avoid Accidental Default Changes

You may create paragraph or character styles directly in their respective dialogs without using selected text as the basis for the new style. In that case, Apply Style to Selection changes the default paragraph style for all new text in the document from [Basic Paragraph] or whatever it had been to the new style you've created. For character styles created with no text selected, selecting Apply Style to Selection will change the default character style of the document from [None] to the newly created style.

INDENTS AND SPACING

Indents differ from tabs in that they're applied automatically and consistently throughout the paragraph with no need for tab characters in the text. Indents are always based on the left and right sides of the column or the text frame (plus frame inset values, if any), not on the page margins.

Alignment. Full paragraphs can be set to one of these values: Left, Center, Right, Left Justify, Center Justify, Right Justify, Full Justify, Toward Spine, or Away From Spine. Except for the last two options, these are all fairly self-explanatory.

Toward Spine and Away From Spine are incredibly helpful alignment options for text that should appear differently depending on if the text falls on the right or left page of a spread. Rather than create two *separate* styles for that text, use either Toward Spine or Away From Spine alignment. As a text frame is moved from one side of a spread to the opposite side, the text in that frame will automatically align properly based on its new position, relative to the spine (FIGURE 1.12).

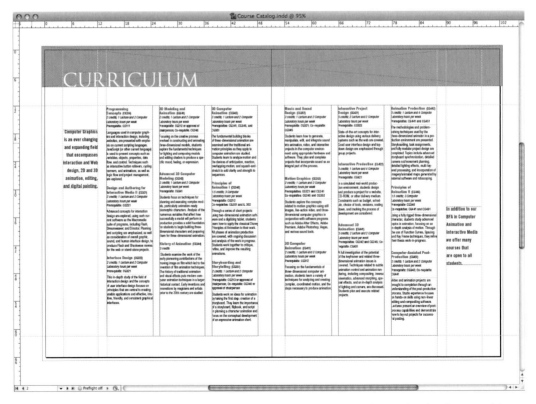

FIGURE 1.12 Text aligned Toward Spine is used to automatically adjust the alignment of the margin callouts on either side of a spread.

A Style Is No Place for Balance Ragged Lines

The Balance Ragged Lines option—which affects left-, right-, and center-aligned text but *not* justified text—evaluates how even (or uneven) the ragged sides of a column are and attempts to minimize the irregularities. Line endings are changed and text is reflowed to create a less jagged appearance. In some cases this can work well. But sometimes Balance Ragged Lines does *too much* averaging out and creates too much distance between the end of a line and the far edge of the column. It's an entirely machine-based decision. There's no intelligence at work deciding if certain phrases should be separated or if your editorial guidelines permit a head-line's second line to begin with short words like "of" or "to."

Another caveat about this feature is that if hyphenation is turned on in the paragraph to which it is applied, InDesign will use hyphenation to achieve even line lengths, needlessly hyphenating words that *can* fit perfectly on a line to achieve what the software considers balance (**FIGURE 1.13**). It is best never to build this attribute into a paragraph style. Only use this as a local override when all other fine-tuning options fail and only on text for which hyphenation is turned off.

Industry Outlook Positive Despite Economic Challenges

Industry Outlook Positive De-spite Economic Challenges

Industry Outlook Positive Despite Economic Challenges

FIGURE 1.13
Original headline (top), Balance Ragged Lines applied with hyphenation turned on (middle), and Balance Ragged Lines applied with hyphenation turned off (bottom).

Ignore Optical Margin. This option is useful for stories threaded through frames to which Optical Margin Alignment is applied. Optical Margin Alignment is a frame-based option that applies to *all* frames through which a story flows, and it's based on a single unit of measurement (typically, the point size of the body copy). For this reason, any text in the story that's significantly larger or smaller than the body copy could end up being poorly aligned (FIGURE 1.14). This is the *only* means by which a local override to Optical Margin Alignment can be achieved in a story, and it's an excellent option for headline or footnote styles, which may use sizes quite different from the body text.

In the top example in Figure 1.14, Optical Margin Alignment adjusts the body copy by pulling items like the quotation mark outside of the column edge, but also pushes the larger headline text farther into the frame. Ignore Optical Margin produces a more satisfactory alignment.

FIGURE 1.14 Applying Ignore Optical Margin to the headline style pulls the headline text closer to the column edge for better alignment.

Going With the
by Joseph O'Reilly

DRIFTING AND DRAFTING ACROSS WY plains with a kayak and bicycle atop you poor aerodynamics and fuel consumptio gusts, the occasional high-wind advisory sign, at the gas pump are constant reminders that, "Equality State" and wind are inseparable.

Going With the
by Joseph O'Reilly

DRIFTING AND DRAFTING ACROSS WY plains with a kayak and bicycle atop you poor aerodynamics and fuel consumptio gusts, the occasional high-wind advisory sign, at the gas pump are constant reminders that, "Equality State" and wind are inseparable.

Left Indent. This option indents the entire paragraph away from the left edge of the text frame or column.

First Line Indent. This option indents only the first line of every paragraph away from the left edge of the text frame or column. To create a hanging indent (where all lines of the paragraph are indented but the first line is not), use a negative value for the first line indent (FIGURE 1.15).

Right Indent. This option indents the entire paragraph away from the right edge of the text frame or column.

Last Line Indent. The Last Line Indent (also called a Last Line Right Indent elsewhere in the application) is essentially a *hanging* right indent and only works when used with two other items: an overall right indent on the paragraph *and* a right-align tab (Shift-Tab) somewhere in the last line. It's ideal for "pushing out" prices in a catalog, page references in a table of contents, or other information in list form. As with a hanging first line indent, the rest of the paragraph is indented to create the effect. The last line uses a negative indentation value to push out text that follows a right-align tab (FIGURE 1.16).

Space Before and Space After. Any paragraph can have a built-in "buffer zone" either above or below it to separate it from other paragraphs. Space Before adds a specified amount of space between the current paragraph and the one that *precedes* it. Space After adds a specified amount of space between the current paragraph and the one that *follows* it.

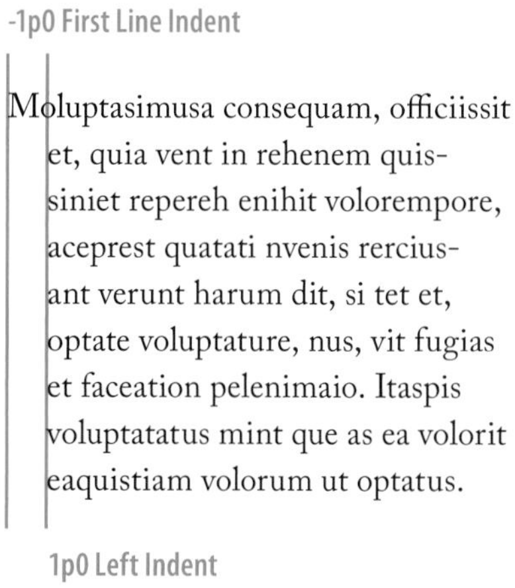

3p0 Right Indent

-1p0 First Line Indent

Moluptasimusa consequam, officiissit
et, quia vent in rehenem quissiniet repereh enihit volorempore,
aceprest quatati nvenis rerciusant verunt harum dit, si tet et,
optate voluptature, nus, vit fugias
et faceation pelenimaio. Itaspis
voluptatatus mint que as ea volorit
eaquistiam volorum ut optatus.

Moluptasimusa consequam,
officiissit et, quia vent in rehenem quissiniet repereh enihit
volorempore, aceprest quatati
nvenis rerciusant verunt harum
dit, si tet et, optate voluptature,
nus, vit fugias et faceation a.
Itaspis voluptatatus mint que as
ea volorit eaquistiam volorum
ut optatus. $29.95

1p0 Left Indent

-3p0 Last Line Indent

FIGURE 1.15 Hanging indents require a left indent setting and a negative first line indent.

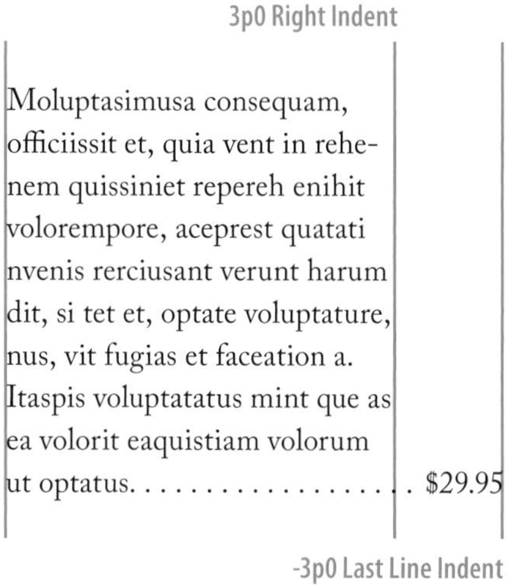

FIGURE 1.16 Last line indents are essentially hanging indents on the last line.

Align to Grid. A paragraph can align entirely to the document's baseline grid (All Lines), ignore the grid altogether (None), or have just its first baseline line "hang" from the grid but ignore it for all subsequent lines (First Line Only) (**FIGURE 1.17**). Full baseline grid alignment overrides any leading values that do not match it. Leading *less* than the increments of the baseline grid is ignored, and leading *greater* than that of the grid—even by a fraction of a point—forces the text to the next line in the grid.

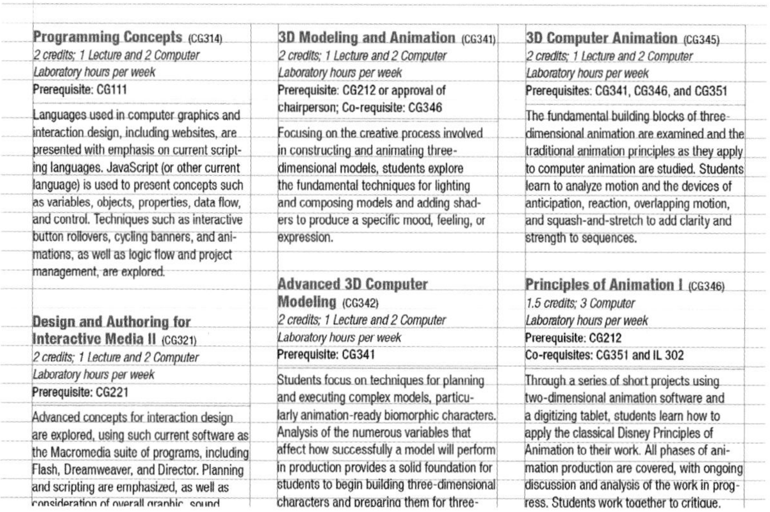

Programming Concepts (CG314)
2 credits; 1 Lecture and 2 Computer
Laboratory hours per week
Prerequisite: CG111

Languages used in computer graphics and interaction design, including websites, are presented with emphasis on current scripting languages. JavaScript (or other current language) is used to present concepts such as variables, objects, properties, data flow, and control. Techniques such as interactive button rollovers, cycling banners, and animations, as well as logic flow and project management, are explored.

Design and Authoring for Interactive Media II (CG321)
2 credits; 1 Lecture and 2 Computer
Laboratory hours per week
Prerequisite: CG221

Advanced concepts for interaction design are explored, using such current software as the Macromedia suite of programs, including Flash, Dreamweaver, and Director. Planning and scripting are emphasized, as well as consideration of overall graphic, sound

3D Modeling and Animation (CG341)
2 credits; 1 Lecture and 2 Computer
Laboratory hours per week
Prerequisite: CG212 or approval of chairperson; Co-requisite: CG346

Focusing on the creative process involved in constructing and animating three-dimensional models, students explore the fundamental techniques for lighting and composing models and adding shaders to produce a specific mood, feeling, or expression.

Advanced 3D Computer Modeling (CG342)
2 credits; 1 Lecture and 2 Computer
Laboratory hours per week
Prerequisite: CG341

Students focus on techniques for planning and executing complex models, particularly animation-ready biomorphic characters. Analysis of the numerous variables that affect how successfully a model will perform in production provides a solid foundation for students to begin building three-dimensional characters and preparing them for three-

3D Computer Animation (CG345)
2 credits; 1 Lecture and 2 Computer
Laboratory hours per week
Prerequisites: CG341, CG346, and CG351

The fundamental building blocks of three-dimensional animation are examined and the traditional animation principles as they apply to computer animation are studied. Students learn to analyze motion and the devices of anticipation, reaction, overlapping motion, and squash-and-stretch to add clarity and strength to sequences.

Principles of Animation I (CG346)
1.5 credits; 3 Computer
Laboratory hours per week
Prerequisite: CG212
Co-requisites: CG351 and IL 302

Through a series of short projects using two-dimensional animation software and a digitizing tablet, students learn how to apply the classical Disney Principles of Animation to their work. All phases of animation production are covered, with ongoing discussion and analysis of the work in progress. Students work together to critique.

FIGURE 1.17 The style for the course name is set to align its first line only to the baseline grid; no other styles used in the course descriptions align to the grid. As a result, each entry starts on the nearest grid line, but no other lines in the entries do.

PARAGRAPH RULES

Paragraph Rules include the same options as underlines for weight, type, color, gap color, and overprinting, but there are some essential differences between underlines and paragraph rules.

Underlines are applied to specific text, which can appear anywhere within a paragraph. Paragraph Rules come in two flavors: Rule Above and Rule Below (FIGURE 1.18). Rules above are attached to the first line in a paragraph, rules below to the last line. There are only a few key differences between these two rule types other than where they appear. I'll cover both rule types simultaneously, pointing out only where the two differ.

FIGURE 1.18 Paragraph Rules at a glance.

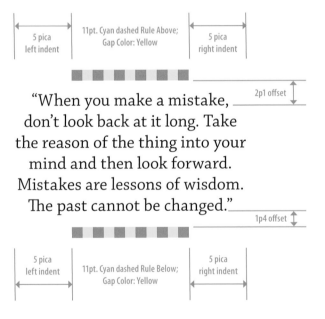

Width. Paragraph rules can span either the width of the text or the width of the column. A rule set to the width of the column (the default setting) spans the full width of the column or text frame, or to the insets of the text frame if applicable. A rule above set to the width of the text is only as wide as the text on the *first* line of the paragraph. Rules below are only as long as the *last* line of text in the paragraph.

Offset. Since rules above and below originate at the baseline of their respective lines, setting a rule above that actually appears *above* a paragraph requires changing its offset value. Increasing the offset value of a rule above moves the rule *up* from the first baseline, whereas increasing the offset value of a rule below pushes the rule *down* below the last baseline.

Rules above can also appear *below* the first line in a paragraph and rules below can appear *above* the last line. A negative offset on a rule above brings the rule down into the text (below the first line's baseline), and a negative offset for a rule below moves it up into the paragraph (above the last line's baseline). For paragraphs with only one line, these rules can be set to overlap one another in very creative ways (FIGURE 1.19). When built into a paragraph style, these complex rule arrangements can be applied in one click to any single-line paragraph.

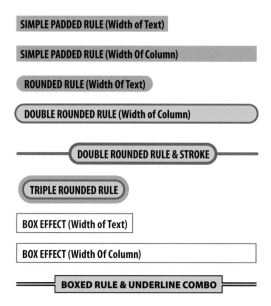

SIMPLE PADDED RULE (Width of Text)

SIMPLE PADDED RULE (Width Of Column)

ROUNDED RULE (Width Of Text)

DOUBLE ROUNDED RULE (Width of Column)

DOUBLE ROUNDED RULE & STROKE

TRIPLE ROUNDED RULE

BOX EFFECT (Width of Text)

BOX EFFECT (Width Of Column)

BOXED RULE & UNDERLINE COMBO

FIGURE 1.19 The level of customization available for a rule's weight, color, position, and indents is especially useful on single-line paragraphs where clever use of offsets and rule weights can produce many "live" border effects without the need for separate strokes or shapes.

Left Indent and Right Indent. Paragraph rule indentation settings are separate from any indents applied to the paragraph. These indents allow rules to extend either *beyond* the edges of the text frame or column (negative left or right indent values) or fall short of the width of the text frame or column (positive indent values).

Keep In Frame. Rules that fall at the top of a text frame will actually "float" outside the top edge of the frame as much as necessary to honor the offset value assigned to them. This behavior can visually throw off the top margin alignment for that column relative to other columns on the page (FIGURE 1.20). Keep In Frame was introduced in CS2 to solve this problem by starting rules at the very top of but still inside the text frame (FIGURE 1.21).

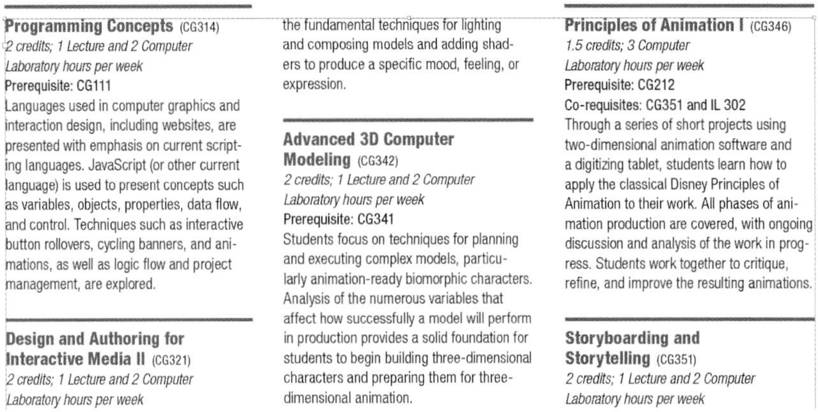

FIGURE 1.20 Paragraph Rules' default appearance with Keep In Frame turned off.

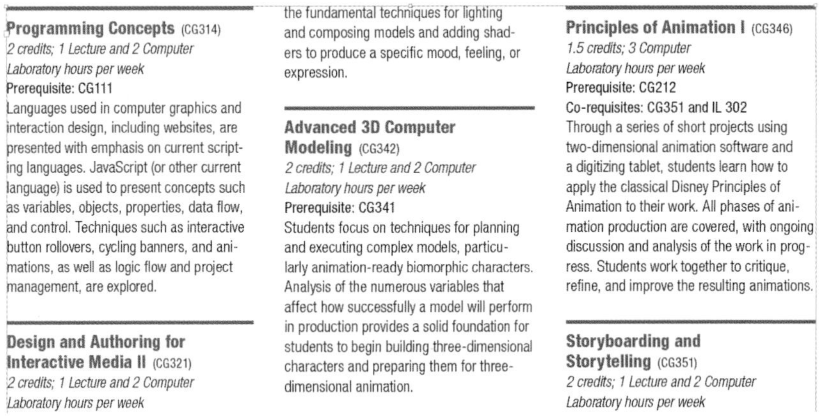

Programming Concepts (CG314)
2 credits; 1 Lecture and 2 Computer Laboratory hours per week
Prerequisite: CG111
Languages used in computer graphics and interaction design, including websites, are presented with emphasis on current scripting languages. JavaScript (or other current language) is used to present concepts such as variables, objects, properties, data flow, and control. Techniques such as interactive button rollovers, cycling banners, and animations, as well as logic flow and project management, are explored.

Design and Authoring for Interactive Media II (CG321)
2 credits; 1 Lecture and 2 Computer Laboratory hours per week

the fundamental techniques for lighting and composing models and adding shaders to produce a specific mood, feeling, or expression.

Advanced 3D Computer Modeling (CG342)
2 credits; 1 Lecture and 2 Computer Laboratory hours per week
Prerequisite: CG341
Students focus on techniques for planning and executing complex models, particularly animation-ready biomorphic characters. Analysis of the numerous variables that affect how successfully a model will perform in production provides a solid foundation for students to begin building three-dimensional characters and preparing them for three-dimensional animation.

Principles of Animation I (CG346)
1.5 credits; 3 Computer Laboratory hours per week
Prerequisite: CG212
Co-requisites: CG351 and IL 302
Through a series of short projects using two-dimensional animation software and a digitizing tablet, students learn how to apply the classical Disney Principles of Animation to their work. All phases of animation production are covered, with ongoing discussion and analysis of the work in progress. Students work together to critique, refine, and improve the resulting animations.

Storyboarding and Storytelling (CG351)
2 credits; 1 Lecture and 2 Computer Laboratory hours per week

FIGURE 1.21 Keep in Frame turned on to improve top margin alignment.

Programming Concepts (CG314)
2 credits; 1 Lecture and 2 Computer Laboratory hours per week
Prerequisite: CG111
Languages used in computer graphics and interaction design, including websites, are presented with emphasis on current scripting languages. JavaScript (or other current language) is used to present concepts such as variables, objects, properties, data flow, and control. Techniques such as interactive button rollovers, cycling banners, and animations, as well as logic flow and project management, are explored.

Design and Authoring for Interactive Media II (CG321)
2 credits; 1 Lecture and 2 Computer Laboratory hours per week

the fundamental techniques for lighting and composing models and adding shaders to produce a specific mood, feeling, or expression.

Advanced 3D Computer Modeling (CG342)
2 credits; 1 Lecture and 2 Computer Laboratory hours per week
Prerequisite: CG341
Students focus on techniques for planning and executing complex models, particularly animation-ready biomorphic characters. Analysis of the numerous variables that affect how successfully a model will perform in production provides a solid foundation for students to begin building three-dimensional characters and preparing them for three-dimensional animation.

Principles of Animation I (CG346)
1.5 credits; 3 Computer Laboratory hours per week
Prerequisite: CG212
Co-requisites: CG351 and IL 302
Through a series of short projects using two-dimensional animation software and a digitizing tablet, students learn how to apply the classical Disney Principles of Animation to their work. All phases of animation production are covered, with ongoing discussion and analysis of the work in progress. Students work together to critique, refine, and improve the resulting animations.

Storyboarding and Storytelling (CG351)
2 credits; 1 Lecture and 2 Computer Laboratory hours per week

KEEP OPTIONS

Not only can paragraph styles determine *how* text is formatted, they can also incorporate rules about *where* text appears. Keep Options allow specific instructions about what text—and how much of it—must stay together, and where text that uses a particular style should begin. When used appropriately in a paragraph style, Keep Options can eliminate the need for manual resizing of text frames to properly distribute text throughout a project.

Keep with Next: [   ] lines. To avoid separating a paragraph using a specific style from a certain number of lines in the *next* paragraph (to minimize awkward breaks at the bottom of columns, for example), designate the desired number of lines here. For instance, a setting of Keep with Next 3 lines would ensure that no fewer than three lines of the following paragraph are effectively "glued" to the current paragraph.

Keep Lines Together. Unlike the Keep with Next option, which connects two paragraphs, the settings here apply within a single paragraph. They control how lines in a paragraph can (or can't) be separated from the rest of the paragraph when text flows into another frame or column, or onto another page.

- **All Lines in Paragraph.** This all-or-nothing option keeps the *entire* paragraph intact. If every line of the paragraph can't fit fully at the bottom of a column, the whole paragraph will jump to the next column (FIGURE 1.22), even if that column appears on another page.

Course Name style (set to keep all lines in paragraph together and keep with next 1 line)

FIGURE 1.22 All paragraphs in this spread are set to keep all lines in the paragraph together, and the first few styles are set to be kept with the next three lines. As a result, all columns automatically start and end cleanly with a full course description, even if room is available for partial paragraph text to fit at the bottom of a given column.

3D Computer Animation (CG345)

Credits/Hours style (set to keep all lines together and keep with next 1 line)

2 credits; 1 Lecture and 2 Computer Laboratory hours per week

Prerequisites style (set to keep all lines together and keep with next 1 line)

Prerequisites: CG341, CG346, and CG351

Course Description style (set to keep all lines together)

The fundamental building blocks of three-dimensional animation are examined and the traditional animation principles as they apply to computer animation are studied. Students learn to analyze motion and the devices of anticipation, reaction, overlapping motion, and squash-and-stretch to add clarity and strength to sequences.

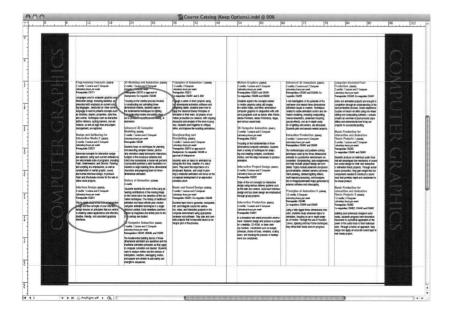

TIP

Your can set any minimums you like for the number of lines that must stay together at Start or End of a paragraph. But it's not possible to have a five-line paragraph that requires three lines be kept together at the *bottom* of the column and three lines be kept together at the *top*. Instead, the *entire* paragraph will jump to the next column.

- **At Start/End of Paragraph.** This option allows more finesse than All Lines in Paragraph. Depending on your style guide, editorial mandates, or personal preference, you may never want to see fewer than three lines of a paragraph at the bottom of a column and no fewer than two paragraph lines at the top of a column.

  - **Start: [ ] lines.** This option establishes a minimum number of lines at the beginning of a paragraph that must be kept together at the bottom of a column or end of a page.

  - **End: [ ] lines.** This option establishes a minimum number of lines at the end of a paragraph that must be present at the top of the next page or column.

Start Paragraph. A style can also include instructions as to *where* a paragraph starts. By default, this option is set to Anywhere, meaning text will flow continuously through all frames. The other options include In Next Column, In Next Frame, On Next Page, On Next Even Page, and On Next Odd Page (**FIGURE 1.23**). If, for example, all topic headings in a story must appear at the top of a column, your topic heading style can be set to In Next Column. Similarly, if all chapters in a book should start on a right-facing page, that book's chapter title style should be set to On Next Odd Page. As text is modified, these styles will still honor their designated location instructions, relieving you of the tedious chore of closing up text frames or adding breaks to reflow text.

HYPHENATION

By default, hyphenation is turned *on* in the Basic Paragraph Style, which means it will be on in every *new* style you create. So you need to decide whether or not you want it on at all. For a headline, where it's unlikely that you'll want *any* words hyphenated, be sure to turn off hyphenation in your headline paragraph style by deselecting the Hyphenate check box.

Proper hyphenation can make or break the appearance of body copy. If you choose to keep hyphenation on, you're faced with a number of additional choices. While these settings are, of course, subjective, there are several hyphenation no-nos built into InDesign by default that you should change.

Words with at Least: [ ] letters. You can limit hyphenation only to words that meet or exceed a minimum length. The default value of five letters means a word like "into" won't be hyphenated, but "input" (or anything longer) will.

After First: [ ] and Before Last: [ ] letters. These values establish a minimum number of letters that must remain together at the beginning of a word or at the end of a word, respectively, before hyphenation is allowed to occur.

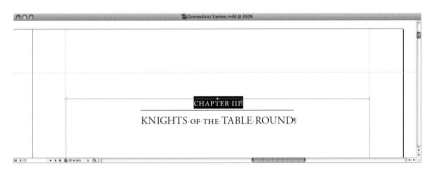

FIGURE 1.23 The Chapter Number style in this book (selected, top) includes the Start on Next Odd Page attribute (right) in its Keep Options, so that all instances of text using this style in the book "jump" to the next right-facing page (left).

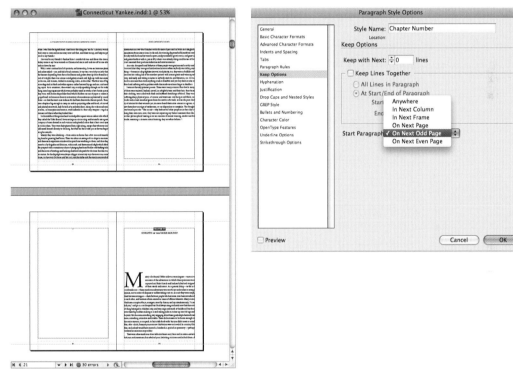

Hyphen Limit: [   ] hyphens. This option establishes the maximum number of hyphens that can appear at the end of consecutive lines, or how many hyphens in a row can appear. A value of 1 means that if a line ends with a hyphenated word, no hyphenation can occur on the line directly above it or the line directly below it.

Hyphenation Zone. The hyphenation zone defines a distance from the column edge within which hyphenation is allowed to occur. Hyphenation Zone settings are meaningless when the default (and preferable) Adobe Paragraph Composer is on. It *only* applies when the Adobe Single-line Composer is assigned to the paragraph, and then only to left- or right-aligned paragraphs.

Better Spacing/Fewer Hyphens slider. In general, InDesign's type engine is programmed with a negative bias toward hyphenation. The algorithms it uses effectively "penalize" hyphenation when calculating optimal line breaks. The Better Spacing/Fewer Hyphens slider enables you to adjust the *severity* of that penalty. Moving the slider toward Fewer Hyphens increases the penalty for hyphenation, in which case the composition engine will rely less on hyphenation and more on varying word and letter spacing to achieve a balanced appearance. Reducing the penalty by moving the slider toward Better Spacing minimizes the composition engine's impact on word and letter spacing (as defined in the Justification dialog) but allows more hyphenation to occur. While this is most noticeable and necessary in justified text, it can also improve the rag and spacing of left- or right-aligned text.

Hyphenate Capitalized Words, Hyphenate Last Word, and Hyphenate Across Column. These three options are on by default, and it mystifies me why that's so. Very few designers or editors I know would allow their paragraphs to hyphenate with these criteria.

Capitalized words like company names, product names, and proper names should rarely be hyphenated but would be with this default setting. With Hyphenate Last Word selected, any paragraph could end on a hyphenated word. Its last line could consist only of the remaining fragment of a hyphenated word, which to me is unacceptable. Hyphenate Across Column may be the worst of the three. It's not good typographic practice to allow a word to start at the end of one column, hyphenate, and end at the beginning of the next. The next column may be on the next page, which is an even more egregious error than hyphenating across columns.

Turn these off, folks, please! Close all documents, go to the Paragraph Styles panel, and then to Hyphenation, and deselect all three boxes. Your editors and your readers will thank you.

JUSTIFICATION

For paragraphs, word and letter spacing can (and should) be controlled independently using the Justification options rather than tracking. Each type of spacing includes three settings: Minimum (the least amount of space allowable between letters or words), Maximum (the greatest amount of space allowable), and Desired (the preferred amount of space) (FIGURE 1.24).

FIGURE 1.24 The
Justification options dialog.

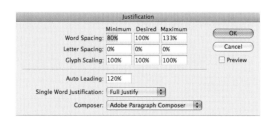

With left-aligned, right-aligned, or centered text, the only value InDesign acknowledges is Desired—and it's used throughout the paragraph consistently. However, in justified text, InDesign considers Desired to be what it should shoot for *wherever possible*. Justifying text requires manipulating the spacing of *all* lines to fit to a uniform column width, so the Desired setting is a target from which InDesign must continually stray. You establish how far it's allowed to stray in either direction by entering a range in the Minimum and Maximum fields. Minimum means the spacing can be *no tighter than* a certain value, and Maximum means the spacing can't be *any looser than* a certain value.

Word Spacing. These values are expressed as percentages, where 100% is *exactly* the word spacing built into the font. Percentages lower than 100 mean tighter word spacing, and higher percentages mean looser word spacing.

Letter Spacing. These values start at 0%, which represents the letter spacing built into the font's metrics. Minimum values are usually negative percentages (any amount below zero to tighten up letter spacing), whereas Maximum values are typically greater than zero.

Glyph Scaling: Good or Bad?

Glyph scaling is on-the-fly horizontal text scaling that InDesign performs only if it needs to and only after exhausting all other justification options available to it. While horizontal scaling of type is never a good design choice, this feature can be helpful in difficult copy-fitting situations where one more option may give the Adobe Paragraph Composer (see "Composer" later in this section) all it needs to produce a better-looking paragraph. The key is to use it sparingly (99% in the Minimum field and 100% in the Desired and Maximum fields) and only in the right situations. At those amounts, the effect is imperceptible.

The benefit of glyph scaling—if you choose to use it—is that you don't have to manually make this adjustment to your text. InDesign does it dynamically but only as needed and only to the specific parts of the paragraph where it will make a difference. If the paragraph changes in any way and glyph scaling is no longer needed, the adjustment is automatically removed.

Why Is My Text Rewrapping?

If you've ever inserted a soft return at the end of a line midway through a paragraph and watched as several lines above it break differently, you've seen the Adobe Paragraph Composer at work. To improve the appearance of *one* line in a paragraph, InDesign may make an adjustment several lines above it if that will keep the spacing of the entire paragraph as consistent as possible. For some, this can be frustrating, but InDesign is continually evaluating the optimal spacing solution, based on your justification and hyphenation settings, when it makes these adjustments. However, you have the option to switch to the Adobe Single-line Composer in those instances where it's more appropriate. This switch should only be made when working with left- or right-aligned paragraphs. Switching to the Single-line Composer for justified text is a recipe for disaster. It disables the precise functionality that justified text requires: consistent and even distribution of text in paragraphs where the text must fit the full width of the column.

The Adobe Paragraph Composer is turned on by default in InDesign. It's unlikely that you'll want to turn off this option application-wide (although you can). However, it may be necessary or appropriate to turn it off in a specific document. To do that, deselect everything in the document, choose the Text tool, open the Paragraph panel, and choose Adobe Single-line Composer from the panel menu. To shut if off application-wide, follow those same steps with no documents open. As with all default changes in InDesign, this will only change the setting for new documents or new text added to an open document. Existing documents, text, and styles remain unaffected.

A more precise strategy for selectively using the Single-line Composer would be to build that composer option into a specific paragraph style. That way, a single-line composed paragraph can exist within a document that otherwise uses the Adobe Paragraph Composer. Better still, you can change the composer on any paragraph as a local override, thereby dealing with problem paragraphs only by exception.

Auto Leading. InDesign uses a default value of 120% of the current point size to establish auto leading if no other leading is specified. You can change the percentage basis for a paragraph's auto leading here. With a setting of 150%, for example, the auto leading for 10-point type would be 15 points, and the leading for 12-point type would be 18 points. However, unless your paragraph style is actually using auto leading, this setting is meaningless.

Single Word Justification. If any line (other than the very last line) in a justified paragraph contains only one word, InDesign can align it in one of four ways.

Full Justify spreads out the word across the width of the column, whereas Align Left, Align Center, and Align Right align that single-word line exactly as their respective names imply.

Composer. One of InDesign's most powerful under-the-hood features is the Adobe Paragraph Composer. Other page layout applications evaluate word and letter spacing one line at a time, adjusting each line of a paragraph with no regard for or awareness of any other part of the paragraph. The result, especially in justified text, can be wild spacing inconsistencies from one line to the next and poor typographic color overall. The Adobe Single-line Composer emulates the line-by-line text flow systems used in other page layout applications. The Adobe Paragraph Composer continuously looks at the paragraph as a whole and optimizes the text flow across each paragraph.

DROP CAPS AND NESTED STYLES

Character and paragraph styles start working together to powerful effect with the options in the Drop Caps and Nested Styles area.

Drop caps

Drop caps are generated automatically using an algorithm that calculates the height required to make the first character (or characters) accurately span a specific number of lines. This calculation is based on the size and leading of the paragraph text. As changes are made to either, the drop cap is automatically resized. Chapter 7 covers drop caps in greater depth.

Nested Styles

Nested Styles allow you to prebuild character styles into your paragraph styles and apply them in a designated order that is "triggered" by specific conditions. In consistently structured text, Nested Styles can automate the formatting of directory listings, run-in heads, tables of contents, page number references, price lists, and almost anything you can think of.

This is where automation and the power of relationships between styles really begins. In fact, Nested Styles convinced *me* to switch to InDesign in the first place. It's *that* important. The next chapter will cover this feature in depth.

Nested Line Styles

New to CS4, this feature works much like Nested Styles, but it has only *one* nesting criteria: the number of lines through which you want the character style to extend. Nested Line Styles are covered in the next chapter.

GREP STYLE

GREP is a text-search feature that describes text or patterns and conditions within text. It is an incredibly powerful addition to InDesign, but that power comes at a cost. You must develop some basic working knowledge of GREP to take advantage of it. Because of GREP's complexity, Chapter 3 is entirely dedicated to GREP styles.

BULLETS AND NUMBERING

The Bullets and Numbering feature received a complete functionality overhaul in CS3. In CS4, the bulleted list feature hasn't changed much, but numbered lists became more powerful. Unfortunately, the dialog from which they're set up also became more daunting and complicated.

Connecting lists to paragraph styles is an essential list management practice, so Chapter 7 covers numbered lists in depth.

Working with Paragraph and Character Styles

Now that you've explored the ins and outs of the available options for paragraph and character styles, let's break down the steps required to create, modify, and apply them.

THE PARAGRAPH STYLES AND CHARACTER STYLES PANELS

All options in the Paragraph and Character Styles panels (FIGURES 1.25 and 1.26) are available from the panel menu, from the icons at the bottom of the panel, or from context menus accessed by Control-clicking/right-clicking a style name. You'll use these panels to do the bulk of your style creation, modification, and organization.

Styles are added to either panel at a position relative to which style is currently selected. If no style is selected, new styles are added to the bottom of the list. You can reorder styles by clicking and dragging the style name to any desired position in the panel or sort all styles by name using the Sort by Name option in the panel menu.

For more orderly style management and to eliminate clutter in the styles panels, you can store similar styles in a folder called a Style Group (see Chapter 11).

Highlight indicates currently selected style in document

Create new style group

Clear overrides in selection

Create new style

Delete selected style/groups

FIGURE 1.25 The Paragraph Styles panel and its menu options.

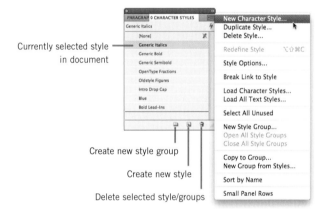

Currently selected style in document

Create new style group

Create new style

Delete selected style/groups

FIGURE 1.26 The Character Styles panel and its menu options are nearly identical to the Paragraph Styles panel and menu but lack the Clear Overrides and Convert [*Style Name*] Bullets and Numbering to Text options.

CREATING PARAGRAPH STYLES

As with most InDesign features, there are several ways to create a paragraph style. You can choose New Paragraph Style from the Paragraph Styles panel menu, Option-click/Alt-click the Create New Style icon at the bottom of the Paragraph Styles panel, or click the Paragraph Style icon in the Control panel (in paragraph mode) and choose New Paragraph Style from that menu.

You can also create paragraph styles in a number of other features' dialogs—Object Styles, Table of Contents, Text Variables, and Cell Styles, for example—where paragraph styles can be selected.

Once in the New Paragraph Style dialog, define all desired attributes for the style, give it a name, and click OK.

Don't Fear the Dialog

One argument I often hear from people unwilling to work with styles is that defining the appearance of their text from a dialog instead of on the page is a less fluid and intuitive process. I completely agree with this argument because I too prefer to work quickly on the page, using the panel options and keyboard shortcuts I'm accustomed to. However, working intuitively *and* taking advantage of styles are not mutually exclusive goals.

A more efficient and intuitive way to define a paragraph style's attributes is to first make the paragraph look the way you want using the methods that work best for you, and then create a new style that picks up all the formatting you've already applied. When any paragraph on a page is selected or the text cursor is within any paragraph, all of its attributes are automatically "pulled in" to the definition when you create a new style. This is a best of both words approach. Designers *can* have their cake and eat it too, so to speak.

APPLYING PARAGRAPH STYLES

To apply a paragraph style, select any text in a story and either click the style name in the Paragraph Styles panel or select the paragraph style from the menu in the Control panel (in paragraph mode). If you've assigned a keyboard shortcut to a style, you can use that shortcut to apply the style, too.

FIGURE 1.27 A plus sign next to any style name indicates the presence of local formatting overrides.

None of these methods removes existing *character-level* formatting (bold, italic, small caps, all caps, etc.) or applied character styles from the selected paragraph(s). Those changes are preserved. When the full paragraph is selected, the Paragraph Styles panel displays a plus sign (+) next to the style name, indicating the presence of local overrides (FIGURE 1.27). Hovering over the style name in the panel displays a tooltip that details the override applied. If more than one override is present, the tooltip shows only (Mixed Overrides).

TIP

InDesign does not consider applied character styles to be overrides, so no plus sign appears if character styles are the only formatting variations in a paragraph.

To apply a paragraph style and remove local character-level overrides (font, size, character color, etc.) and paragraph-level overrides (indents, space after, leading, etc.) but *not* applied character styles, do one of the following:

- Option-click/Alt-click the style name in the Paragraph Styles panel.

- Control-click/right-click the desired style name and choose Apply [*Style Name*], Clear Overrides.

- Click the Clear Overrides in Selection icon at the bottom of the Paragraph Styles panel.

To apply a paragraph style and *only* remove applied character styles, Control-click/right-click the desired style name and choose Apply [*Style Name*], Clear Character Styles.

To apply a paragraph style and simultaneously remove all paragraph- and character-level overrides *and* all applied character styles, you can do either of the following:

- Control-click/right-click the desired style name and choose Apply [*Style Name*], Clear All (FIGURE 1.28).

- Shift-Option-click/Shift-Alt-click the style name in the panel.

TIP

When you create a new paragraph style, you can apply it immediately to any selected text from the General options area of the New Paragraph Style dialog by selecting the Apply Style to Selection check box.

FIGURE 1.28 Removing all local overrides and character styles when applying a paragraph style.

MODIFYING PARAGRAPH STYLES

You can easily modify paragraph styles via a dialog in the following ways:

- Double-click the style name in the Paragraph Styles panel.

- Select the style name in the Paragraph Styles panel and choose Style Options from the panel menu.

- Control-click/right-click on the style name in the Paragraph Styles panel and choose Edit [*Style Name*] (FIGURE 1.29).

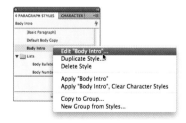

FIGURE 1.29 Best practice is to Control-click/right-click a style name to edit its attributes without applying it to selected text.

Of the preceding three methods, the latter is the safest option. It's the only way to avoid unintentionally applying the style to other text (if your cursor is in text with different formatting) or setting that paragraph style as the Text tool's default (if the cursor is not placed in *any* text).

Keeping It Loose: Creating Adaptable Character Styles

Often, a character style's *only* difference from the paragraph's overall formatting is one attribute (italic or bold instead of regular, or red instead of black). Everything else—size, font family, tracking, case, and so on is identical to the rest of the paragraph. In that case, your character style should be as "undefined" as possible. If, for example, your "Italics" character style just uses the italic version of your body copy, leave *every other option* in that style undefined. The character style will inherit all other formatting changes made to the paragraph it is applied in but remain italicized.

As changes occur in that paragraph, a minimally defined character style absorbs all those changes as well, retaining only its "unbreakable" defined attribute(s). A character style that's *specifically* defined as Adobe Garamond Pro Italic, 10 points with 13-point leading will be less adaptable if the font, point size, or leading of the paragraph change.

The trickle-down benefit of this functionality is that a character style with only Bold defined as the Font Style will work on almost *any* paragraph, provided the paragraph's font uses Bold and not Heavy or some other nonstandard naming convention. Whether you use Caslon or Garamond, Myriad or Helvetica, this *one* bold character style will work for all of them (**FIGURE 1.30**).

The following is a list of my "must-have" flexible character styles. All InDesign users should build *some* of these into their document defaults.

- Generic Italics (only Italic is defined in the Font Style field; a variation on this could be Generic Oblique for fonts that use that designation)

- Generic Bold (only Bold is defined in the Font Style field)

- Generic Semibold (only Semibold is defined in the Font Style field)

- Knockout (only the character fill is defined, using the Paper swatch in the Character Color area of the dialog)

- All Caps (only the All Caps option is selected under Basic Character Formats)

- No Break (only the No Break option is selected under Basic Character Formats)

- Small Caps (only the Small Caps option is selected under Basic Character Formats)

- OpenType Fractions (only the Fractions option is selected under OpenType features)

Not *all* of these generic styles will work for all fonts, depending on the complexity of a font and how its particular variations are named. For example, applying an Italic attribute to Myriad Pro Semibold will change the font to Myriad Pro Italic. The Semibold attribute is dropped. In that font (as in many others), the variation is named Semibold Italic.

Keeping It Loose: Creating Adaptable Character Styles (continued)

To set up an adaptable character style:

1. Be sure that no text is selected in your document

2. Choose New Character Style from the Character Styles panel menu. The resulting dialog should have *nothing* defined for any attribute. Pull-down menus should have no options selected, check boxes should have a small dash through them (Mac) or show a small box (Windows), text fields should be empty, and Character Color settings should show question marks instead of assigned swatches.

3. If for some reason some attributes are specified that you don't want as part of the style, select (Ignore) from any pull-down menu, click any active check box until it appears as described in the previous step, and delete all text from any dialog field. To remove a swatch that may be applied, Command-click/Ctrl-click the swatch name in the Character Color area to leave the character fill and stroke undefined.

4. Define *only* the attribute(s) you want in this dialog (Italic or Bold under Font Style, for example), and make sure the style is based on [None].

5. Name the style appropriately and click OK.

To have these adaptable styles available in *all* new documents, follow the same procedure but do it with *no* documents open. Character styles added in this manner become part of your document defaults. But they will not be added to any existing documents.

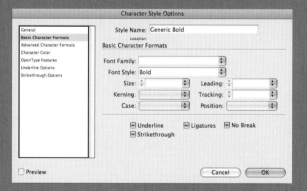

FIGURE 1.30 The fewer options defined for a character style, the more versatile it is. This style will act as the bold character style for every typeface that uses Bold (but not Semibold or Heavy). All character formatting represented by empty fields, unspecified menu choices, and neutral check boxes is inherited from the paragraph or paragraph style.

Redefine Style: The Indecisive Designer's Best Friend

There's another method for modifying paragraph styles that I highly recommend because it's more likely in tune with how you work in your layouts. When you want to experiment with changes to styled text, modify the necessary attributes for one paragraph right on the page, and then use the Redefine Style feature to transfer your modifications into the established style definition. This allows you to see your small local change cascade throughout all text defined by that style and immediately see its impact on your entire document. If you're not satisfied with the results, a simple undo (Command/Ctrl-Z) restores the style, and if you want to make additional adjustments, you can redefine the style over and over as often as you want without ever opening a dialog.

The Redefine Style option is available from several places but *only* if the cursor is within text using a style other than [No Paragraph Style], and then only if some attribute of the selection differs from the paragraph style definition. Wherever there's a styling + (plus sign), you can use this feature. Under those circumstances, you can redefine a style in the following ways:

- Choose Redefine Style from the Paragraph Styles panel menu.

- Control-click/right-click on the style name in the Paragraph Styles panel and choose Redefine Style (**FIGURE 1.31**).

- Click the Paragraph Style icon in the Control panel (in paragraph mode) and choose Redefine Style from the menu.

- Use the keyboard shortcut Shift-Command-Option-R/Shift-Ctrl-Alt-R.

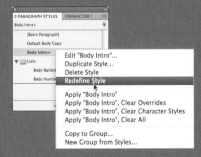

FIGURE 1.31 The Redefine Style option accessed from the Paragraph Styles panel.

CREATING CHARACTER STYLES

You can also create character styles by multiple means. Typically, you'll start building character styles in the following ways:

- Choose New Character Style from the Character Styles panel menu.

- Option-click/Alt-click the Create New Style button at the bottom of the Character Styles panel.

- Choose New Character Style from the Character Style icon in the Control panel (in character mode).

The New Character Style command is also available in many dialogs throughout the application including Drop Caps, Nested Styles, Nested Line Styles, GREP Styles, Bullets and Numbering, Text Variables, and others. Almost anywhere that a character style can be *selected*, a new character style can be created.

APPLYING CHARACTER STYLES

To apply a character style, select the text you want to style and click the name of the desired style in the Character Styles panel or click the Character Style button in the Control panel (in character mode) and choose the desired style from the menu. If you've assigned a keyboard shortcut to the style, you can also invoke that shortcut to apply the style.

Applying a character style will not change any existing character-level formatting unless that formatting conflicts with an attribute defined by the character style. In other words, applying a character style that only changes the color of the text to red will not remove local formatting like italics. The text will simply become red *and* italicized. However, if the character style definition specifies that the text should be red *and* bold, the italic attribute that had been applied locally will be removed in favor of the character style's bold font style.

MODIFYING CHARACTER STYLES

Because character styles inherit much of their formatting from the paragraph and may include very few unique attributes, modifying them is a bit different from modifying paragraph styles.

The Redefine Style option in particular behaves quite differently for character styles. Changes to attributes not originally defined as part of the character style are considered local overrides to the *paragraph*, not to the character style. In other words, if a character style that only changes a character's color is applied to some text and you later make that text bold, the Redefine Style option will be grayed out in the Character Styles panel since the Font Style attribute was never

NOTE
If you have text formatted with a character style selected and choose Redefine Style from the Paragraph Styles panel menu, the paragraph style will be redefined to include the character-level attributes defined by the character style. All paragraph-level attributes (and character-level attributes undefined in the selected character style) will be preserved.

a part of the applied character style. If, however, you change the color of the text in this example, the character style name will appear with a plus sign next to it and the Redefine Style option will be available in the Character Styles panel menu. Because of this behavior, I prefer to use the Character Style Options dialog, with Preview turned on, to modify character styles.

DISASSOCIATING TEXT FROM A STYLE

At some point in a project, you may want to use an existing style's formatting as the basis for an entirely new style, but sever the connection between the original style and the new style. If you place your cursor in the styled text and create a New Paragraph Style or New Character Style, InDesign automatically bases the new style on the applied style. That keeps the two styles bound to one another, no matter how many changes you make to the new style.

To create a new style that branches off *completely* from an existing style, change the Based On style setting of the new style to [No Paragraph Style] for paragraph styles or [None] for character styles. To simultaneously apply that style to the selected text, select the Apply Style to Selection check box.

To disassociate any selected text from the paragraph or character style applied to it *without* creating a new style, choose Break Link to Style from the panel menu or click the Paragraph Style or Character Style buttons (whichever is appropriate) in the Control panel and choose Break Link to Style from the drop-down menu (FIGURE 1.32).

FIGURE 1.32 The Break Link to Style option selected from the Control panel.

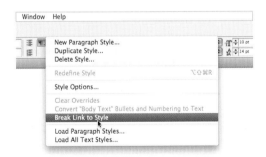

DUPLICATING STYLES

Duplicating a style creates an *identical* but unrelated copy of the selected style with "copy" appended to the style name. Unlike a new style created from styled text, a duplicated style does not base the new style on the selected style. Instead, it exactly duplicates any Based On settings in the source style.

To duplicate a style from selected text:

- Choose Duplicate Style from the panel menu.

- Choose Duplicate Style from the Paragraph Style or Character Style menu (whichever is appropriate) in the Control panel.

To duplicate any paragraph or character style whether or not text to which it's applied is selected, Control-click/right-click the style name in the panel and choose Duplicate Style from the context menu.

DELETING STYLES

After a while, you may find you've created a number of styles you no longer need. To remove any paragraph or character style:

- Select the style in the appropriate panel and choose Delete Style from the panel menu.

- Control-click/right-click the style name in the panel and choose Delete Style from the context menu.

If the selected style is not used anywhere in the document, it will be deleted from the list of styles in the panel immediately. However, if the style is used anywhere in the document (including as a nested style in a paragraph style, even if that paragraph style is not used), a dialog will pop up asking you which style should replace the deleted style. The default is [Basic Paragraph], which I don't recommend using. You can choose to replace the outgoing style with any other existing style in the document from the menu in this dialog or choose [No Paragraph Style].

If you select the latter, an active Preserve Formatting check box appears in the dialog (FIGURE 1.33). This deletes the style but does not change the appearance of any text in the document to which it was applied. Deselecting Preserve Formatting changes *all* text formatted with the outgoing style to [No Paragraph Style], removing any formatting that does not match that style definition.

FIGURE 1.33 Preserve Formatting maintains the appearance of text when its style is entirely deleted and not replaced with another style.

FINDING AND REMOVING UNUSED STYLES

For faster style panel housecleaning, you may want to find and delete any styles not presently used in a document. From either the Paragraph Styles panel menu or the Character Styles panel menu, choose Select All Unused to highlight all styles in the panel that do not appear on any document page (FIGURE 1.34). Then go back to the panel menu and choose Delete Style. Since the styles are not used, they will be deleted immediately with no interim dialog.

Character styles that are nested in a paragraph style are *not* selected when selecting all unused styles from the Character Styles panel, even if the paragraph styles in which they're nested are not used. InDesign considers nested character styles "in use" by the paragraph style whether or not the paragraph style is applied to text.

If during this process you want to keep an unused style in a document, Command-click/Ctrl-click its name to deselect it before deleting the other selected styles.

FIGURE 1.34 Unused styles highlighted in the Paragraph Styles panel with the Select All Unused feature.

IMPORTING TEXT STYLES FROM OTHER DOCUMENTS

You can load styles from any existing InDesign document from either the Paragraph Styles or Character Styles panel menus, or from the corresponding menus in the Control panel.

To import styles from another document:

- Choose Load All Text Styles from either the Paragraph Styles panel menu or the Character Styles panel menu to load both paragraph and character styles, or choose the more specific option in each panel's menu (Load Paragraph Styles and Load Character Styles, respectively) to load only one kind of style.

- Choose the document containing the styles you want from the Open a File dialog and click Open.

The resulting Load Styles dialog lets you get more selective about which specific styles will be loaded from the source document (FIGURE 1.35). Only styles with checked boxes next to their names will be imported. When loading *all* styles, paragraph styles are listed first, followed by character styles.

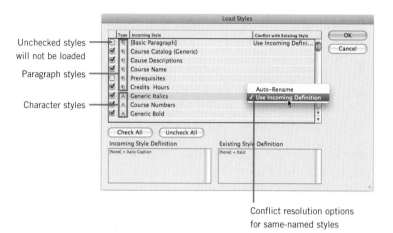

Unchecked styles will not be loaded

Paragraph styles

Character styles

Conflict resolution options for same-named styles

FIGURE 1.35 Any incoming styles can be included or excluded in the Load Styles dialog, and same-named styles can either redefine a style in the destination document or be added as duplicate styles but applied to nothing.

There will always be at least one conflict when loading paragraph styles, because every InDesign document contains [Basic Paragraph Style]. A conflict is any incoming style name that matches a style name in the destination document. Each conflict can be resolved in one of two ways:

- Use Incoming Definition redefines the existing style in the document to match the incoming style.

- Auto-Rename loads the incoming style with "copy" appended to its name, changing nothing in the destination document.

There is no formal method for exporting styles. If you want to add styles to another document, you must open that document and load styles from another document. Also, when you copy styled text from one document and paste it into another, all styles used by the copied text are added to the destination document. However, there's a downside to this method that is covered in Chapter 11.

NOTE
When you select Load All Paragraph Styles, any character styles nested in an incoming style are also imported.

CHAPTER 2

Nesting and Sequencing Styles

THE CONCEPT OF *separate* paragraph and character styles was around long before InDesign in applications like PageMaker, QuarkXPress, and Microsoft Word. QuarkXPress had a close-but-no-cigar implementation of character styles when they were added to that application. They were, undeniably, a great way to save attributes for text that varied from a paragraph's overall formatting and to make fast changes in a document by modifying a style instead of tracking down what could amount to hundreds of local overrides. But that's as far as it went. The two styles—paragraph and character—were completely independent of one another. In other applications, character styles still had to be applied one by one to any text that required them.

With InDesign CS, Adobe's engineers did something that, it seems, had never occurred to anyone before: They made character styles work *within* paragraph styles using a feature called Nested Styles. This concept was so simple, and it made perfect sense. How had someone not thought of it before?

Nested Styles

In the simplest terms, the Nested Styles feature is a way to prebuild (or nest) one or more character styles into a paragraph style (FIGURE 2.1). Those character styles are automatically applied in a predetermined order that is "triggered" by specific conditions (e.g., "through 2 commas" or "up to 1 En Space"). What character styles are nested in the paragraph, in what order, and what triggers the switch between them is entirely customizable.

FIGURE 2.1 Basic nesting at work in a dictionary definition. A bold, blue, sans-serif character style is applied through the colon, followed by an italic character style through a closing parenthesis. The paragraph's default formatting then takes over.

nest: *(verb)* to place an object or element in a hierarchical arrangement, typically in a subordinate position.

style: *(noun)* a particular, distinctive, or characteristic mode or form of construction or execution in any art or work.

When the Nested Styles feature was introduced in InDesign CS, it provided designers with an unprecedented level of formatting power, and it has been continuously improved from CS2 through CS4. In consistently structured text, nested styles can automate the formatting of bulleted and numbered lists, run-in heads, page number references, price lists, and much more.

Nested styles are appropriate for *any* project. For large jobs like directories and catalogs with great quantities of text or cyclical publications like magazines and newsletters where a look and feel is established in advance and reused month to month, they are the best way to improve productivity, ensure consistency, and maintain the highest level of flexibility throughout the design and production process. While they may be less critical for smaller or stand-alone projects like advertisements and packaging, they are no less useful.

THE NESTED STYLES WORK AREA

The Nested Styles work area is where you select character styles to include in a paragraph or paragraph style, establish how far the nested style or styles extend in that paragraph, and—in the case of multiple nested character styles—establish in what order the character styles appear.

You can access the Nested Styles options in several ways. With your cursor in any paragraph of text, use the keyboard shortcut Command-Option-R/Ctrl-Alt-R to open the dedicated Drop Caps and Nested Styles dialog. Alternately,

TIP

You can navigate any InDesign dialog that has a pane of options on the left via some standard keyboard shortcuts. Press Command/Ctrl-1 to access the first option in the pane, press Command/Ctrl-2 to access the second, and so on. To jump directly to Drop Caps and Nested Styles (the tenth option in the Paragraph Style Options dialog), press Command/Ctrl-0. Unfortunately, anything that follows the tenth option in that list does not benefit from these shortcuts and must be clicked normally.

you can either open the Paragraph panel (Command-Option-T/Ctrl-Alt-T) and choose Drop Caps and Nested Styles from the panel menu (FIGURE 2.2), or choose the same option from the context menu at the far right of the Control panel (in text mode).

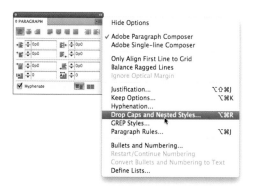

FIGURE 2.2 Choose Drop Caps and Nested Styles from the Paragraph panel menu to access Nested Styles options.

Nested styles can be applied directly to any paragraph, but it's better to build your nested styles into a new or existing paragraph style so that you can later capitalize on your efforts and instantly apply a nested style as often as needed in your document. In the Paragraph Style Options (or New Paragraph Style) dialog, click Drop Caps and Nested Styles in the left pane (FIGURE 2.3).

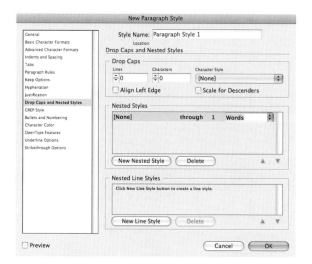

FIGURE 2.3 The Drop Caps and Nested Styles area of the Paragraph Style Options dialog includes settings for Nested Styles along with Drop Caps and Nested Line Styles.

Below the Drop Cap options is the Nested Styles work area (FIGURE 2.4). When you edit an existing paragraph style that has no nested styles, the work area contains only the text "Click New Nested Style button to create a nested style." When you create a new paragraph style, the default settings of "[None] through 1 Words" are already set up in the Nested Styles work area. These defaults amount to the same thing as not having any nested styles—no variation from the defaults of the paragraph style.

3. Designate whether the selected style extends through or up to the delimiter.

4. Specify the number of instances of the delimiter to include before changing styles.

5. Select a delimiter from the pull-down menu, or type the desired delimiter in the delimiter field.

FIGURE 2.4 The various fields and menus available for nested styles in the Drop Caps and Nested Styles area.

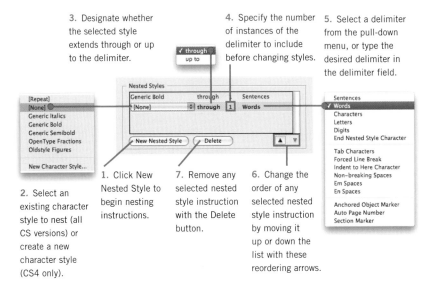

1. Click New Nested Style to begin nesting instructions.

2. Select an existing character style to nest (all CS versions) or create a new character style (CS4 only).

7. Remove any selected nested style instruction with the Delete button.

6. Change the order of any selected nested style instruction by moving it up or down the list with these reordering arrows.

The Nested Styles work area is composed of the following option menus, fields, and buttons:

New Nested Style button. Click this button to begin nesting character styles within a paragraph or paragraph style, or if one or more nested styles already exist and you want to add another. Once clicked, the four options required to set up a nested style become active.

Character Style pull-down menu. Any character styles already present in your document are immediately available from this menu. In CS4, new character styles can be created without having to leave this dialog by using the New Character Style option at the bottom of the menu:

- The **[None]** option leaves the paragraph formatting unchanged, which is useful if your nested style occurs somewhere other than at the very beginning of your paragraph. None doesn't mean "no formatting"; it simply means no variation from the paragraph's normal appearance.

Unless more nesting will occur later in the same paragraph, there is no need to end each sequence of nested styles with [None]. Once all nesting instructions have been completed, the paragraph automatically returns to its default appearance.

- The **[Repeat]** option lets you set up a "formatting loop" for your nested styles that applies character styles in a certain sequence and then repeats that sequence (or a part of it) again and again through the remainder of the paragraph. See the section "Repeating Nested Styles in a Loop" later in this chapter for step-by-step instructions for repeating nested styles.

- Choose **New Character Style** to add a style that does not already exist in the document. The New Character Style dialog opens on top of the Paragraph Style Options dialog. If the Preview check box is selected and you choose New Character Style, preview will be disabled while the New Character Style dialog is active. Once the style is defined and you click OK, preview is automatically restored. Character styles built while in the Nested Styles work area are added to the document after the paragraph style is saved.

Through or up to pull-down. Nested styles have a fixed range of either through or up to a specific character called a delimiter. Delimiters trigger the change to the next style. The through or up to option determines whether the nested character style includes the delimiter character (through) or stops just short of it (up to). For example, a bold style applied *through* one em dash will also make the em dash bold, but if *up to* is chosen, the bold style is not applied to that em dash (FIGURE 2.5).

SURVEY OF GRAPHIC DESIGN—Surveys visual communication from its earliest forms to its present visualized conceptions. Emphasizes links between society and the development of advertising art. Analyzes and compares major stylistic trends and influences.

SURVEY OF GRAPHIC DESIGN—Surveys visual communication from its earliest forms to its present visualized conceptions. Emphasizes links between society and the development of advertising art. Analyzes and compares major stylistic trends and influences.

FIGURE 2.5 The paragraph on the left uses an all caps blue style through one em dash, resulting in a blue em dash. The paragraph on the right applies the style up to one em dash, so the dash does not have the nested style applied.

Number of instances field. The number (1 or more) in this field establishes how many instances of the delimiter must occur before the style change is invoked (through 2 sentences, for example). Change this number by typing or using the up or down arrow keys with your cursor in the field.

Delimiter field and menu. Delimiters complete the instructions for each nested style by specifying what single character either triggers a switch to another nested style or returns to the paragraph's default formatting.

Any character can be a delimiter, and preset options like sentences, words, and some marker characters are available from the menu at the end of each nested style instruction. There are, of course, many other characters you might want to use as a delimiter. If the particular option you need is not available in the delimiter menu, you can type it into the delimiter field. For example, if you have a run-in heading in your paragraph that should use a nested style through one colon, simply type a colon in the delimiter field. If, however, the delimiter character you want cannot actually be entered in a dialog (a tab or soft return, for example), you can use its metacharacter equivalent (a code that represents the character or symbol). For a tab, that metacharacter would be ^t. See Chapter 3, "Automatic Styling with GREP," for more on using metacharacters.

Delete. Select any nested style from the list and delete it using this button. Only the selected use of the style is removed from the nesting instruction. The styles are not deleted from the document, even if they were created from this dialog with the New Character Style option.

Reordering arrows. Multiple character styles can be nested within any paragraph style, and the top-to-bottom order in which they appear in the Nested Style settings is the left-to-right order in which they'll appear in the paragraph. To change the order of the nested styles, select any style in the sequence and click either the up or down arrow as often as necessary to move the style to the appropriate position.

ANATOMY OF NESTED STYLES

Each of the following paragraphs represents a range of nested style scenarios, increasing from very simple to somewhat complex. FIGURE 2.6 shows the simplest nesting scenario: A character style starts formatting the paragraph and then switches back to the basics. The bold, sans-serif, blue character style (Course Name) is nested at the start of a paragraph through one en space, which applies different formatting only to the course name.

FIGURE 2.6 A single character style nested at the start of a paragraph.

SURVEY OF GRAPHIC DESIGN Surveys visual communication from its earliest forms to its present visualized conceptions. Emphasizes links between society and the development of advertising art. Analyzes and compares major stylistic trends and influences.

Building on the previous example, FIGURE 2.7 nests a Course Number character style through one en space *before* the course name. Another style (Prerequisites) is applied *after* the course name through one closing parenthesis. In both examples so far, the paragraph automatically returns to its default formatting after the nested style instructions have been completed.

GD214 **THE CORPORATE IMAGE** *(Prerequisite: AD213)* Students develop corporate identity logos with emphasis on exploring creative solutions that define a corporation's image. Logo application is extended to a complete corporate business system and finished to presentation form.

FIGURE 2.7 Three styles nested in sequence at the beginning of a paragraph.

FIGURE 2.8 adds two more nested styles at the *end* of the course description. After the Prerequisites style, [None] is selected to revert to the default paragraph formatting since more nesting will follow it. The text continues with that default paragraph style format, and then nesting starts up again after one right indent tab (indicated by the metacharacter ^y). Next, the Credit/Hour Lead-ins character style is nested through one colon, followed by a Credits/Hours style for the numbers following that colon.

This last style can continue until the end of the paragraph. Oddly enough, there's no "end of paragraph" option available in the delimiter menu. If you enter the ^p metacharacter that represents a hard return at the end of a paragraph, it is automatically replaced with the End Nested Style Character option. This nesting instruction terminates with an End Nested Style Character for that reason and because:

- *Something* must be entered in this field to finish the instruction.

- It's the least likely character to appear anywhere in this particular text. As such, it will *never* be found and the last style in the sequence will remain applied through the end of the paragraph.

GD342 **PUBLICATION DESIGN** *(Prerequisites: CD172 and GD214)* The conceptual and technical abilities required to design magazines and other publications are emphasized. Students learn the impact of marketing objectives, research, and technology on publication design.   **CREDITS: 3**

FIGURE 2.8 Adding [None] to the nesting instructions reverts to the paragraph's normal appearance until the next nested style.

FIGURE 2.9 reverts to [None] to format the vertical divider, and then adds a [Repeat] instruction to continuously apply its last three styles. In other words, the style ends with: Credit/Hour Lead-ins through one colon, then Credits/Hours up to one vertical divider, then [None] through that same character, and then start over from Credit/Hour Lead-ins in a nonstop loop until the end of the

paragraph. This successfully formats the credits, studio hours, and so on using that three-style sequence as often as necessary. With [Repeat] as the final instruction, there's no need to "end" the sequence. It will never end until the paragraph does.

FIGURE 2.9 The [Repeat] option formats the text at the end of the paragraph in a continuous loop of nested styles.

GD441 ENVIRONMENTAL GRAPHICS *(Prerequisite: GD312)* Examines the creative development and use of environmental graphics as public informational tools and projections of identity. Students learn to work with scale, construct models, prepare presentation boards, and design flow charts. **CREDITS: 2 | STUDIO HRS: 2 | LECTURE HRS: 1**

Character Styles Used:
COURSE NUMBER
COURSE NAME
Prerequisites
CREDIT & HOUR LEAD-INS
Credits & Hours

Paragraph Styles Used:
Course Description

FIGURE 2.10 Styles used in Figures 2.6 through 2.9.

FIGURE 2.10 shows the component styles, both character and paragraph, used to build these examples.

THE DOWNSIDE OF NESTING STYLES

Although a nested character style is applied within a paragraph and will reflect any changes made to that character style, the actual style remains, in a way, hidden. In **FIGURE 2.11**, the two paragraphs look the same, but their respective formatting was achieved by different means. The top paragraph had its character styles applied manually, so the name of the character style applied to the selected text is highlighted in the Character Styles panel. The bottom paragraph uses nested styles to accomplish the same look. But since the character styles are built into the paragraph style, no character style name is highlighted in the panel. This is more than a curious bit of InDesign trivia, it's an important behavior to be aware of.

All this automation power and instant formatting is fantastic when you're working *exclusively* in InDesign. However, in today's publishing environment, the printed page is not the only venue for your projects. Often, designers are asked to export content to other formats for repurposing on the Web or elsewhere. Unfortunately, those other formats aren't hip to all the cool stuff built into InDesign, so your automatic formatting may be lost on the other end and have to be reapplied manually.

Character styles applied manually

GD342 PUBLICATION DESIGN *(Prerequisites: CD 172 and GD 214)* The conceptual and technical abilities required to design magazines and other publications are emphasized. Students learn the impact of marketing objectives, research, and technology on publication design. **CREDITS: 3 | STUDIO HRS: 6**

Character styles nested in a paragraph style

GD441 ENVIRONMENTAL GRAPHICS *(Prerequisite: GD312)* Examines the creative development and use of environmental graphics as public informational tools and projections of identity. Students learn to work with scale, construct models, prepare presentation boards, and design flow charts. **CREDITS: 2 | STUDIO HRS: 2 | LECTURE HRS: 1**

FIGURE 2.11 Manually applied character styles are identified in the Character Styles panel when selected (top), but nested character styles are not (bottom).

Even *within* InDesign, you may use other features that need to call on a character style you've nested, but those features will only recognize a manually applied character style, not a nested one. This is also true of character styles used by Nested Line Styles (see "Nested Line Styles" later in this chapter) and GREP styles (see Chapter 3). It's important to know what these potential pitfalls are and plan accordingly. Watch out for the following InDesign features in which the character styles in a nested style are not recognized:

Select All Unused. The Select All Unused option in the Character Styles panel is a fast and easy way to clean out styles you may no longer need in your document. When a paragraph with nested character styles is present on any page in your document, those nested characters styles are considered "in use" and will not be selected with this option. However, if a paragraph style with character styles nested in it is just *defined* in the document but *not* applied to any text, the character styles nested in it are also considered to be in use and will be ignored by the Select All Unused function. (See Chapter 11, "Style Management.")

Find/Change. Styles can vastly extend the power of InDesign's many Find/Change (Command/Ctrl-F) query options, but a search for text formatted with a particular character style will only deliver matches for manually applied instances of that style. Nested occurrences of the style are not found. (See Chapter 8, "Advanced Find/Change with Styles.")

RTF export. When exporting text (File > Export) from InDesign to the Rich Text Format (.rtf), InDesign's styles and their attributes (as many as are supported by the Rich Text Format) are also exported. If character styles are nested in a paragraph, the nested formatting is *not* preserved in the resulting RTF file. Interestingly, however, the character style *definitions* are exported to and available in the RTF document when it's opened in Microsoft Word. They must then be selected from the styles area of the Word document and reapplied to each instance in the exported file.

Running Header Text Variables based on a Character Style. When using the Text Variables feature to generate running headers that "pull in" text formatted with a specific character style, nested line styles and GREP styles are not recognized. This feature only recognizes standard nested styles and locally applied character styles. (See Chapter 9, "Generating Dynamic Content with Styles.")

Export for Dreamweaver. InDesign's HTML export feature (File > Export for Dreamweaver) does not recognize nested styles or GREP styles. Text formatted with manually applied character styles will be enclosed in `<span>` tags in the resulting HTML file, but no tagging will be added around text formatted via nested or GREP styles. Instead, the whole paragraph is marked only with a single `<p>` tag. (See Chapter 10, "Styles, CSS, and XML.")

Advanced Nesting Techniques

One of your jobs as designers is to impose order and structure on the text you're provided, making it easily digestible by your intended audience. But not all of that structure is 100 percent consistent, nor does it always conform to the easiest of nested style scenarios. However, there are ways to push the envelope in a nested style and establish complex formatting results that can be applied over and over with a single click.

NESTING AT THE END OF A PARAGRAPH

Typically, nesting occurs at the beginning of a paragraph and then gives way to the default formatting of the paragraph. But nesting can also occur anywhere within a paragraph or at the end of the paragraph. However, the end of a paragraph is harder to define than the beginning. These types of nesting situations require a bit more thought about which delimiters will successfully accomplish the desired formatting switch at the end of a paragraph.

When nesting occurs anywhere other than the beginning of a paragraph, you must start with the [None] option in the Character Style pull-down menu to delay the application of a nested character style until the appropriate delimiter is encountered. The [None] option actually means "no character style." When [None] is chosen, InDesign uses the default formatting of the paragraph style without modification.

Take for example a catalog containing product descriptions that each end with an item number (FIGURE 2.12). All item numbers must be in a different character style than the rest of the text. But just how many sentences make up each paragraph? The "through 1 sentence" delimiter would work only if all the descriptions were a single sentence. Even if the catalog initially comes to you with single-sentence descriptions, there's no telling what will happen in the editing process. You want to be prepared for the unexpected and build a nested style that's flexible enough to deal with one *or more* sentences.

Lightweight Denim Jeans

This breezy alternative to traditional blue jeans is perfect for warm summer days. A fashionable low-rise cut and classic five-pocket styling offer all the casual versatility of standard jeans with the comfort of a lightweight khaki. Available in both relaxed and traditional fit. ***Item #DL44968***

Boot-cut Stretch Jeans

A tapered leg makes for a flattering silhouette, and a touch of Lycra makes these fitted jeans feel as good as they look. Triple-washed for extra softness and comfort. ***Item #DS57865***

FIGURE 2.12 Two product listings, each made up of a different number of sentences, but both properly handling the nested item number style.

To automate a style switch in this instance, there must be a delimiter after the end of the description but before the start of the item number that triggers the style change. You could use an en dash or put the item number in parentheses, but there might be en dashes or parentheses in the description and InDesign will respond to the first trigger it finds. You shouldn't be forced to put in dashes and parentheses you don't want just to trigger a nested style change.

The solution should be invisible to the reader and guaranteed not to appear anywhere else in your text. A handful of special characters in InDesign fit this description nicely: white spaces, the right indent tab, and the End Nested Style character.

White spaces. InDesign includes 12 kinds of white spaces (FIGURE 2.13), not including the space you get when you press the spacebar. Beyond their intended use—to provide a range of spaces of varying widths—they're also great style triggers because they're invisible, and the odds are very slim that they'll appear anywhere within normal paragraph text. That makes them unobtrusive, unique, and therefore ideal as delimiters.

TIP
The flush space (^f) is a great hidden delimiter option. Flush spaces "expand" to fill any gap in a given line, but only when used in paragraphs formatted with the Justify All Lines option. If Justify All Lines is not in use, a flush space looks and behaves exactly like a normal spacebar space, making it a perfect delimiter.

FIGURE 2.13 A dozen white space characters are available by choosing Type > Insert White Space.

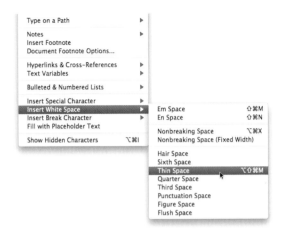

A few white space metacharacters supported in Find/Change and elsewhere are not recognized as nested style delimiters. Specific exceptions are the third space (^3), quarter space (^4), and sixth space (^%). These are ignored in the delimiter field when typed as metacharacters. However, the sixth space will work as a delimiter when copied and pasted from the layout into the delimiter field.

Right indent tab. The oh-so-useful right indent tab simultaneously positions text *and* acts as a unique nested style delimiter. Like white spaces, it's invisible and unlikely to be used anywhere else in a single paragraph. The right indent tab character aligns whatever follows it to the right edge of the column (FIGURE 2.14). It eliminates the need to physically set a right-aligned tab at the farthest edge of a column and keeps your formatting flexible because it will continue to adapt to any changes in the width of the column or frame, keeping any text that follows it aligned to the right edge. Insert a right indent tab in text by either pressing Shift-Tab or choosing Type > Insert Special Character > Other > Right Indent Tab. To designate a right indent tab character as a delimiter, type the metacharacter ^y in the delimiter field.

End Nested Style Character. When there's no other foolproof, consistent delimiter you can use to trigger a style change, the End Nested Style Character will get the job done. Because I love a nesting challenge, I try to use this as infrequently as possible because it means I've run out of any better options and I'll need to manually insert the End Nested Style Character in my text everywhere a nested style needs to change. Avoiding repetitive work is the goal of a style-based approach, so this is the last resort option. But sometimes, no matter how clever you are, there's no choice but to use this character to accomplish your formatting objectives.

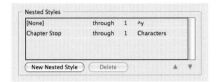

Within ten short minutes after we had opened fire, armed resistance was totally annihilated, the campaign was ended, we fifty-four were masters of England. Twenty-five thousand men lay dead around us.

But how treacherous is fortune! In a little while—say an hour—happened a thing, by my own fault, which—but I have no heart to write that. Let the record end here.   ❧

FIGURE 2.14 The right indent tab is used to align a story stop character at the end of this paragraph as well as change its formatting to the Chapter Stop character style.

To designate an End Nested Style Character as a nested style delimiter, choose End Nested Style Character from the delimiter menu (**FIGURE 2.15**), or type the metacharacter ^h into the delimiter field. Like white spaces and the right indent tab, this character is invisible. It is also a zero-width character. Most white spaces occupy a fixed amount of space, and the right indent tab and flush space occupy all the space between the text that precedes and follows them, but a zero-width character occupies no space. Other zero-width characters in InDesign include the anchored object marker, index marker, and cross reference marker.

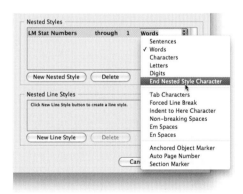

FIGURE 2.15 Completing a nested style instruction with the End Nested Style Character.

The End Nested Style Character is the best option for triggering style changes in situations where a nested style needs to be applied but the number of words, types of punctuation, and spacing in the text are so inconsistent that the varying conditions rule out any other option (**FIGURE 2.16**).

FIGURE 2.16 With no consistent structure to rely on in these paragraphs, each statistic switches styles via manually inserted End Nested Style Characters.

USING MULTIPLE DELIMITERS

For additional flexibility, you can specify several characters in the delimiter field as potential triggers for a nested style change (FIGURE 2.17). If you enter more than one character as a delimiter, *any* of them will cause the style formatting change. If you want the bold lead-in of a paragraph to switch back to the normal paragraph style after *either* a colon or any ending punctuation like a period, question mark, or exclamation point, you can type all those characters, one after another, in the delimiter field. Whichever character is encountered first will trigger the style change (FIGURE 2.18).

FIGURE 2.17 Multiple delimiter options in a Nested Styles instruction.

Through one period. That triggers the style change.

Through one colon: also gets the job done.

Through one em dash — works like a charm.

Through one ellipse…is recognized as well.

Through one question mark? Yes, that, too.

Through one exclamation point! All this from one style!

FIGURE 2.18 Style changes triggered by multiple delimiters.

InDesign also recognizes multiple metacharacters. If you want a nested style used through either a standard tab or a right indent tab (whichever comes first), the application recognizes ^t^y as a tab or a right indent tab. You can also combine standard characters and metacharacters as delimiters. For example, :^_ is interpreted as a colon or an em dash. Unfortunately, specific words or letter combinations cannot act as delimiters. You can't trigger a style change with an instruction such as "up to the word 'phone'." InDesign can't process this. The word phone in the delimiter field is read as "p *or* h *or* o *or* n *or* e, whichever comes first."

When none of these delimiters will do the job, it's time to break out the big guns and move up to a GREP style, which is discussed in the next chapter. GREP styles are more flexible and do not depend on any specific order or even specific words or letters to be invoked. However, their implementation is more complex, and there's a learning curve involved for those new to GREP.

REPEATING NESTED STYLES IN A LOOP

Prior to InDesign CS3, repeating a sequence of style changes within a paragraph meant setting up those steps multiple times. Every style, range, and delimiter option had to be added one by one in the rather small work area of the dialog. This made things particularly difficult if the number of required repetitions was uncertain. You would need to add more loops than might be needed in the longest-case scenario to ensure that the style would not "run out" of nesting instructions.

In CS3 and later, a sequence only needs to be set up once, and then followed by an instruction of "[Repeat] last 2 Styles" (or whatever the appropriate number for your purposes would be). InDesign continues to apply those styles over and over until it either runs out of matching criteria or reaches the end of the paragraph.

In FIGURE 2.19, the track numbers and names for a CD label run in one continuous paragraph rather than on separate lines. Each song title is preceded by the track number, which is formatted with a Track Numbers character style that uses a custom underline. Punctuation Spaces on either side of the track number

TIP

Multiple delimiters are similar to the logic going on behind the scenes when Sentences is chosen from the delimiter menu. A sentence is anything that ends in a period, question mark, or exclamation point, but InDesign is smart enough to know that closing quotation marks are considered part of a sentence, even though they appear after the ending punctuation mark. That's beyond the scope of any trigger you could set with a range of characters in the delimiter field.

serve two purposes: They complete the "boxed" effect around the numbers, and they serve as delimiters to trigger the change between the Track Numbers character style and the default paragraph style used for the song titles.

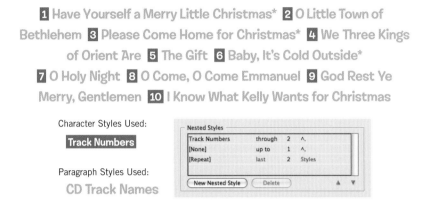

The sequence is Track Numbers *through 2 Punctuation Spaces (^.), and then [None]* (meaning the paragraph style with no changes) *up to 1 Punctuation Space*. The last setting is to *repeat those last 2 styles*, which handles the formatting for every remaining number and song title in the paragraph.

Nested Line Styles

A common typographic treatment in books and magazines is to use a particular style through the first few lines of text in a chapter or an article. Maintaining this formatting throughout the design process—while text is still being revised and column widths are subject to change—can be a chore. Nested style changes are triggered by specific characters. Since a line is not a character, criteria such as "through 3 lines" are not available via regular nesting. InDesign CS4 remedied that shortcoming with the addition of Nested Line Styles, which dynamically maintain a particular nested style through a specified number of lines (e.g., All Caps for 3 lines). As lines rewrap due to text edits or column width resizing, the nested line style automatically adapts to those changes (FIGURE 2.20).

Nested Line Styles work seamlessly in combination with Nested Styles, Drop Caps, and GREP styles, which can all exist within the same paragraph (FIGURE 2.21) provided they do not conflict with one another (see the sidebar "When Styles Collide").

IT WAS IN WARWICK CASTLE THAT I CAME ACROSS THE CURIOUS STRANGER WHOM I AM GOING TO TALK ABOUT. HE ATTRACTED ME BY THREE THINGS: his candid simplicity, his marvelous familiarity with ancient armor, and the restfulness of his company—for he did all the talking. We fell together, as modest people will, in the tail of the herd that was being shown through, and he at once began to say things which interested me. As he talked along, softly, pleasantly, flowingly, he seemed to drift away imperceptibly out of this world and time, and into some remote era and old forgotten country; and

IT WAS IN WARWICK CASTLE THAT I CAME ACROSS THE CURIOUS STRANGER WHOM I am going to talk about. He attracted me by three things: his candid simplicity, his marvelous familiarity with ancient armor, and the restfulness of his company—for he did all the talking. We fell together, as modest people will, in the tail of the herd that

FIGURE 2.20 A nested line style through three lines adapts to any column width.

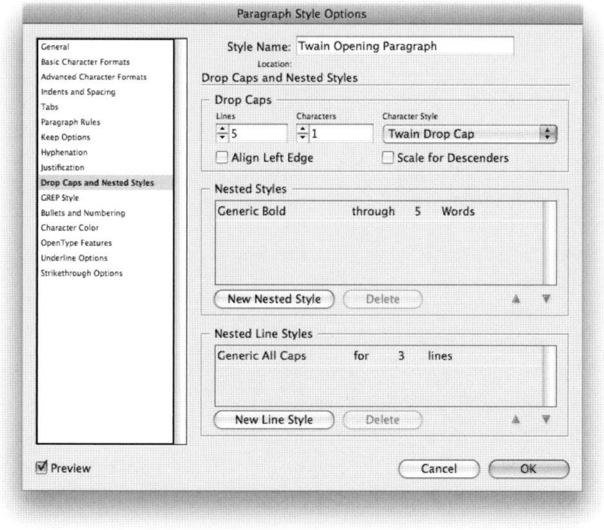

IT WAS IN WARWICK CASTLE THAT I CAME ACROSS THE CURIOUS STRANGER WHOM I AM GOING TO TALK ABOUT. HE ATTRACTED ME BY THREE THINGS: HIS CANDID SIMPLICITY, HIS MARVELOUS FAMILIARITY WITH ANCIENT ARMOR, AND THE RESTFULNESS OF HIS COMpany—for he did all the talking. We fell together, as modest people will, in the tail of the herd that was being shown through, and he at once began to say things which interested me. As he talked along, softly, pleasantly, flowingly, he seemed to drift away imperceptibly out of this world and time, and into some remote era and old forgotten country; and so he gradually wove such a spell about me that I seemed to move among the

FIGURE 2.21 Drop Caps, Nested Styles, and Nested Line Styles can be applied simultaneously to a single paragraph.

Setting up a nested line style is essentially the same as setting up a regular nested style. In the Nested Line Styles work area, select a character style to span a given number of lines. You can also set up multiple nested line styles in a specific sequence and repeat line styles just as you can with nested styles. For example, to alternate the formatting of every other line in a paragraph, set a style through 1 line, then another style through 1 line, and then repeat the last 2 lines with the [Repeat] option (FIGURE 2.22).

FIGURE 2.22 Two nested line styles set to repeat continuously.

I'm not quite sure why anyone would deliberately choose this kind of line style. It seems like a cruel trick to play on the reader, but this is an example of what you can do with multiple nested line styles using the Repeat option.

When Styles Collide

With lots of automatic formatting at work, there could be instances where the different settings for GREP styles, Nested Styles, and Nested Line Styles conflict with one another in a paragraph. You can set a drop cap to use a particular character style and span a certain number of letters and lines, and then set a nested style through the first word, add a nested line style through a given number of lines, and include a GREP style to handle text that matches a particular pattern. All these styles are designed to co-exist. If there are no clashes among the character styles, all styles will be applied properly. In other words, if a bold character style and an all caps character style overlap one another, both styles will be applied. The text will be both bold and set in all caps.

If, however, a nested style calls for all caps and a nested line style calls for small caps, or a GREP style calls for blue text and a nested style calls for red text, those are conflicts. To resolve these contradictory settings, InDesign follows a specific order for which styles it will honor first. GREP styles get top priority, Nested Style settings are obeyed next, and Nested Line Styles are applied last (or ignored first, depending on how you choose to look at it).

Paragraph Styles in Sequence: The Next Style Option

You've seen how customized sequences of nested character styles can be applied and repeated within a single paragraph style. Similar sequencing is also possible from paragraph to paragraph with the Next Style option, which provides one-click formatting for multiple paragraphs with different styles.

When a series of paragraph styles will follow one another in a consistent pattern, including a Next Style setting in each style instructs InDesign to change formatting to the next designated style after a paragraph break.

For example, if a newsletter story consistently starts with a headline, followed by a by-line, then a first paragraph with unique formatting, and then standard body copy, each of those four styles can contain instructions about which style follows it (FIGURE 2.23). When that text is flowed in one thread, you can apply all four styles in that specific order in a single step.

Headline Style
By-Line Style

INTRO PARAGRAPH STYLE USES a drop cap and nested line style for the first paragraph.

Body Copy style used through the remainder of the article because "Same Style" is chosen as the next style setting.

Every paragraph from this point on continues to use the Body Copy style...

Going With the Wind
by Joseph O'Reilly

DRIFTING AND DRAFTING ACROSS WYOMING'S EXPOSED HIGH plains with a kayak and bicycle atop your car, you learn quickly why poor aerodynamics and fuel consumption are a real drag. Recurring gusts, the occasional high-wind advisory sign, and all-too-frequent stops at the gas pump are constant reminders that, all things being equal, the "Equality State" and wind are inseparable.

For U.S. businesses moving cargo across the Great Plains, aerodynamic angst is markedly more refined than the barrels of diesel trucks hemorrhage in fuel-siphoning headwinds. Blowing snow, poor visibility, trailer-toppling squalls, and road closures are further indications that wind alone is a force to be reckoned with.

But as the monolithic turbines sprouting up from the remote, arid flats of the Foote Creek Rim and the more fertile foothills of Medicine Bow National Forest alternatively suggest, wind is a valuable commodity — and one that is harvested with increasing regularity.

FIGURE 2.23 Four styles applied in sequence using the Next Style option.

The Next Style setting is a pull-down menu located in the General area of the Paragraph Style Options dialog, just below the Based On pull-down menu (FIGURE 2.24). The menu contains all existing paragraph styles in the current document and a New Paragraph Style option if the style you need has not yet been created. Three other options are also in this menu: one that is very useful for sequencing styles (Same Style), one you'll *probably* never use (No Paragraph Style), and another you should definitely *not* use (Basic Paragraph). See the section "Establishing Relationships: Based-on Styles" later in this chapter for explanations of No Paragraph Style and Basic Paragraph.

TIP

If you know you'll be relying on Next Style settings, a handy time-saver is to start with the last style in the sequence, and then work backward. By doing so, the desired next style will already be available. If you start from the first style and then define all the successive styles, you'll have to go back into each previous style definition and select the newly created next style from the menu.

FIGURE 2.24 The Next Style menu in the General options area of the Paragraph Style Options dialog.

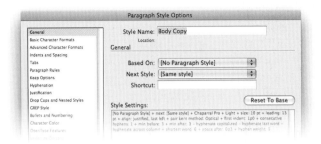

Choose Same Style, which is the default, if a style is used for many paragraphs in a row (body copy for instance). Each time a hard return is typed, the new paragraph picks up the style of the previous one. To designate a different next style for any paragraph style, select the name of an existing style from the Next Style pull-down menu (FIGURE 2.25) or use the New Paragraph Style option to create a style. In that situation, the style will switch to the designated next style when a hard return is typed.

FIGURE 2.25 An existing Intro Paragraph style assigned as the next style for an article by-line.

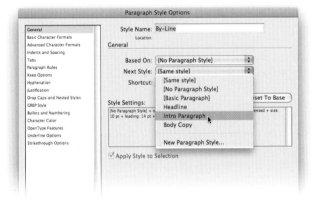

APPLYING STYLES IN SEQUENCE

To apply paragraph styles in sequence, select two or more paragraphs that include Next Style settings. In the Paragraph Style Options dialog, Control-click/right-click on the name of the *first* style in the sequence and choose the Apply "*Style Name*" then Next Style option from the context menu (FIGURE 2.26). All paragraphs will be formatted consecutively based on those Next Style settings.

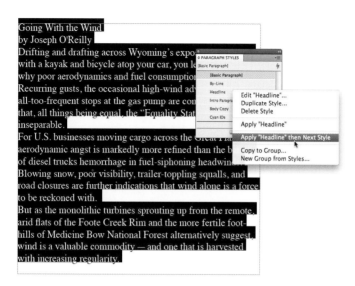

FIGURE 2.26 Applying multiple styles to multiple paragraphs.

If local overrides have been made or character styles have been applied manually to the selected text, the context menu will include these additional options (FIGURE 2.27):

- **Apply "*Style Name*" then Next Style, Clear Overrides** removes all local overrides in the selection with the exception of character styles applied manually.

- **Apply "*Style Name*" then Next Style, Clear Character Styles** does the opposite of the preceding option. Character styles are removed, but local overrides are preserved.

- **Apply "*Style Name*" then Next Style, Clear All** strips out all overrides and character styles, applying the chosen styles in their unmodified form.

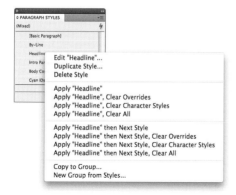

FIGURE 2.27 Additional options in the context menu when overrides or character styles are present in selected text.

REPEATING A SEQUENCE OF PARAGRAPH STYLES

In projects like catalogs or directories, where a series of paragraph styles repeats in a consistent sequence, you can boost efficiency by setting up a formatting loop. To make this work, modify the *last* style used in the sequence so that its Next Style setting calls on the *first* style in the sequence. The entire formatting routine is then applied continuously until InDesign runs out of paragraphs to which it can apply styles.

In FIGURE 2.28, the Product Name style has a Next Style setting of Product Manufacturer. That style has a Next Style setting of Product Platform. Product Platform has a Next Style setting of Product Description, which has a Next Style setting of Product URL. That ends the sequence of five paragraphs that make up each product entry. The Product URL style's next style is set to Product Name (the first style in the sequence), which starts the formatting pattern all over again.

FIGURE 2.28 A Next Style sequence repeats when the last paragraph style calls on the first paragraph style to start the pattern again.

ScreenFlow

Telestream	Nevada City, CA

PLATFORM: Mac OSX Leopard 10.5 or later
Quickly captures screen activity and both internal or external audio for screencasts and demos. Simple interface allows for transitions, zooms, and screen highlighting. Multiple export formats.

www.telestream.net

BBEdit 9

Bare Bones Software	Bedford, MA

PLATFORM: Mac OSX 10.4 or later (Universal Binary)
Award-winning product provides an abundance of features for editing, searching, and manipulation of text and professional-level HTML editing. Includes GREP pattern searching, save to FTP, and scripting support.

www.barebones.com

FileMaker Pro 10

FileMaker, Inc.	Santa Clara, CA

PLATFORM: Mac OSX 10.4.11 or later; Windows Vista Ultimate, Bussiness & Home; Windows XP Professional and Home Edition
Easy-to-use database software helps you manage people, projects, assets and more. Intuitive point-and-click interface helps you customize solutions and share them with ease. Robust reporting and data export features.

www.filemaker.com

NOTE

Useful as the Next Style type of paragraph sequencing is, it relies on 100 percent consistency in the number of paragraphs in each sequence. Any missing or extra paragraphs will cause a cascade of incorrectly applied styles. Another caveat is that no style in the sequence can use "Same Style" as its Next Style setting if you intend to repeat the style sequence. Once "Same Style" is encountered, that style is applied through the remainder of the selection.

Establishing Relationships: Based-on Styles

Paragraph and character styles can be connected in ways other than sequentially. Any paragraph or character style can be based on another style, so that changes to one "parent" style cascade down through all variations of it, yet any unique attributes applied to those "child" styles—a change in color, case, or size, for example—are preserved.

This is extraordinarily useful in long documents where different paragraph styles may be offshoots of the main body copy, such as an opening paragraph with a drop cap or bulleted and numbered lists. Each variation relies on common attributes handed down from the parent body copy style. For this reason, it's best to create and fine-tune your parent style first, and then define any child styles you want based on it.

FIGURE 2.29 shows some fairly common parent-child styles relationships. The column on the left is the parent that's used for the majority of the text. The column on the right includes three child styles based on that body copy style including an introductory paragraph that eliminates the first line indent but includes a drop cap, a bulleted list, and a numbered list with a bold run-in first sentence.

Icaectum seque ma dolent vendi tota et, unt magnatem res quibuscipis vollabo reribus sit fuga. Itatis nos alibus molorem etustrum ides peritatis re prae neturem faccatemquo berspid ulliquas aspere, tenihitatias dolorae.

Que del modi renecumque que nienime cor sende volorem quatend untiberiti officaes ent plabo. Tibus eum, qui accumenem invellu ptatur aceptus maiorpor rem velist velit, nimenis itionse porunt, sitatin cimusapedi re pro te nobiscit dit, sinullor sam, comnimodi tempost, sedit volor aute.

Seque ma dolent vendi tota et, unt magnatem res quibuscipis vollabo reribus sit fuga. Itatis nos alibus molorem etustrum ides peritatis re prae neturem faccatemquo berspid ulliquas aspere, tenihitatias dolorae. Que del modi renecumque que nienime cor sende volorem quatend untiberiti officaes ent plabo.

- Tibus eum, qui accumenem invellu ptatur aceptus maiorpor rem velist velit, nimenis itionse porunt, sitatin cimusapedi

- Nobiscit dit, sinullor sam, comnimodi tempost, sedit volor aute volessitem aut autem inctiam que autectam quo dolorepudi soluptium

1. **Imiliti busant volupta si soloritatem lam fuga.** Nam quodi conempo rectotat iditatatur aliquas piduscia nam reius ea dolorpore eos est, sinumquodis.

2. **Maximi, suntios es voluptatusae.** Velic te eum quam utat enia culpa dolor ate qui re plabore consequid molupta abo.

FIGURE 2.29 A body copy style (left column) and some child styles based on it (right column).

FIGURE 2.30 shows those same paragraphs after the typeface, font size, and leading were changed *only* in the body copy style. The changes have been passed down to the child styles, but no unique settings—drop cap, bullet formatting, nested styles, or indents—have changed.

Icaectum seque ma dolent vendi tota et, unt magnatem res quibuscipis vollabo reribus sit fuga. Itatis nos alibus molorem etustrum ides peritatis re prae neturem faccatemquo berspid ulliquas aspere, tenihitatias dolorae.

Que del modi renecumque que nienime cor sende volorem quatend untiberiti officaes ent plabo. Tibus eum, qui accumenem invellu ptatur aceptus maiorpor rem velist velit, nimenis itionse porunt, sitatin cimusapedi re pro te nobiscit dit, sinullor sam, comnimodi tempost, sedit volor aute.

Seque ma dolent vendi tota et, unt magnatem res quibuscipis vollabo reribus sit fuga. Itatis nos alibus molorem etustrum ides peritatis re prae neturem faccatemquo berspid ulliquas aspere, tenihitatias dolorae. Que del modi renecumque que nienime cor sende volorem quatend untiberiti officaes ent plabo.

■ Tibus eum, qui accumenem invellu ptatur aceptus maiorpor rem velist velit, nimenis itionse porunt, sitatin cimusapedi

■ Nobiscit dit, sinullor sam, comnimodi tempost, sedit volor aute volessitem aut autem inctiam que autectam quo dolorepudi soluptium

1. **Imiliti busant volupta si soloritatem lam fuga.** Nam quodi conempo rectotat iditatatur aliquas piduscia nam reius ea dolorpore eos est, sinumquodis.

2. **Maximi, suntios es voluptatusae.** Velic te eum quam utat enia culpa dolor ate qui re plabore consequid molupta abo.

FIGURE 2.30 Changes applied to the formatting of the body copy style (left column) are passed down to all styles based on it (right column).

InDesign only looks at the *differences* between the parent and the child style. A comparison of the two occurs at all times. Those differences are indicated in the Style Settings box at the bottom of the General options in the Paragraph Style Options dialog (FIGURE 2.31). The parent style is identified by name, followed by the details of each specific attribute that's unique to the child style. Any attributes indicated with plus signs following the parent style name are unique to the child style and will be immune from any parent style changes.

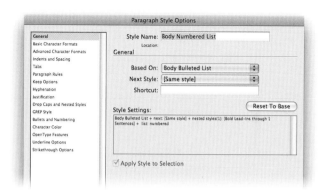

FIGURE 2.31 The Style Settings box lists any deviations from the parent style attribute by attribute.

BASING ONE STYLE ON ANOTHER

To base a paragraph or character style on an existing style, create a new style and choose the desired parent style from the Based On pull-down menu. All styles in your current document are available in the Based On pull-down menu along with two other options: Basic Paragraph and No Paragraph Style.

Basic Paragraph. This is InDesign's default setting, which is typically Times Roman. You should never use this, not just because Times Roman is a ubiquitous and unimaginative typeface, but for all the reasons detailed in the sidebar "The Dangers of the Basic Paragraph Style."

No Paragraph Style. Usually, the attributes of No Paragraph Style are the same as Basic Paragraph but are not associated with the Basic Paragraph style. No Paragraph Style is automatically selected for new paragraph styles unless your cursor is already within text to which a paragraph style is applied. In that case, InDesign assumes you intend to make your new style a child of the current style, so it automatically selects the current style in the Based On menu. Keep an eye out for this as you create new styles. You may want to pick up the selected formatting but not necessarily link your new style to the existing one.

Once you've selected your base style, simply modify any attribute—size, color, leading, and so on—within the new style and save it.

RESETTING A STYLE TO ITS BASE

All text styles—even [Basic Paragraph]—are based on *some* other style, whether or not you specifically make a choice from the Based On menu. By default, new paragraph styles are based on [No Paragraph Style] and new character styles are based on [None].

The Dangers of the Basic Paragraph Style

Every InDesign document contains a style called Basic Paragraph that can be modified but not deleted. On the Mac platform, that style is defined as Times Regular, 12 points, with automatic leading. While it's *possible* to redefine that style with other formatting that you prefer, I strongly recommend against doing so. All InDesign users should beware of relying on Basic Paragraph in any way.

The inherent problem with Basic Paragraph is that every InDesign document includes it. However, there's no guarantee that *your* document's modified Basic Paragraph style matches either the out-of-the-box InDesign default or the Basic Paragraph style defined (or, perhaps, redefined) on someone else's computer. If you apply Basic Paragraph, modify it to your liking, or base any styles in your document on it, your chances of encountering a style conflict between documents become quite high. When copying and pasting from document to document, the incoming text is reformatted to match the definition of the style in the destination document if any styles have the same name. Since Basic Paragraph exists in *every* InDesign document, your modified version of that style—and any incoming styles based on it—will change. It is, quite literally, an accident waiting to happen.

I recommend adhering to these two rules:

- Pretend Basic Paragraph isn't even an option and always start with new, uniquely named styles of your own.

- When creating Paragraph Styles, be sure that [Basic Paragraph] is not selected from the Based On menu in the General options of the New Paragraph Style dialog. Instead, stick with InDesign's default [No Paragraph Style] option unless you have specific paragraph styles from which you want to produce slight variations.

InDesign considers the "base" style to be whatever the *current* style is based on, even if that style is itself based on another style. The Reset to Base button in the General area of the Paragraph Style Options dialog removes all unique attributes from a style based on another style, but it only resets a style one level back. In other words, if a numbered list style is based on a bulleted list style, which in turn is based on a body copy style (**FIGURES 2.32** and **2.33**), clicking Reset To Base in the numbered list's style options reverts its appearance only as far back as the bulleted list style. It does not reset all the way back to the body copy style.

Seque ma dolent vendi tota et, unt magnatem res quibuscipis vollabo reribus sit fuga. Itatis nos alibus molorem etustrum ides peritatis re prae neturem faccatemquo berspid ulliquas aspere, tenihitatias dolorae. Que del modi renecumque que nienime cor sende volorem quatend untiberiti officaes ent plabo.

Icaectum seque ma dolent vendi tota et, unt magnatem res quibuscipis vollabo reribus sit fuga. Itatis nos alibus molorem etustrum ides peritatis re prae neturem faccatemquo berspid ulliquas aspere, tenihitatias dolorae.

- Tibus eum, qui accumenem invellu ptatur aceptus maiorpor rem velist velit, nimenis itionse porunt, sitatin cimusapedi

- Nobiscit dit, sinullor sam, comnimodi tempost, sedit volor aute volessitem aut autem inctiam que autectam quo dolorepudi soluptium

1. **Imiliti busant volupta si soloritatem lam fuga.** Nam quodi conempo rectotat iditatatur aliquas piduscia nam reius ea dolorpore eos est, sinumquodis.

2. **Maximi, suntios es voluptatusae.** Velic te eum quam utat enia culpa dolor ate qui re plabore consequid molupta abo.

Style: Body Intro
(based on Default Body Copy)

Style: Default Body Copy

Style: Body Bulleted List
(based on Default Body Copy)

Style: Body Numbered List
(based on Body Bulleted List)

FIGURE 2.32 The first paragraph with the drop cap is based on the body copy style in the second paragraph.

Seque ma dolent vendi tota et, unt magnatem res quibuscipis vollabo reribus sit fuga. Itatis nos alibus molorem etustrum ides peritatis re prae neturem faccatemquo berspid ulliquas aspere, tenihitatias dolorae. Que del modi renecumque que nienime cor sende volorem quatend untiberiti officaes ent plabo.

Icaectum seque ma dolent vendi tota et, unt magnatem res quibuscipis vollabo reribus sit fuga. Itatis nos alibus molorem etustrum ides peritatis re prae neturem faccatemquo berspid ulliquas aspere, tenihitatias dolorae.

- Tibus eum, qui accumenem invellu ptatur aceptus maiorpor rem velist velit, nimenis itionse porunt, sitatin cimusapedi

- Nobiscit dit, sinullor sam, comnimodi tempost, sedit volor aute volessitem aut autem inctiam que autectam quo dolorepudi soluptium

1. **Imiliti busant volupta si soloritatem lam fuga.** Nam quodi conempo rectotat iditatatur aliquas piduscia nam reius ea dolorpore eos est, sinumquodis.

2. **Maximi, suntios es voluptatusae.** Velic te eum quam utat enia culpa dolor ate qui re plabore consequid molupta abo.

FIGURE 2.33 When the first paragraph is reset to the base style, it loses all unique formatting and looks identical to the body copy in the second paragraph.

However, clicking Reset To Base on the body copy style (the style on which the two list styles are based) will strip out all formatting on the body copy that doesn't conform to [No Paragraph Style], and *that* formatting change will radiate out to the two list styles based on it (FIGURE 2.34).

FIGURE 2.34 When the body copy style is reset to base, it takes on the appearance of [No Paragraph Style]. All styles based on the body copy style—the intro paragraph, bulleted list, and numbered list—inherit that change.

Seque ma dolent vendi tota et, unt magnatem res quibuscipis vollabo reribus sit fuga. Itatis nos alibus molorem etustrum ides peritatis re prae neturem faccatemquo berspid ulliquas aspere, tenihitatias dolorae. Que del modi renecumque que nienime cor sende volorem quatend untiberiti officaes ent plabo. Icaectum seque ma dolent vendi tota et, unt magnatem res quibuscipis vollabo reribus sit fuga. Itatis nos alibus molorem etustrum ides peritatis re prae neturem faccatemquo berspid ulliquas aspere, tenihitatias dolorae.

■ Tibus eum, qui accumenem invellu ptatur aceptus maiorpor rem velist velit, nimenis itionse porunt, sitatin cimusapedi

■ Nobiscit dit, sinullor sam, comnimodi tempost, sedit volor aute volessitem aut autem inctiam que autectam quo dolorepudi soluptium

1. **Imiliti busant volupta si soloritatem lam fuga.** Nam quodi conempo rectotat iditatatur aliquas piduscia nam reius ea dolorpore eos est, sinumquodis.

2. **Maximi, suntios es voluptatusae.** Velic te eum quam utat enia culpa dolor ate qui re plabore consequid molupta abo.

CHAPTER 3

Automatic Styling with GREP

WHEN GREP WAS ADDED to Find/Change in InDesign CS3, an unprecedented level of text processing and manipulation became part of the application. In CS4, that power can now be built directly into a paragraph with GREP styles.

GREP (General Regular Expression Parser) is a means of *describing* text—or patterns and conditions within text—and it need not include one word or character of *actual* text. GREP's origins are in computer programming, a world that most designers find cryptic and off-putting. But GREP is not as formidable as it may initially seem, and once you understand its potential, any resistance you may have toward learning it will rapidly disappear.

GREP has historically been used for powerful search-and-replace operations. A standard, text-only find/change query looks for exact text and replaces it with other exact text (find every instance of "dog" and replace it with "cat," for example). A single GREP query, on the other hand, can search for every instance of "dog *or* cat *or* hamster *or* parakeet" and replace them all with "pet" in one step. That's an example of a conditional search. "Or" is a condition—this *or* that *or* another thing *or* something else. The ability to analyze text in this manner is called parsing.

Primarily, GREP parses text for patterns, and that's where its usefulness as style criteria really comes into play. Consider how you would describe a paragraph. One possible description could be *the beginning of a line, followed by an unspecified number of characters up to the end of a line.* That's a pattern, and patterns are everywhere. After you've used GREP a few times, you'll start to see patterns where you never noticed them before.

GREP Styles vs. Nested Styles

Nested styles, as powerful as they are, apply character styles in a very precise order, and a specific delimiter must trigger the style change (this style through one colon, then another style through one sentence, and so on). GREP styles have no such limits. They make style changes based on matching *patterns* within your text. The specific *words* that make up that pattern don't matter, and it makes no difference to GREP styles where or in what order those patterns appear. They require no unique triggers, and they can apply the desired character style as many times as necessary within a paragraph without a "repeat" instruction.

Chapter 2, "Nesting and Sequencing Styles," mentioned that nested styles can't be triggered by or attached to a specific word. If you put the word "phone" in the nested styles delimiter field, it's interpreted as "p *or* h *or* o *or* n *or* e, whichever comes first." A GREP style, however, *can* automatically format a specific word or group of words with a character style regardless of where or how many times it appears in your text. And that's the simplest example of what a GREP style can do that a nested style can't.

The main advantage of GREP styles is that they're at work *all the time*—looking for patterns in the background so you don't have to. If new text that matches your pattern is added to a paragraph with a GREP style applied, it is formatted automatically.

So, how are GREP styles built? How are patterns and conditions described? What instructions ensure that text is parsed for the desired results? All of this GREP magic is accomplished through special characters (or combinations of characters) called metacharacters.

Metacharacters

You've probably seen metacharacters many times when using special characters in a text search or nested style instruction in InDesign. For instance, to indicate a right-align tab as a nested style delimiter you must use the ^y metacharacter. The combination of the two characters *describes* a right-align tab. This is InDesign's metacharacter convention. All InDesign metacharacters begin with a caret (^), so a tab is represented as ^t, a paragraph return as ^p, and a soft return as ^n, just to name a few.

WHAT MAKES A GREP METACHARACTER?

GREP metacharacters are expressed differently than InDesign metacharacters. GREP was around long before InDesign, and its established syntax uses a backslash to define metacharacters. In a GREP expression, a tab is represented as \t, a paragraph return as \r, and a soft return as \n.

However, there are a great many characters unique to InDesign that GREP was never intended to deal with. Anchored object markers, flush spaces, and current page number markers are just a few examples. These InDesign-specific characters are described by metacharacters that begin with a tilde (~). So in a GREP expression, ~= describes an en dash, ~f describes a flush space, and ~N describes a current page number character.

While most metacharacters are made up of two or more characters, some are composed of only one character. For example, a period in a GREP expression means "any character other than a hard return." If you need to include an *actual* period as part of a GREP expression, you must "escape out" the period by adding a backslash before it (\.). Similarly, since backslashes typically *start* a GREP metacharacter, you also need to escape out a backslash (\\) if you want to include a *literal* backslash in a GREP expression.

This can seem a bit confusing at first, since the same character that makes a normal character into a metacharacter is also used to make a metacharacter into a normal character.

Alphanumeric characters (a–z, A–Z, 0–9) in a GREP expression match themselves exactly. There's no need to pair them with backslashes or any other metacharacter syntax.

TABLE 3.1 lists all *single-character* metacharacters, their GREP meaning, and how to match them literally, if necessary.

TABLE 3.1 **Single-character Metacharacters**

Metacharacter	Type	What It Matches	To Find the Actual Character
. period	Wildcard	Any character (except a hard return)	\.
^ caret	Location	Beginning of paragraph	\^
$ dollar sign	Location	End of paragraph	\$
? question mark	Repeat	Zero or one time	\?
* asterisk	Repeat	Zero or more times	*
+ plus sign	Repeat	One or more times	\+
| vertical divider	Match	Or	\\|
(opening parenthesis	Match	Begin marking subexpression	\(
) closing parenthesis	Match	End marking subexpression	\)
[opening square bracket	Match	Begin character set definition	\[
] closing square bracket	Match	End character set definition	\]

Every nonalphanumeric character in InDesign has a corresponding metacharacter, and there are several types of metacharacters totally unrelated to specific characters that perform a number of different functions. Some describe the location of text (the beginning of a line or the end of a line, for example), how often something repeats (one or more times, exactly three times, etc.), conditions like "Or" (this *or* that), and whether or not the text being described appears within a certain context (*only if preceded by* this or *only if not followed by* that).

Full descriptions of each metacharacter type follow in the next section, and every one of them will be used in specific examples later in the chapter, so you can see them all in context.

METACHARACTER TYPES

The metacharacter types are grouped into submenus in the Special Characters for Search menu, which is located at the end of the To Text field in the GREP Style area of the Paragraph Style Options dialog (FIGURE 3.1). The first 11 options in that menu (from Tab through the Other submenu) provide access to metacharacters for specific characters like punctuation, bullets, and dashes, as well as unique InDesign metacharacters like variables, markers, and white spaces. The remaining metacharacter types in this menu (from Wildcards through Posix) are where the real power of GREP styles lies.

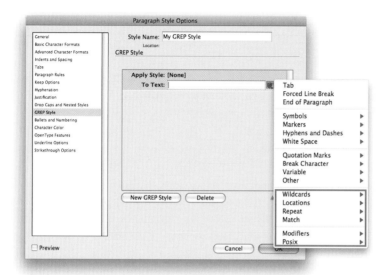

FIGURE 3.1 The most powerful and GREP-specific metacharacters are located in the last two groups (starting with Wildcards) in the Special Characters for Search menu.

Wildcards

The simplest of the metacharacter types is the wildcard. Examples of wildcards are any character (.), any digit (\d), or any white space (\s). TABLE 3.2 lists all wildcard metacharacters and what they match.

TABLE 3.2 **Wildcard Metacharacters**

Metacharacter	What It Matches
\d	Any digit
[\l\u]	Any letter (this is, technically, a character class made up of any uppercase or lowercase character)
.	Any character (except a hard return)
\s	Any white space (all spaces, including custom InDesign white spaces, tabs, forced line breaks, and paragraph returns)
\w	Any word character (including uppercase and lowercase letters, the digits 0–9, and the underscore character)
\u	Any uppercase letter
\l	Any lowercase letter
\d	Any digit

InDesign's basic Find/Change operation for text and the delimiter menu for Nested Styles include *some* wildcards, but they describe only one instance of what they represent, so "any digit" or "through 1 digit" will work for 0 through 9 but not for multidigit numbers like 10 or 100. To find two digits requires using two "any digit" metacharacters in Find/Change or specifying an exact number for a nested style. When that's done, 10 will be found, but 1 and 100 will not. This proves very limiting very quickly.

Technically, GREP wildcards also describe a single instance of a type of character, but they can be paired with repeat metacharacters to define repetition in very specific or very powerful and flexible ways.

Repeat metacharacters

Repeat metacharacters control how many or how few times a character occurs in the text being parsed. Examples of repeat metacharacters are zero or one time (?), zero or more times (*), and one or more times (+). Combined with wildcards, repeat metacharacters form the foundation of common and useful GREP expressions such as *any character one or more times* (.+), *any digit zero or more times* (\d*), or *any white space character zero or one time* (\s?).

Repetition can be as general as the preceding examples or controlled more precisely by quantifying the number of matches with specific numeric ranges surrounded by curly brackets ({ }). For instance, \d{3} refers to *any three digits in a row* and \d{3,6} means *at least three digits in a row but no more than six digits in a row*. TABLE 3.3 lists all repeat metacharacters and what they define.

TABLE 3.3. **Repeat Metacharacters**

Metacharacter	What It Defines
?	Zero or one time
*	Zero or more times
+	One or more times
??	Zero or one time (shortest match)
*?	Zero or more times (shortest match)
+?	One or more times (shortest match)
{3}	A specific number (in this case, 3)*
{2,4}	A minimum and maximum range (at least 2 but no more than 4, as shown here)*

* This option does not appear in the Special Characters for Search menu. The exact number or numeric range must be typed between curly brackets directly into the To Text field.

Wrapping Your Head Around Zero

You may be asking, why on Earth would I want to find something that occurs *zero* times? The zero or one time and zero or more times repeat metacharacters serve a very useful purpose. They allow for the possibility that something *may* (one time or more times) *or may not* (zero times) be there.

Not all the patterns you define will be simple and consistent. GREP expressions can account for potential inconsistencies with this *may or may not be there* concept. If your GREP style is set up to look for any digit zero or more times, you can consider of this as instructing InDesign as such: "If you find one or more digits, that's great! But if you don't, that's OK, too. I know some of the text being parsed is inconsistent."

When it comes to repetition, GREP expressions will always try to make the longest possible match. For example, if you're using GREP to describe any text that's enclosed in parentheses, you might describe it as *an opening parenthesis, followed by any one or more characters, followed by a closing parenthesis.* In GREP terms, that would look like this: \(.+\). Notice that the parentheses have been "escaped out" with backslashes because the actual parenthesis character is a GREP metacharacter with a specific meaning.

Unfortunately, the criterion *any one or more characters* (.+) includes the parenthesis character, so if there is more than one piece of information in the paragraph that's enclosed in parentheses, the expression \(.+\) will match *everything* from the very first opening parenthesis to the very last closing parenthesis in the paragraph and everything in between (**FIGURE 3.2**). To prevent this, the "shortest match" limiter (?) must be added to the pattern just before the closing parenthesis, changing the meaning of the search to: *an opening parenthesis, followed by any one or more characters and stopping at the first closing parenthesis found.*

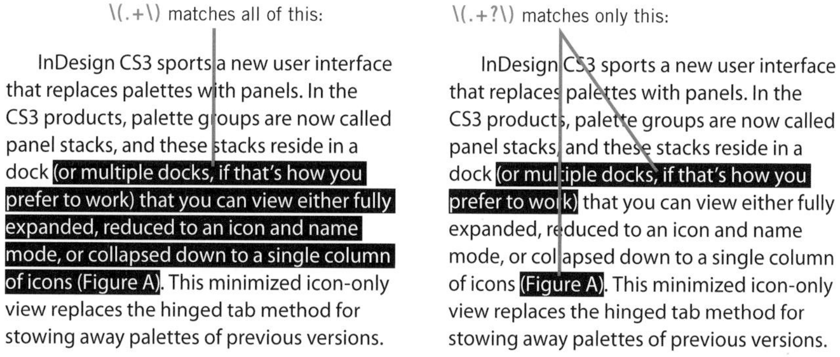

\(.+\) matches all of this:

InDesign CS3 sports a new user interface that replaces palettes with panels. In the CS3 products, palette groups are now called panel stacks, and these stacks reside in a dock (or multiple docks, if that's how you prefer to work) that you can view either fully expanded, reduced to an icon and name mode, or collapsed down to a single column of icons (Figure A). This minimized icon-only view replaces the hinged tab method for stowing away palettes of previous versions.

\(.+?\) matches only this:

InDesign CS3 sports a new user interface that replaces palettes with panels. In the CS3 products, palette groups are now called panel stacks, and these stacks reside in a dock (or multiple docks, if that's how you prefer to work) that you can view either fully expanded, reduced to an icon and name mode, or collapsed down to a single column of icons (Figure A). This minimized icon-only view replaces the hinged tab method for stowing away palettes of previous versions.

FIGURE 3.2 A "greedy" GREP expression (left) is reined in by the shortest match limiter (right).

Location metacharacters

GREP expressions not only describe characters and how many of them to match, but they can also refer to a location such as the beginning of a word (\<), beginning of a paragraph (^), end of a word (\>), end of a paragraph ($), or a word boundary (\b). Here again, combining these metacharacters with others makes search queries even more specific and powerful. For instance, the query ^\d+?\. describes *any one or more digits* (\d+?) *at the beginning of a paragraph* (^), *followed by a period* (\.).

Location metacharacters help fine-tune a GREP pattern when the description of the text to be found might occur several places in a paragraph, but your goal is to only apply a GREP style to the matching text in a specific part of that paragraph.

It's important to note that none of these location metacharacters find an actual character in the text they are searching. They match a zero-width *position* at the desired location. Think of these zero-width positions as the space the cursor occupies when you're working with text. When the cursor is at the beginning of a word, it's occupying a space between the first character in that word and whatever precedes it. That same principle applies to all location metacharacters.

Beginning of word (\<). This is *not* the first character in a word. It's the position between the first character in a word and any nonword character (a space, punctuation mark, or the start of a new line) that precedes it.

End of word (\>). Similarly, this is not the *last* character in a word but the position after that character and before any nonword character that follows it.

TIP
A useful but undocumented location metacharacter doesn't appear in the Special Characters for Search menu: the End of Story metacharacter (\Z). This metacharacter finds the very last position in an InDesign story (a single, unthreaded text frame or any number of threaded text frames).

Word boundary (\b). This is another, more general, way of referring to that zero-width position *between* a word character and a nonword character, but it can be used interchangeably for either the beginning or end of a word. When you do a Find/Change operation and turn on the Whole Word option, a word boundary character is added at the beginning and end of whatever you're searching for.

Beginning of paragraph (^). Whether your paragraph is one line or dozens of lines, this metacharacter defines the position just before the first character in it.

End of paragraph ($). This is the position *after* the last character in any paragraph but before the return (if there is one).

Match criteria

Greater specificity can be built into GREP styles with match metacharacters, which establish a custom range of valid matching characters, define required conditions, or isolate portions of an overall pattern as smaller subpatterns.

Marking subexpression (( )). Wrapping text or metacharacters within parentheses has a very significant function in GREP. It defines (or marks) what's within the parentheses as a subexpression, also known as a subpattern. Marking portions of a regular expression as a subexpression allows that subexpression to be remembered and recalled for later use. This is profoundly useful in Find/Change operations but less so in GREP styles. GREP styles only *format* what matches the expression; they can't change the text any other way.

However, subexpressions also "group" parts of a pattern so that they may be considered as a whole that must appear together, as you'll see in the examples later in this chapter.

Nonmarking subexpression ((?:)). Nonmarking subexpressions are a useful way to isolate portions of a pattern, but they are not remembered and cannot be called on in a Find/Change operation. Their use in GREP styles is therefore quite limited.

Character set ([ ]). Character sets, also called character classes, are ranges or groups of characters to be matched. Any characters that appear within square brackets are part of the character set, so `[aeiou]` translates as "any vowel" when built into a regular expression. Character sets can be defined in several ways. In addition to specific letters (like the vowel example), *ranges* of characters can be defined. A character set for all digits from 0 to 5 could be represented as `[012345]` or more efficiently as `[0-5]`. Other ranges might include `[a-zA-Z]`, which represents any uppercase or lowercase letter.

TIP
The ability to define ranges using a dash requires a bit of caution when trying to include an *actual* dash in a character set. To guarantee that a dash will be recognized as just a dash, it should be the very first character in the character set immediately following the opening square bracket.

Other metacharacters can be part of a character class as well. In fact, the *any uppercase or lowercase letter* example just mentioned can be expressed more efficiently as `[\l\u]` using the any lowercase letter and any uppercase letter wildcards instead of actual letters. However, the brackets that define a character set act like kryptonite on some metacharacters, causing them to lose their special powers. When a period is used in a regular expression, it means *any character*, but when a period is used within a character set, it just means a period. The same holds true for question marks, asterisks, and other single-character metacharacters. Unfortunately, putting a backslash before these characters in a character set does not restore their wildcard status. It just includes the backslash in the character set.

Or (|). The vertical divider character establishes the "Or" condition between what precedes and follows it. For example, the GREP query for finding the words dog *or* cat *or* goldfish *or* parakeet would be

```
\<cat\>|\<dog\>|\<parakeet\>|\<goldfish\>
```

Only the | metacharacter is *required* to establish the "Or" condition, but notice that before each word in the query is a beginning of word metacharacter (\<)

and following each is an end of word metacharacter (\>). This additional location metacharacter prevents the parser from accidentally finding "cat" in a word like "location" or "dog" in "boondoggle." It could probably be left out for parakeet and goldfish, but why take the chance?

Positive lookbehind ((?<=*something*)). This cryptically named match criterion means *only if the match is preceded by* something in particular. The expression must look behind (or, more accurately, before) the matching text to verify that what's defined after the equal sign is present. If it's not, the match is disqualified. The positive lookbehind statement must be placed *before* the text to be matched in the GREP pattern.

Positive lookahead ((?=*something*)). This performs a function similar to positive lookbehind but looks *ahead* of the matching text to make sure it's *followed by* whatever is defined after the equal sign. The lookahead criteria must be present or the match is disqualified. The positive lookahead statement must be placed *after* the text to be matched in the GREP pattern.

For example, if you want a character style applied to all the figure references in a book that appear within parentheses but don't want the style applied to the parentheses, you would create a GREP style that finds *any one or more characters, but only if there's an opening parenthesis before them, and a closing parenthesis after them.* The full search query would look like this:

```
(?<=\().+?(?=\))
```

Note that the opening and closing parentheses in the lookahead and lookbehind expression are escaped out with backslashes (\(and \), respectively) because parentheses are specific GREP metacharacters. Also, the expression representing *any one or more characters* within the parentheses (.+?) uses the shortest match metacharacter (?) to avoid the problem illustrated in Figure 3.2.

Negative lookbehind ((?<!*something*)). As its name suggests, negative lookbehind means only if the match is *not* preceded by something in particular.

Negative lookahead ((?!*something*)). Similarly, negative lookahead means only if the match is *not* followed by something in particular.

Modifiers

Modifiers change the rules that apply to a GREP expression or portion of that expression. By default, all GREP operations in InDesign are case sensitive. If however, your pattern requires both uppercase and lowercase characters to be considered matches, start your expression with the Case-insensitive On ((?i)) modifier, which turns off case sensitivity for the entire pattern. If you need only a *portion* of a pattern to be case insensitive, place the Case-insensitive On metacharacter before that specific part of the expression, and then add the Case-insensitive Off metacharacter ((?-i)) at the point where you want case sensitivity to resume.

The Multiline and Single-line modifiers apply to Find/Change operations across multiple paragraphs. Since a GREP style only parses text one paragraph at a time, these options are not relevant to GREP styles.

Posix

Posix classes are an alternate means of defining character sets that, interestingly, must appear *within* a character set (in other words, within square brackets). For example, the Posix-style character class [[:alnum:]], which includes any alphanumeric character, is the same as the character set [a-zA-Z0-9]. Most Posix character classes duplicate options available with regular character sets.

Posix support is included in InDesign to make the application's GREP options consistent with established GREP standards, but I have yet to find a use for them. To keep an already complex subject as simple as possible, Posix will not factor into any GREP style definitions in this chapter.

Special Characters for Search Menu Caution

At the end of each To Text field in the GREP Style work area is the same Special Characters for Search icon found in the GREP tab of the Find/Change box. Clicking the icon opens a menu containing more than 100 GREP metacharacters grouped by type. When selected from the menu, the metacharacters are inserted automatically in the field. This is an enormously helpful way to construct GREP expressions piece by piece without having to memorize numerous cryptic metacharacters.

However, there is a limitation to be aware of when using this menu to build expressions that use metacharacters in the match category. Except for the "Or" option, all match metacharacters need to be "wrapped" around the text or the condition they describe to work properly. For example, choosing Positive Lookbehind from the menu just puts the *structure* of that metacharacter ((?<=)) in the To Text field. But to actually *use* positive lookbehind to verify that, for example, the word NEW appears before the text you're describing, the expression needs to be (?<=NEW). The menu only supplies the shell, requiring you to move your cursor back into the correct position to define the parameters of the condition. The same applies to all other lookahead and lookbehind operations, subexpressions, and character sets. You can't select a part of the pattern you've already defined, and then choose one of these match metacharacters to wrap it around the selection. Doing so *replaces* the selection, so be sure to insert the match metacharacter's "structure" first, and *then* add your specific parameters.

REMEMBERING METACHARACTERS

One of the intimidating aspects of starting to work with GREP styles is the sheer number of metacharacters available. The any character and any digit wildcards, as well as the one or more times repeat metacharacter will probably be used most often and are worth committing to memory. Over time, the more you use metacharacters, the more they'll stick with you. Although the Special Characters for Search menu is a very helpful tool for building patterns without having to memorize metacharacters, there are a few metacharacters that are not listed in that menu.

A list of metacharacters—both for GREP and InDesign's caret-based syntax—is available from the application's Help files. Choose InDesign Help from the Help menu and search for the word "metacharacter," or just type "metacharacter" in the search field of InDesign CS4's application bar (**FIGURE 3.3**). The first matching help entry will be "Adobe InDesign CS4 * Metacharacters for searching," which links to a (nearly) complete table of available metacharacters.

FIGURE 3.3 Searching InDesign's Web-based Community Help (or local Help files if you're offline) for the word metacharacter provides access to a full table of InDesign and GREP metacharacters.

The table is a better and more at-a-glance reference, but it is still not 100 percent complete. The online Community Help could be updated by Adobe any time, but here are a few metacharacters that are currently missing from that list:

- **End of Story.** As noted earlier in the chapter, the End of Story metacharacter (\Z) is not listed in the Special Characters for Search menu, nor is it listed in the Help files.

- **Exact/Minimum/Maximum repeat ranges.** The repeat metacharacter convention of enclosing a specific number in curly brackets ({2} for example) to define an exact number of instances or to establish a minimum and maximum number of instances to match (such as {2,4}, which means no fewer than two but no more than four) is entirely undocumented.

- **Tilde.** Since the tilde (~) is used to define InDesign-specific characters like custom white spaces, the only way to include an *actual* tilde in a GREP expression is to escape it out with a backslash (\~).

- **Wildcard opposites.** Certain wildcards, such as any digit also have metacharacter "opposites" that define, in this example, any character that's *not* a digit (\D). Other wildcard opposites include any character that's not a white space (\S), any nonword character (\W), any character that's not uppercase (\U) or not lowercase (\L), and any character that's not a word boundary (\B). Notice that all of these are uppercase versions of the metacharacter for which they have the opposite meaning.

Creating a GREP Style

The step-by-step process of adding a GREP style to a paragraph style is simple enough. The GREP Style work area in the Paragraph Style Options dialog consists of very few actual options (FIGURE 3.4).

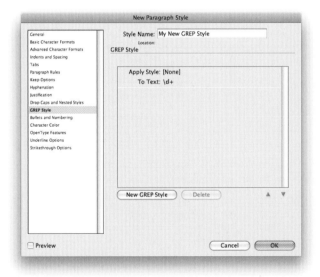

FIGURE 3.4 The GREP Style work area.

To add a GREP style to a paragraph style, follow these steps in the GREP Style area of the Paragraph Style Options dialog:

1. Click the New GREP Style button.

2. Select an existing character style to be used on any matching text in the paragraph—or define a new character style by choosing New Character Style—from the Apply Style menu (FIGURE 3.5).

3. Define your GREP pattern in the To Text field by either typing it in (if you're familiar with GREP) or by constructing each piece of the expression using the Special Characters for Search menu at the end of the field. See the next section, "Defining Expressions for GREP Styles," for some sample GREP scenarios.

FIGURE 3.5 Existing document character styles are available to GREP styles from the Apply Style menu.

Like Nested Styles and Nested Line Styles, more than one GREP style can be attached to a paragraph style and arranged in a specific order using the up and down arrows at the bottom of the list.

Defining Expressions for GREP Styles

Selecting a character style to apply with your GREP style is the easy part of the GREP style creation process. It's the GREP expression that requires more effort and practice. Learning what GREP can and can't do is a continuous process. There's definitely a learning curve, but even if you start small with some basic GREP, you can accomplish a lot. There's no need to master it all at once.

The individual metacharacters and what each one does was covered earlier in the chapter. Now it's time to start putting them together. The following examples are intended to familiarize you with GREP patterns in practical situations. The expressions start off simple and then become more complex as more GREP features are added to each subsequent example.

SPECIFIC WORDS OR NAMES

A GREP style can apply a character style automatically to a specific word or group of words. Suppose you have a product named Super Widget in a brochure that must always have a particular character style applied to it. Applying the character style manually to every instance is tedious work. Using Find/Change to locate Super Widget in your text and apply the character style at the same time (see Chapter 8, "Advanced Find/Change with Styles") speeds things up, but what happens when the text changes and more instances of the name get added? You'd either have go back and manually format them or perform another Find/Change operation.

A simple GREP style can eliminate the need for either of those two formatting options. Click the New GREP Style button to add a new GREP style to the paragraph style, choose your Product Name character style from the Apply Style menu, and then type Super Widget into the To Text field (FIGURE 3.6). The GREP style will parse the paragraph continuously, detecting and automatically formatting every existing instance of Super Widget in a paragraph and any that may get added later (FIGURE 3.7).

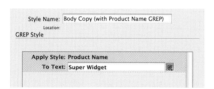

FIGURE 3.6 Literal text used as GREP style criteria.

Announcing the latest in modern convenience: the **Super Widget** all-purpose device! From the people who brought you the Wonder Tool and the Miracle Product comes this latest time- and money-saving product. Once you've used the **Super Widget**, you'll wonder how you ever got along without one. It's *that* good!

FIGURE 3.7 Multiple matches of the same product name in a single paragraph, formatted with a GREP style.

But suppose you have *several* product names that require the same treatment. There's no need to create a GREP style for *each* product name. A single GREP style can just as easily format every instance of Super Widget *or* Miracle Tool *or* Wonder Product with the same character style (FIGURE 3.8). You just need to use the match metacharacter for "Or" (|). Place that vertical divider character between each product name (with no space around it) to create this GREP expression:

Super Widget|Wonder Tool|Miracle Product

This applies the character style to *each* name, wherever and however often each appears in the paragraph.

Announcing the latest in modern convenience: the **Super Widget** all-purpose device! From the people who brought you the **Wonder Tool** and the **Miracle Product** comes this latest time- and money-saving product. Once you've used the **Super Widget**, you'll wonder how you ever got along without one. It's *that* good!

FIGURE 3.8 Literal text plus the "Or" condition (|) used in a GREP style to format three possible options in the paragraph as often as they occur.

PRICES

Detecting prices in text is another task that's tailor-made for a GREP style. In abstract terms, a price is made up of a dollar sign (\$), a dollar amount consisting of one or more digits (\d+), a decimal point (\.), and an amount in cents consisting of two digits (\d\d). Note that the metacharacters for the dollar sign and the decimal point (period) have been escaped out with backslashes so they are not treated as the special GREP metacharacters they would be without the backslashes. When put together, the GREP pattern for a price would look like this:

`\$\d+\.\d\d`

Unfortunately, something's missing from this pattern. Although it correctly describes a price, it doesn't describe *every* price—specifically, any price greater than $1,000.00 that contains a comma. The pattern will work fine for every price from $1.00 to $999.99, but nothing in this pattern accounts for the *possibility* that a comma may be present.

To fix this pattern requires a different way of describing the dollar amount. Instead of *any digit* one or more times, the pattern needs to look for *any digit or comma* one or more times. The any digit metacharacter (\d) describes a range of numeric characters from zero through nine, as does the character set `[0-9]`. The range of any character set can be expanded simply by including the desired character within the square brackets. A character set that describes any digit or comma could be written either as `[0-9,]` or more simply as `[\d,]`. The correct pattern for a price that can include a comma is:

`\$[\d,]+\.\d{2}`

Note that the two digits after the decimal point in this revised expression are described as `\d{2}` instead of `\d\d`. Both expressions are correct. They do the same thing, but when you start describing a number of more than two or three digits, the multiple \d metacharacters start to clutter the pattern. For example, describing a nine-digit U.S. zip code as `\d\d\d\d\d-\d\d\d\d` is far more cumbersome than `\d{5}-\d{4}`. Since the field for working with GREP expressions in the GREP Style work area is very small, using the latter method might be a good habit to get into.

FIGURE REFERENCES IN PARENTHESES

Figure references in a book (like this one) are often presented in parentheses with some kind of unique formatting—bold, italic, a color, and so on—to make them stand out. Typically, however, it's only the text *inside* the parentheses that's formatted this way, not the parentheses characters. When creating a GREP style for a situation like this, the parentheses need to be included to identify the references to format, but they need to be ignored when applying the desired character style. Simply describing your desired GREP style as `\(Figure \d+\)` will also apply the selected character style to the parentheses.

Using the parentheses as part of the GREP expression in a way that *doesn't* include them in the style change requires changing the context of the expression. Describing just the reference is simple. Figure references like "Figure 1" would appear as `Figure \d+` using the literal word "Figure," a space, the *any digit* metacharacter (`\d`), and the *one or more times* match metacharacter (`+`). To describe it as a match *only if preceded by* an opening parenthesis and *only if followed by* a closing parenthesis requires the positive lookbehind (`?<=`) metacharacter at the beginning of the expression and the positive lookahead (`?=`) metacharacter at the end of it. The lookbehind expression must specify an opening parenthesis (`(?<=\()`), and the lookahead expression must specify a closing parenthesis (`(?=\))`). With these expressions in place, the GREP style matches Figure whatever, but *only* if it's preceded by an opening parenthesis and followed by a closing parenthesis. The parentheses are not considered part of the match. They only establish a *requirement* for the match. So, the final pattern would be

`(?<=\()(Figure \d+)(?=\))`

When assigned a character style that uses a different font, size, weight, and color, the formatted text within the parentheses would appear as it does in **FIGURE 3.9**.

Barrel-organs (**FIGURE 1**) have been made with as many as three or four cylinders set in a circular revolving frame, but these more elaborate instruments were mainly used in churches and chapels (**FIGURE 2**), a purpose for which they were in great demand for playing hymns, chants and voluntaries during the 18th and early 19th centuries.

FIGURE 3.9 A GREP style applied to text *within* parentheses but not to the parentheses.

E-MAIL ADDRESSES

Although each e-mail address is unique, all e-mail addresses must adhere to a specific syntax to function properly. That syntax starts with the addressee's name, followed by the @ symbol, which is followed by the domain name, then the domain extension. Domain extensions can be as few as two letters, like *.de* or *.tv*, but no more than four, like *.name*. There are also double domain extensions like *.co.uk* that need to be accounted for.

Let's start with the recipient's name, which can only contain alphanumeric characters, periods, underscores, and dashes. This can be defined with a character set

([ ]) of any one or more uppercase or lowercase letters, digits, dashes, underscores, or periods. That character set would look like this: [-\u\l\d_]+. The plus symbol *outside* the character set adds the one or more times repeat criterion to every character in the set. Also, note that the dash appears *first* within the character set to avoid being confused for a range definer such as 0–9 or a–z.

The @ symbol can be used literally, because it has no special meaning in GREP.

The domain name can be defined by a character set that's *nearly* identical to the recipient's name. Domain names can't include periods, so the character set that defines it would be [-\u\l\d_]+. Copying the first portion of the pattern, pasting it after the @ symbol in the To Text field, and then deleting the period in the character set is a much faster way to define the domain name than building it from the menu or retyping it.

The period after the domain name must be escaped out with a backslash (\.) to prevent it from acting as the any character metacharacter.

The domain extension has more restrictions, so it's much easier to define. Domain name extensions can only contain letters, and although most domain extensions are three letters (.com or .edu, for example), there must be *at least* two letters but *no more than* four for it to be a valid extension. You might be tempted to use *any character one or more times* (.+) to describe the extension, but this is dangerous. Remember, GREP is greedy. "Any character one or more times" will continue to make matches of every space, letter, digit, and punctuation mark through the remainder of the paragraph. In the price example, the cents portion of the price was defined as *exactly* two digits (\d{2}). The curly brackets can specify an exact number, but they can also define a minimum and maximum number. For the domain extension, the minimum is two letters and the maximum is four letters, so the expression [\u\l]{2,4} defines the domain extension as *no fewer than two, but no more than four uppercase or lowercase letters.*

Now comes the tricky part, defining domains with double extensions, like .co.uk. It may be rare that you'll encounter this e-mail format, but it doesn't mean you can't allow for the possibility in the same GREP expression. In other words, this extra extension *may or may not* be there, and that's where the *zero or one time* (?) repeat metacharacter is useful.

The extra domain extension would be described much the same way as the standard extension \.[\u\l]{2,4}, but because *none* of it may actually be a part of the e-mail address, it needs to be isolated from the overall pattern. Placing a question mark after the {2,4} only applies the zero or one time instruction to the two or four letters. It doesn't include the period that may or may not be there. Placing a question mark after the \. *and* after the {2,4} creates another problem.

It treats the period and the letters that follow it as separate when they need to be considered together. If the e-mail address appears at the end of a sentence and is followed by a period, this method will also include the ending period of the sentence in the GREP style.

To define this troublesome extra domain possibility as a complete unit of the period and letters, it must be marked as a subexpression. Subexpressions isolate a portion of a larger pattern. Anything defined as a subpattern will be parsed as a complete and stand-alone unit *within* the overall expression. Sub-expressions are defined by simply placing the relevant metacharacters within parentheses. In this case, that subexpression would appear as (\.[\u\l]{2,4}). This encapsulates the additional domain extension as a whole, not as separate pieces. Now, when zero or one time metacharacter (?) appears after the subex-pression, it applies to the period *and* the letters. They have to appear together, or they won't be considered a match.

The GREP pattern for e-mail addresses, when all these pieces are put together, looks like this:

```
[-\u\l\d._]+@[-\u\l\d_]+\.[\u\l\d]{2,4}(\.[\u\l]{2,4})?
```

FIGURE 3.10 diagrams this *entire* expression to provide an easier visual reference for what each piece of the pattern represents and what it will match. When this GREP pattern is the basis of a GREP style built into a paragraph style, all e-mail addresses in text using that style will automatically have a character style applied to them.

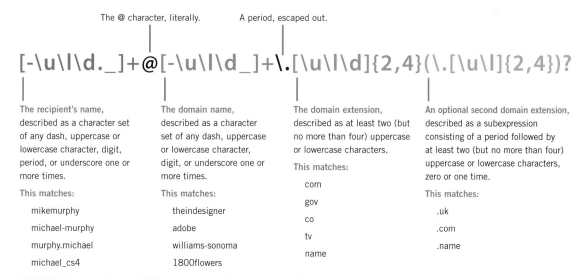

FIGURE 3.10 A bullet-proof GREP pattern that will match any e-mail address, foreign or domestic.

FIND AND FORMAT FRACTIONS

GREP styles are a great way to dynamically "switch on" the OpenType Fractions attribute for anything that looks like a fraction in a paragraph. A character style with no other attributes defined *except* OpenType Fractions handles this formatting beautifully for *any* OpenType font (see the sidebar "Keeping it Loose: Creating Adaptable Character Styles" in Chapter 1).

If you're feeling confident in your grasp of GREP so far, you might think that describing a fraction is a pretty easy task. After all, a fraction is just one or more numbers followed by a slash, followed by one or more numbers (⅔, ¼, ⁷⁄₁₆, etc.). That simple GREP expression would look like this:

```
\d+/\d+
```

But it's not that simple. While this *does* describe a fraction, it also describes parts of a date like 9/26/2008. One concern about describing text in the abstract is that you may be describing text you hadn't planned to. Understanding metacharacters and finding patterns isn't nearly as challenging as planning for the unexpected match and writing a pattern that finds only what you really want.

So, how do you distinguish between dates and fractions? It requires imposing conditions on the pattern using negative lookbehind and negative lookahead. You define the fraction by stating that a match exists *only if it is not preceded by or followed by* other specific characters.

In this case, the beginning of the fraction can't be preceded by *any one or more digits and a slash*, and the end of the fraction can't be followed by *a slash and any one or more digits*. Unfortunately, the lookahead and lookbehind functions don't recognize repeat metacharacters like *one or more times* (+). This limitation requires adding a second lookbehind and a second lookahead condition.

NOTE
Not all OpenType fonts support fractions the same way. Most handle standard fractions like ½ and ¾ without a problem, but some (like Warnock Pro and Adobe Jenson Pro) don't translate "unusual" fractions like 4/5 or 7/16 at all. If the font doesn't support it, neither will your GREP style.

This is a bit complicated, so I'll simplify it by describing the *idea* behind the pattern first. A fraction, as opposed to a date, is any one or more digits, followed by a slash, then followed by any one or more digits (\d+/\d+), but *only if it's not preceded by* a digit and a slash and *that* digit and slash are not preceded by a digit either ((?<!\d)(?<!\d/)), and *only if it's not followed by* a slash and a digit and *that* slash and digit are also not followed by a digit ((?!/\d)(?!\d)). **FIGURE 3.11** diagrams the complete pattern that successfully describes a fraction without matching a date.

All that just to describe a fraction may seem like a lot, but this GREP expression can be built into *any* paragraph that uses an OpenType font with fraction support—Adobe Caslon Pro, Garamond Premiere Pro, Minion Pro, and many others. After you write it once, you never have to write it again (**FIGURE 3.12**).

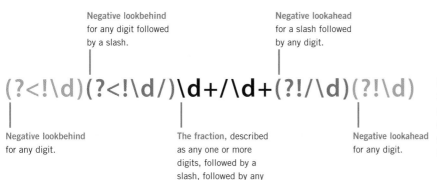

Negative lookbehind for any digit followed by a slash.

Negative lookahead for a slash followed by any digit.

Negative lookbehind for any digit.

The fraction, described as any one or more digits, followed by a slash, followed by any one or more digits.

Negative lookahead for any digit.

FIGURE 3.11 Strategic use of negative lookbehind and negative lookahead conditions prevents portions of a date from being mistaken for a fraction.

Adobe Garamond Pro

Never manually format fractions like ½, ⅔, or ¾ again, and do it with the peace of mind that a date like 9/26/08 won't get confused for a fraction in the process.

FIGURE 3.12 A GREP style that detects fractions and applies the OpenType Fractions attribute using a character style can work for multiple typefaces.

Minion Pro Semibold

Never manually format fractions like ½, ⅔, or ¾ again, and do it with the peace of mind that a date like 9/26/08 won't get confused for a fraction in the process.

Adobe Caslon Pro Semibold Italic

Never manually format fractions like ½, ⅔, or ¾ again, and do it with the peace of mind that a date like 9/26/08 won't get confused for a fraction in the process.

U.S. PHONE NUMBERS

Another GREP expression that seems easy enough to write is for U.S. phone numbers, which are all ten digits divided into three groups: a three-digit area code, a three-digit exchange, and a four-digit suffix. Describing that pattern is as simple as this:

`\d\d\d-\d\d\d-\d\d\d\d` or `\d{3}-\d{3}-\d{4}`

But these patterns make a few assumptions: The separate parts of the phone number are separated by a dash instead of the more trendy period, the area code isn't enclosed in parentheses as it often is, and there's no number 1 preceding the area code. This requires a closer look at how to truly describe *any* U.S.

phone number, no matter how it's formatted. The only true constant is that the phone number is ten digits. The rest is a laundry list of potential inconsistencies that must be accounted for. Here's where repeat metacharacters—specifically the zero or one time (?) metacharacter—prove extraordinarily useful.

Let's first deal with the dashes between the numbers. Let's assume that there could be a dash or a period between the numbers, or that there could be nothing between them. That means creating a character set to account for the dash or the period ([-.]) and adding a zero or one time metacharacter (?) to that character set, just in case neither of the two options is present. That changes the pattern to:

`\d{3}[-.]?\d{3}[-.]?\d{4}`

Now let's deal with the different ways the area code might be presented. It *could* have a 1 and a dash before it, or a 1 and a space, or neither of those. It *could* be enclosed in parentheses or not. If it *is* enclosed in parentheses, it will more than likely have a space after the closing parenthesis rather than a dash or a period. This requires accounting for a number 1 that may or may not be there or, in GREP terms, occurs *zero or one time* (1?), a dash, period, or space that *may* follow that 1 ([-.\s]?), an opening parenthesis that *may* precede the area code (\(?), a closing parenthesis that *may* follow it (\)?), and a dash, period, or space that may follow that ([-\s.]). That changes the pattern to:

`1?[-.\s]?\(?\d{3}\)?[-.\s]?\d{3}[-.]?\d{4}`

This one GREP pattern, diagrammed in **FIGURE 3.13** for greater clarity, will successfully identify and format 1-800-555-1234, 1 (800) 555-3456, 1.800.555.0124, (800) 555-0987, 888.555.5678, and 888-555-3210. But it *won't* find an acronym-style phone number like 1-800-FLOWERS.

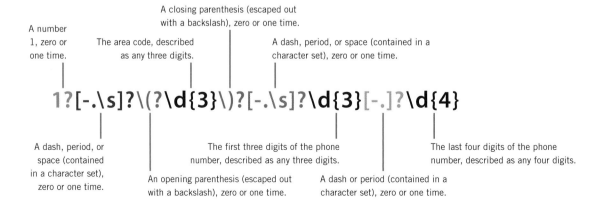

FIGURE 3.13 A GREP expression that correctly matches all of the most common ways a U.S. phone number might be presented.

CHAPTER 4

Auto-styling Imported Word and Excel Files

WHATEVER YOUR FEELINGS MAY BE about Microsoft and its Office products, there's one fact that can't be avoided: They're everywhere. It is nearly impossible to work collaboratively with writers, editors, and clients without having to work with, at the very least, content provided as Word and Excel documents.

Fortunately, InDesign works with the Word and Excel formats quite well, and it includes tools specifically geared toward maximizing compatibility between its features and theirs. Two InDesign dialogs—Microsoft Word Import Options and Microsoft Excel Import Options—are tailor-made for working with these Microsoft applications. With them you can peer into aspects of the incoming file, ignore or preserve certain features they support, and associate relationships between their styles and InDesign's styles.

This cross-application compatibility allows InDesign users to capitalize on work already done in Word and Excel, thereby reducing repetition and eliminating the potential for human error.

Working with Word Files

When I need to write, I use a text editor, and when I need anything more power-ful than that, I use InDesign. However, the times that I've been *required* to use Word, I've been surprised by how many similarities there are between Word styles and InDesign styles.

Like InDesign, Word has a complex and powerful set of text styling features that include paragraph and character styles. Word styles can be based on other styles, just as InDesign styles can, and a Word paragraph style can include a "Style for following paragraph" instruction that performs the same function as InDesign's Next Style setting.

Fortunately, the two applications part company dramatically in their imple-mentation of these common features with InDesign soundly trumping Word in the ease-of-use department and affording advanced style features like Nested Styles, Nested Line Styles, and GREP styles for which Word has no equivalent.

The connections between the two applications are managed in the Microsoft Word Import Options dialog, which you can access whenever you import a Word document by choosing File > Place. By default, this dialog will not appear unless you select the Show Import Options check box in the Place dialog (FIG-URE 4.1) before clicking Open.

FIGURE 4.1 Select the Show Import Options check box when placing Word documents to access Word-specific import settings.

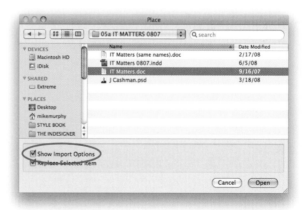

There's no way to access this dialog when dragging and dropping a file from the Finder (Mac) or Windows Explorer (PC), or when choosing File > Place > In In-Design in Adobe Bridge. It is only accessible from within the destination docu-ment by choosing File > Place.

When you import Word files *without* using this dialog, InDesign, by default, imports all styles from the Word document along with all table formatting, inline graphics, and page breaks. You'll always be able to tell what styles came in from Word by their appearance in the Paragraph and Character Styles panels (FIGURE 4.2). Imported Word styles have a small disk icon next to their names in the panel. Those disk icons will appear until the style is modified (or if you just view its attributes in the Style Options dialog) in InDesign.

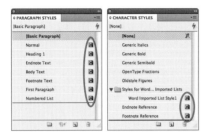

FIGURE 4.2 Imported Word styles in the Paragraph Styles and Character Styles panels.

WORD IMPORT OPTIONS

From the Microsoft Word Import Options dialog (FIGURE 4.3), you can choose what to bring in from the Word document being placed and what to strip out during the import process. Word's formatting capabilities pale by comparison to InDesign's, and its lack of CMYK support makes it unlikely that you'll want to preserve colors applied to text in Word. But there may be a number of other things you *will* want to keep.

NOTE
Except for its name, the Microsoft Word Import Options dialog is identical to the RTF Import Options dialog that appears when Show Import Options is selected when importing a Rich Text Format file.

FIGURE 4.3 The Microsoft Word Import Options dialog shown with its default settings.

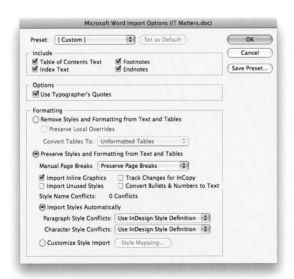

In the **Include** area of the dialog, you can choose to include or exclude any of the following:

- **Table of Contents Text.** Note the word "Text" in this option. A Word Table of Contents (TOC) is much like an InDesign TOC. It tracks text in the document that uses a particular style, collects that text, and presents it along with the page number where that text is found in the document (see Chapter 9, "Generating Dynamic Content with Styles"). But this option does not preserve that dynamic link between text styles and a TOC. It only brings in the text that was generated by the TOC process in Word. All associations with a "live" TOC are broken, and only static text gets placed in the InDesign file.

- **Index Text.** Here again, all the associations between a dynamically generated Word index and the references within the text are lost. Just the index text that was generated within the Word file comes into InDesign. No index markers or topics are preserved in the import process.

- **Footnotes.** Word footnotes *do* transition smoothly when placed into an InDesign document. The footnote reference numbers and their link to the footnote text are preserved.

- **Endnotes.** InDesign does not have an endnotes feature. Nonetheless, the text of any endnotes from an incoming Word file can be preserved. The reference numbers are imported at the same place in which they appear in the Word document, and the endnote text is placed at the end of the story. However, there will be no link between the endnotes and the reference numbers in the text. Deleting a reference number will not delete the endnote, nor will it renumber subsequent references in the imported text.

In the **Options** area the *only* option is Use Typographer's Quotes. Even if you opt to strip out all other Word formatting, keep this option selected to ensure that proper "curly" quotes and apostrophes appear when the imported text is placed in InDesign.

The **Formatting** area of the dialog is where you choose to either eliminate *all* Word styles and formatting, or most of it with a few exceptions, or to preserve styles and formatting in either of two ways:

- **Remove Styles and Formatting from Text and Tables.** This first option does just what its name implies. Every style and all manual formatting is stripped out of the Word file, and all incoming text comes in formatted with No Paragraph Style applied to it. With this option chosen, you're also given an option to bring in any tables in the Word document as either unformatted tables or unformatted tabbed text. Word tables cannot be mapped to InDesign table styles on import.

While this setting *does* get you off to a clean start, it removes all bold and italics from the Word document, too, which requires you to reapply those attributes in the InDesign file. It also strips out bullets and numbers from bulleted and numbered lists. These can be unacceptable losses in many workflows, so there are options for preserving select formatting or creating associations between incoming Word styles and your destination InDesign document's styles.

The simplest of these—Preserve Local Overrides—is available when Remove Styles and Formatting from Text and Tables is selected. This preserves bold, italics, and underlines but also preserves some unwanted attributes, like colors applied to text in the Word document. It will not preserve the bullets or numbers in bulleted and numbered lists.

- **Preserve Styles and Formatting from Text and Tables.** The greatest control you can exercise over incoming Word files is to choose Preserve Styles and Formatting from Text and Tables. This option gives you access to two different methods of Word-to-InDesign style conversion: automatic or custom.

Importing Word styles automatically

The only option to establish when importing styles automatically is how InDesign will handle "conflicts" between the incoming Word styles and any styles in the InDesign document that have the same name (FIGURE 4.4). The so-called conflicts are, in fact, exact matches. For paragraph and character styles, you simply decide whether to use the existing InDesign style's attributes (Use InDesign Style Definition) or to rewrite that InDesign style with the attributes of the incoming Word style (Redefine InDesign Style). A third option, Auto Rename, will bring in the Word style with "_wrd_1" appended to the style name (FIGURE 4.5) and leave the existing InDesign style unchanged. Imported RTF files behave the same way but instead append "_rtf_1" to the style name. When Auto Rename is chosen, the renamed styles will be applied to the imported text.

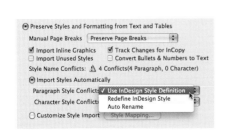

FIGURE 4.4 Automatic style import options.

FIGURE 4.5 Auto renamed Word styles in the Paragraph Styles panel.

Customizing Word style import

Automatic style importing assumes that the style names in your InDesign file match the styles in your Word file. This will not likely be the case in most situations. In all likelihood you'll need to make associations between Word and InDesign styles that have completely different names. For that you'll need to take advantage of Style Mapping.

To map Word styles to specific InDesign styles:

1. Select a Word file to import by choosing File > Place.

2. Be sure to either select the Show Import Options check box or hold down the Shift key before you click Open.

3. Choose Customize Style Import in the Microsoft Word Import Options dialog (FIGURE 4.6).

FIGURE 4.6 Style Mapping allows style-by-style relationships to be established between incoming Word styles and existing InDesign styles.

4. Click the Style Mapping button.

5. In the Style Mapping dialog (FIGURE 4.7), all paragraph and character styles in the Word file are listed on the left, paired with InDesign Style pull-down menus that appear on the right.

FIGURE 4.7 The customized Style Mapping dialog.

NOTE
Whether or not you preserve formatting for imported Word tables, you cannot map those tables to any InDesign table style, even if you've applied a Word table style. Only Excel files can be mapped to Table Styles in the import process. But you can map any paragraph or character styles used in a Word table to InDesign's paragraph and character styles.

6. For each incoming Word style, select any of the current InDesign document's styles from the corresponding menu (FIGURE 4.8) or define a new style by choosing New Paragraph Style.

FIGURE 4.8 An existing InDesign paragraph style mapped to an incoming Word paragraph style.

Important Importing Behavior

When you import a bulleted or numbered list from an incoming Word file, a style group called Styles for Word/RTF Imported Lists gets added to the Character Styles panel. This group contains a character style named Word Imported List Style1. Additional imported lists will be added to this group as Word Imported List Style2, Style3, and so on (**FIGURE 4.9**). These styles are applied as local overrides to the bullets and numbers in these lists, and sometimes to the entire list item, even if your list paragraph style contains specific character style settings for the bullets or numbers.

There's no way to prevent these overrides in the import process. It's a translation error between the automatically generated bullets and numbers in each application. You can only remove the overrides *after* the text is placed. To clear them from your document, delete the imported character style and choose your preferred character style as its replacement in the Delete Character Style dialog (**FIGURE 4.10**).

Another small anomaly is how footnote styles are handled between the two applications. If you map an incoming Word footnote style to an existing InDesign footnote style, you may find that the footnote formatting you selected is not applied when the text is placed. That's because footnote paragraph styles cannot be applied directly to footnote text. They must be assigned in the Document Footnote Options dialog (Type > Document Footnote Options). Once that's done, all footnotes will be properly styled.

FIGURE 4.9 Unwanted character styles are imported along with bulleted and numbered lists.

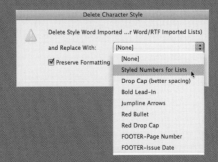

FIGURE 4.10 Replacing the Word Imported List Style with your preferred style is the only way to resolve the list formatting issue between Word and InDesign.

SAVING WORD IMPORT OPTIONS AS PRESETS

Whatever method for importing Word files you choose, there's no need to repeat the preceding steps every time you bring in Word documents. Once you've selected all your desired import options, you can create an import preset by clicking the Save Preset button and saving those options with the name of your choice (FIGURE 4.11). Like other InDesign presets—Document Presets, Print Presets, and Adobe PDF Presets, to name a few—your import preset is added to the Preset pull-down menu at the top of the Microsoft Word Import Options dialog.

FIGURE 4.11 Any configuration of Word import options can be saved as a preset for later reuse.

You can create as many presets as you like, and any preset can be established as your importing default if you click the Set as Default button with the desired preset selected in the menu (FIGURE 4.12). For example, if you prefer to bring in Word content completely clean most of the time, create a default preset that turns off all incoming Word formatting and only has the Use Typographer's Quotes option selected.

FIGURE 4.12 Any import preset can be established as the default for handling Word files.

MAINTAINING LINKS TO WORD FILES

Unlike imported graphics, imported Word files do not, by default, maintain a link back to the original document once they're placed in InDesign. All ties to the original Word file are broken when the text is placed. This default behavior can be changed by turning on the Create Links When Placing Text and Spreadsheet Files option in InDesign's preferences (Preferences > File Handling) (FIGURE 4.13). When the Word file is placed with this option on, it will appear in the Links panel just as placed images do (FIGURE 4.14).

This option is off by default, and for good reason. If, after the initial import, the Word file is modified and then updated in InDesign, all formatting applied or edits made in InDesign will be wiped out when the linked Word file is updated.

TIP

If you *do* turn on text and spreadsheet linking before importing a specific file, it's best to go back to the Preferences dialog and immediately turn it off again after the file is imported. The linked file will remain linked, but you'll eliminate the risk of unintentionally establishing links to all future text and spreadsheet imports.

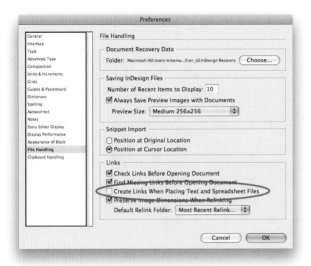

FIGURE 4.13 Imported Word and Excel files are handled similarly to linked images when Create Links When Placing Text and Spreadsheet Files is selected in the Links area of InDesign's File Handling Preferences.

There's only one instance where any real benefit can be gained by linking to an external Word file, and it requires an almost impossibly perfect workflow. First, all Word styles and InDesign styles must be identically named, and those styles must be mapped using the Import Styles Automatically option when the file is placed. Second, no edits to that text whatsoever can take place in InDesign if the linked Word file will be subsequently updated.

Even under those circumstances, this is still something of a pipe dream. Word's bold and italics are not "true" styles. If you use a character style in InDesign for bold and italics, there's no Word equivalent to map them to when you establish the relationship between the two application's styles. All bold and italics applied in Word will be local overrides in the InDesign document.

FIGURE 4.14 A linked Word file in the Links panel.

GETTING INDESIGN STYLES INTO WORD

It bears mentioning that the style import and mapping process depends on a critical factor: human cooperation. Maximizing the value of Word and InDesign compatibility requires communication between the content provider (editors, writers, clients, etc.) and the designer. The more collaboratively these two sides work together, the better and faster the workflow will be.

The compatibility between Word styles and InDesign styles is not a one-way street. It's also possible to get your InDesign styles *into* a Word document. Why would you want to do this? Consider magazines, newsletters, and other publications that use standardized formatting in templates from issue to issue. These workflows could be vastly streamlined if the editors and writers were applying styles in Word that corresponded to the InDesign styles used by the designers.

In the real world, the task of establishing that style consistency is less likely to fall on editors or writers than it is on designers, but setting up Word styles and templates is hardly high on any designer's list of desirable tasks. However, there are two fast, easy ways to get your InDesign styles into Word:

- Copy styled text from InDesign and paste it into a Word document. Any InDesign styles applied to the copied text are added to the Word document Style list.

- Select the text in an InDesign story that contains the desired styles, export it to the Rich Text Format (File > Export), and then open the RTF file with Word (FIGURE 4.15). The InDesign styles are now available in Word.

FIGURE 4.15 InDesign text exported to the Rich Text Format (.rtf) preserves all InDesign paragraph and character styles applied to it.

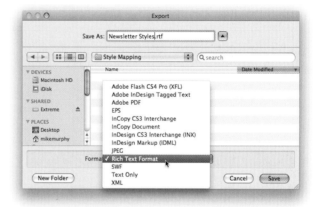

The style names and their formatting are brought into Word using both methods, but that's not all. Based On settings are preserved from InDesign to Word as are Next Style settings. However, Word lacks advanced formatting like Nested Styles, Nested Line Styles, and GREP styles, so don't expect that level of support.

Once the styles are in the Word document, delete the text and save the new document as a Word Document Template (.dot) that can be distributed to your writers and editors. They can author in this template with all the transferred styles available to them and return a compatibly styled Word document to the design team.

In all likelihood your InDesign styles will use fonts unavailable to those who provide your text, so you may want to take the additional step of simplifying the styles in Word for maximum compatibility. If you use Adobe Caslon Pro for your serif body copy, consider changing the style definition in Word to Times New Roman or Georgia. If your sans-serif headings use ITC Franklin Gothic, change the Word style to Verdana or Arial for maximum compatibility with different users and across operating systems.

With common style names and hierarchies established in the Word files you receive and the InDesign templates you work with, you can then create an import
preset that matches styles automatically using InDesign's style definitions and
use that preset every time you import Word files into specific project templates.

Working with Excel Files

When you import Excel spreadsheets using any of InDesign's normal means—
dragging and dropping a file icon from the Finder (Mac) or Windows Explorer
(Windows), or choosing File > Place—they arrive on your page as unformatted
tabbed text. Instead of columns, the placed Excel file has tabs between each
cell in a row, and each row is presented as a single line of text. This is easily converted to a table in InDesign by selecting the placed text and choosing Convert
Text to Table from the Table menu.

You can *temporarily* change this behavior when you import tables using File >
Place by selecting the Show Import Options check box before clicking Open. This
opens the Microsoft Excel Import Options dialog (FIGURE 4.16), where you can
switch from Unformatted Tabbed Text to either Formatted Table (which preserves
Excel formatting) or Unformatted Table (which strips out Excel formatting) from
the Table menu in the Formatting options. A third option, Formatted Only Once,
is applicable when maintaining links between the placed tables in InDesign and
their Excel source documents (see Chapter 6, "Table and Cell Styles").

> **TIP**
> InDesign only imports the
> first sheet in an Excel work-
> book when you drag an Ex-
> cel document into a layout
> or don't select Show Import
> Options in the Place dialog.
> Importing anything other
> than Sheet 1 (or whatever
> it's named in your file) re-
> quires selecting the desired
> sheet in the Microsoft Excel
> Import Options dialog.

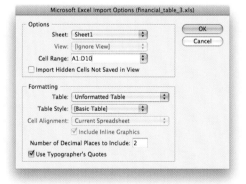

FIGURE 4.16 The Microsoft
Excel Import Options dialog.

Any adjustment to Excel import behavior is retained only for the length of your
current InDesign session. Once you quit and relaunch InDesign, the setting reverts to the default of importing Excel files as unformatted tabbed text. Unfortunately, this dialog lacks a Save Preset option, so there's no way to redefine the
default behavior for importing spreadsheets.

MAPPING SPREADSHEETS TO STYLES

In the Microsoft Excel Import Options dialog are a number of very useful options—selecting a range of cells or designating a particular sheet to import from the incoming file, for example—but only *one* style-related choice: the Table Style pull-down menu (FIGURE 4.17), which allows you to apply a table style to an Excel file as it is placed. Mapping styles to incoming Excel files is a much more limited process than mapping Word styles. An imported Excel file can only be mapped to a single InDesign table style.

FIGURE 4.17 An incoming Excel file can have an InDesign table style assigned to it as it's imported.

The default choice is Basic Table, which is the table equivalent of the Basic Paragraph style. Other choices are No Table Style and any table styles extant in the current document. You can also create a new table style from this menu and, from the New Table Style dialog, create any necessary cell styles for that table style. While this is *technically* possible, it's hardly practical due to the complexity and sheer number of options associated with a table.

The differences between cell styles and table styles, and the relationship between imported Excel files and table and cell styles, are covered in detail in Chapter 6.

CHAPTER 5

Object Styles

SO FAR YOU'VE LOOKED exclusively at text and the time-saving benefits of building multiple text attributes and behaviors into a style. But text isn't the only element that makes up an InDesign layout, nor is it the only asset in a project to which you can assign multiple attributes. Frames, shapes, and strokes—collectively known as objects—potentially have at least as many attributes as text.

InDesign CS2 introduced Object Styles to extend the style concept (a reusable set of stored attributes) beyond text. Nearly any object attribute—fill, stroke, corner options, text wrap, transparency, and more—can be saved to an object style, making complex object formatting a one-click process.

One-stop Shopping for Attributes

Nearly 100 distinct object attributes can be specified in an object style, not counting the independent object-, fill-, stroke-, and text-level transparency options. A complete exploration of these attributes would require a detailed account of how anchored options work, the ins and outs of text wrap, frame fitting, and many other tangential subjects that would require many more pages than this chapter—perhaps even this entire book—contains.

The Object Style Options dialog (**FIGURE 5.1**) is the Walmart of object attributes. You can find just about everything you want there. This one dialog includes six separate panels and as many dialogs in their entirety. Represented here is every option you would find in the following panels and dialogs:

TIP
New swatches can be created in the Fill and Stroke areas of the Object Style Options dialog by double-clicking on either swatch proxy and defining a new solid swatch (adding gradients and tint swatches is not supported here) in the resulting dialog.

- Swatches panel and Swatch Options dialog (except modifying existing swatches or creating gradient swatches)

- Stroke panel

- Corner Options dialog

- Text Frame Options dialog

- Story panel

- Text Wrap panel

- Attributes panel (or rather all options from the Attributes panel distributed across the Fill, Stroke, and Text Wrap & Other areas of the Object Style Options dialog)

- Anchored Object Options dialog

- Frame Fitting Options dialog

- Effects panel and each Effects dialog (shadows, glows, feathering, etc.)

FIGURE 5.1 The Object Style Options dialog.

WHAT OBJECT STYLES CAN DO

An itemized breakdown of the different settings in the Object Style Options can't possibly convey just how much an object style can do in a single click once it's style is defined. Instead, let's look at a representative example.

The first spread in FIGURE 5.2 includes a sidebar text frame placed over the image on the left page. The second spread has an unformatted frame containing unformatted text over the image on the right page that needs the same formatting. That finished frame on the first spread includes a significant amount of formatting (FIGURE 5.3), including a sequence of paragraph styles and transparency effects applied independently to the fill and stroke. Every one of those attributes is part of a single object style. With one click, the unformatted frame in the second spread can be assigned *all* of those attributes (FIGURE 5.4).

This, in a nutshell, is what an object style can do for you—apply multiple attributes and effects with a single click to any stroke, shape, graphic frame, or text frame (including the text in that frame). There are very few features in InDesign that offer more possibilities.

FIGURE 5.2 A text frame with complex styling (top spread, left) and an unformatted frame that must match it (bottom spread, right).

FIGURE 5.3 Attribute-by-attribute breakdown of this frame's formatting.

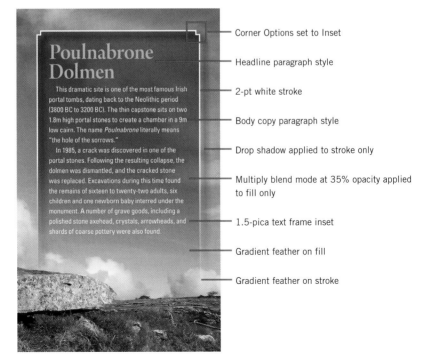

Corner Options set to Inset

Headline paragraph style

2-pt white stroke

Body copy paragraph style

Drop shadow applied to stroke only

Multiply blend mode at 35% opacity applied to fill only

1.5-pica text frame inset

Gradient feather on fill

Gradient feather on stroke

FIGURE 5.4 All attributes from Figure 5.3 applied in one click with an object style.

WHAT OBJECT STYLES CAN'T DO

For all of their formatting power, there are a few key tasks object styles can't do. An object style cannot define anything about an object's geometry—that is, its size, proportion, dimensions, scale, or shape (ellipse, rectangle, polygon), nor can it define an object's physical location (with the exception of an object style applied to an anchored object).

Object styles can't fundamentally change an object, either. For example, assigning either of the "basic" object styles (see the next section, "Default Object Styles") will not convert a frame to that content type. You can apply Basic Graphic Frame to a text frame, Basic Text Frame to a graphic frame, and *either* can be applied to an unassigned frame. The appropriate attributes will be applied, but the frame's content type will not change.

Default Object Styles

Three object styles are built into every InDesign document that cannot be renamed or deleted. Two of them—Basic Graphic Frame and Basic Text Frame—can have their attributes modified, but the None style cannot be edited in any way.

The Basic Graphic Frame default has no fill, a 1pt black solid stroke, and all transparency set to the Normal blend mode at 100% opacity. All other attribute categories are shut off for this style.

The Basic Text Frame default is a single-column frame with a 1-pica (.1667") gutter, no inset spacing, no fill or stroke, vertically justified to the top, and a first line baseline offset of Ascent. All transparency is set to the Normal blend mode at 100% opacity. Paragraph Styles, Story Options, Text Wrap & Other, Anchored Object Options, and Frame Fitting Options are ignored by this style.

By default, new text frames are created with the Basic Text Frame style applied unless you specifically change that setting. New graphic and unassigned frames, strokes, shapes, and objects drawn with the Pen tool, however, are assigned the None style, not Basic Graphic Frame.

ASSIGNING DEFAULT OBJECT STYLES

Object styles have a unique take on the default style concept. Paragraph styles default to Basic Paragraph, and character styles default to None. As you'll see in the next chapter, table styles and cell styles have their own defaults, too. Since objects can be text *or* graphic frames, object styles have two "assignable" defaults.

In the Object Styles panel (Window > Object Styles or Command/Ctrl-F7), the basic styles have an icon next to their names (FIGURE 5.5) indicating one as the default object style for text frames 🅣 and one as the default object style for graphic frames 🔲. Any object style can be assigned as the default text frame style or the default graphic frame style, or both (FIGURE 5.6). To assign a default, select a style from the Object Styles panel, and from the panel menu, choose Default Text Frame Style or Default Graphic Frame Style (whichever is appropriate) and select the desired style from the submenu.

> **TIP**
>
> An easier way to reassign defaults is to drag the appropriate icon to the desired object style in the panel to make it the current text or graphic frame default. You can also reassign a graphic frame by switching to the Selection tool, deselecting all objects on the page, and clicking the desired style name in the panel. The text frame default style can be assigned the same way but only with the Text tool selected.

FIGURE 5.5 Text and graphic frame defaults are indicated by an icon next to the style name.

FIGURE 5.6 Text and graphic frame defaults both set to None.

Similarities Between Object Styles and Text Styles

In many ways, object styles are merely an extension of paragraph and character styles, exhibiting much of the same behavior and controlled by similar means. For example:

- Object styles have a dedicated panel, and the Control panel contains an Object Style icon and an object style drop-down menu.

- When an object is selected while a new object style is created, the selected object's attributes are used as the basis for the style definition.

- Control-clicking/right-clicking an object style name in the panel menu displays a context menu from which you can choose Edit *YourStyleName* without accidentally applying the style.

- Copying a styled object from one document to another adds the style to the destination document. Similarly, you can load object styles from other documents by choosing Load Object Styles from the panel menu. If an incoming object style includes paragraph styles as its attribute, those paragraph styles (and any character styles defined within them via nesting or GREP) are also added to the destination document.

- Object styles can be organized into Style Groups (see Chapter 11, "Style Management").

Differences Between Object Styles and Text Styles

Beyond their association with objects rather than text, object styles have some other distinct differences in behavior that don't conform entirely to the conventions of their text style counterparts.

SELECTIVE ATTRIBUTE INCLUSION

Like other style dialogs, the Object Style Options dialog contains a left pane with a list of different attribute categories. However, this is the only dialog where an entire category can be disregarded by the style and all of its related attributes ignored. In the top-left pane of the dialog, each category name has a check box next to it. If the check box is not selected (which appears as a small box on Windows and a hyphenated box on the Mac), all attributes in that category are ignored by the style (FIGURE 5.7). In other words, an object style in which the Fill category is set to "ignore" will never change the fill color, tint, gradient angle, or fill overprint setting of an object to which it's applied.

FIGURE 5.7 Selected items are considered "defined" in a style; deselected items are ignored by the style and left "as is" when the style is applied.

This makes object styles less absolute than paragraph styles, where *every* attribute is included in the style definition. It's not quite like character styles, where unspecified attributes are inherited from the paragraph. There is no "top level" style for an object that's akin to a paragraph style. Ignored settings simply honor any attribute already applied to an object on a page. Those attributes are not considered overrides to the style, either, because they're not defined by it.

Adding Effects? Add One More State

The pane containing the transparency-specific options (below the Effects for menu), has *three* possible states for any effect: On, Off, and Ignore (**FIGURE 5.8**).

Using the Drop Shadow effect as an example, On "forces" the drop shadow onto the object (it must be included) and Off removes any existing drop shadow settings. Ignore will leave any existing drop shadow in place, but it won't *add* a drop shadow to the object. The general Transparency category at the top of this list—where opacity and blend modes are assigned—has only the On and Ignore states available to it.

FIGURE 5.8 The three available states of the Effects options: Ignore (hyphenated or small check box), On (selected), and Off (deselected).

Object styles also honor the object-level transparency options introduced in CS3, where different transparency settings can be applied independently to an object's fill, stroke, and text. The default choice in the Effects for menu is Object, but that can be changed to assign transparency and effects to any specific component of the object.

OVERRIDE REMOVAL

When you apply a paragraph style by clicking its name, no overrides are removed. You must either choose Apply *YourStyleName*, Clear Overrides or Option-click/Alt-click the style name. The Object Style panel, however, is *pre-set* to remove overrides. By default, the Clear Overrides When Applying Style option is selected in the panel menu (FIGURE 5.9), meaning that any object formatting that does not match a defined attribute of the object style is removed in favor of the style's setting for that attribute. However, since not all attributes have to be assigned to a style, that doesn't mean *every* unique attribute of the object is cleared—only those specifically activated in the object style.

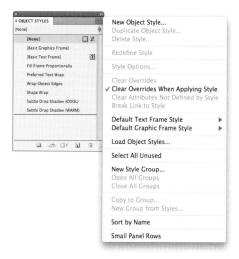

FIGURE 5.9 Overrides are cleared by default when object styles are applied.

For paragraph styles, Shift-Option-clicking/Shift-Alt-clicking a style name removes *every* attribute that doesn't match the paragraph style's definition. The same keyboard shortcut works for object styles, but it's potentially as dangerous as it is convenient. Since an object style need not include settings for every object attribute, reducing an object to only the style's defined attributes can have unintended results.

FIGURES 5.10 through 5.14 demonstrate the potential for Shift-Option-clicking/ Shift-Alt-clicking to act as an "attribute killer." In FIGURE 5.10, the text frame has *some* attributes (fill, text inset, paragraph style, etc.) applied to it, but no object style assigned to it. If an object style that *only* includes text wrap options (see "Flexible Object Styles Every InDesign User Should Have" later in this chapter) is applied to that frame by clicking the style name in the panel, the text wrap setting will be added, but nothing else about the object changes (FIGURE 5.11).

When the frame is selected, the highlighted object style in the panel will not have a plus after it because the unique attributes are not considered overrides.

FIGURE 5.10 An unstyled text frame with a specific fill and inset, and paragraph style.

FIGURE 5.11 Text wrap settings added to the frame by an object style.

If the object style is applied by Shift-Option-clicking/Shift-Alt-clicking the style name or choosing Apply Style, Clear Attributes Not Defined By Style from the panel menu (FIGURE 5.12), the frame's fill and text inset will be removed (FIGURE 5.13) because text wrap is the only attribute actually defined by the object style. The text within the frame may *appear* unchanged, but if the paragraph is selected, the Paragraph Styles panel reveals that the style is no longer applied. Although the text formatting is preserved, it's reduced to No Paragraph Style with overrides (FIGURE 5.14).

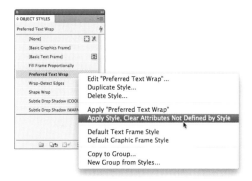

FIGURE 5.12 The Apply Style, Clear Attributes Not Defined By Style command can remove more formatting than expected.

UPCOMING EVENTS

COMPUTER CLASSES: Learn to use Word, Excel, or Photoshop at one of the various computer classes the library offers. Call for dates, rates, and details. **MOVIE MONDAYS:** Why go to the multiplex when the library is free! Children's movies are screened the first and third Monday of the month at 6:30 p.m. **SPEAK IN TONGUES:** The Vernon County Library now offers an online Learn a Language program. Go to the electronic resources page on our web site and click on Tell Me More. Enter your libarary card number and you're ready to learn a language in the comfort of your home.

FIGURE 5.13 Fill and inset attributes removed from the frame by the "pure" application of the object style.

FIGURE 5.14 Text formatting is preserved, but style associations are broken.

FIGURE 5.14 Text formatting is preserved, but style associations are broken.

The only undefined formatting that is preserved when an object style is applied with the Clear Attributes Not Defined By Style option is character styles.

Combining Paragraph Styles and Object Styles

Any individual style is useful, but when styles are combined, they become exponentially more powerful. The one option that's off by default for every new object style is the same one that adds the greatest amount of increased functionality to a text frame's object style: the ability to designate a paragraph style for the frame. It seems that the engineers were so determined to require you to deliberately activate the option that it even gets turned off *again* if you create a new object style based on an object style where it's already been turned on.

Once you *do* commit a paragraph style to an object style, you potentially add much more than one attribute. The Paragraph Style category in the Object Style Options dialog contains not only a menu of existing styles to choose from (and the option to create a new style), but also an option to honor that style's Next Style setting (see Chapter 2, "Nesting and Sequencing Styles") when the object style is applied to the text frame (**FIGURE 5.15**).

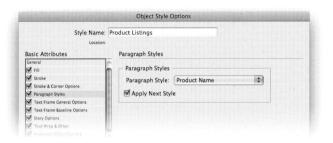

FIGURE 5.15 Multiple
paragraph style application
is enabled with Apply Next
Style selected.

But wait, it gets better! The Apply Next Style check box enables the Next Style setting for *every* paragraph in the text frame, so each subsequent paragraph's Next Style instruction is also honored. Using this method, a complete *sequence* of text formatting can be built into the frame's object style. If that sequence is meant to repeat, as described in the "Repeating a Sequence of Paragraph Styles" section in Chapter 2, any consistent series of paragraph styles can be applied with a single click along with all other attributes of the text frame (FIGURE 5.16).

ScreenFlow
Telestream   Nevada City, CA
Platform: Mac OSX Leopard 10.5 or later
Quickly captures screen activity and both internal or external audio for screencasts and demos. Simple interface allows
for transitions, zooms, and screen highlighting. Multiple
export formats.
www.telestream.net
BBEdit 9
Bare Bones Software   Bedford, MA
Platform: Mac OSX 10.4 or later (Universal Binary)
Award-winning product provides an abundance of fea-
tures for editing, searching, and manipulation of text and
professional-level HTML editing. Includes GREP pattern
searching, save to FTP, and scripting support.
www.barebones.com
FileMaker Pro 10
FileMaker, Inc.   Santa Clara, CA
Platform: Mac OSX 10.4.11 or later; Windows Vista Ul-
timate, Bussiness & Home; Windows XP Professional and
Home Edition
Easy-to-use database software helps you manage people,
projects, assets and more. Intuitive point-and-click interface
helps you customize solutions and share them with ease.
Robust reporting and data export features.
www.filemaker.com

FIGURE 5.16 Paragraph
styles are applied in
sequence when Apply Next
Style is selected.

The one limitation of this otherwise fantastic feature is that it only works on single, unthreaded text frames. However, it will work perfectly on multicolumn frames.

Flexible Object Styles Every InDesign User Should Have

In Chapter 1, "The Fundamentals: Paragraph and Character Styles," I covered "flexible" character styles that could be applied in many different situations and still work consistently. Character styles are "tacked on" to paragraph styles, allowing for two levels of style formatting. Object styles don't work quite this way. There's no character style equivalent for an object. But their ability to selectively include or exclude entire categories of attributes does allow you to employ a similar technique. Flexible object styles can apply a particular attribute to many frames while retaining their other unique formatting. The following examples describe a handful of these flexible object styles.

AUTO-FIT FRAMES

InDesign CS4 added proportional image placement and scaling when an imported graphic is placed on the page into a newly created graphic frame via the click-and-drag method. But when an image is placed in an existing frame—a placeholder frame on a master page, for example—it's placed in that frame at 100% (FIGURE 5.17).

FIGURE 5.17 An object placed in an existing frame at InDesign's default of 100%.

While the cropping and positioning of an image in a frame is always subject to fine-tuning, it helps to actually *see* the image in the frame, not a small portion of it, before making those adjustments. Using Frame Fitting Options in an object style for placeholder frames, you can set that frame to scale the image so that it fills the frame proportionally, starting from the top-left corner of the frame (FIGURE 5.18). Placed image proportions can vary dramatically, so the height of the frame may need to be adjusted or the image repositioned to its best advantage. But this is an ideal way to quickly size images upon import into an existing frame (FIGURE 5.19).

FIGURE 5.19 The same image from Figure 5.17 when placed in a pre-fit frame.

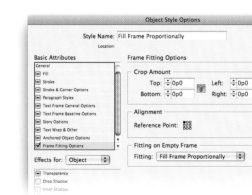

FIGURE 5.18 Frame Fitting Options in the Object Style Options dialog set a graphic frame to resize any image placed in it.

PREFERRED TEXT WRAP OPTIONS

The only way to change InDesign's text wrap settings is to turn one of the wrap methods *on* by default (by making the change with all documents closed) and set your desired values. Unfortunately, when text wrap is on by default, every object you add to the page has a text wrap applied to it. This is a recipe for instant frustration and is not a viable option.

Instead, define an object style for which all other options are ignored and define only your preferred text wrap offsets. Rather than start off with no offsets, choose the Wrap Around Bounding Box option and add a preferred offset of, for example, one pica (FIGURE 5.20).

FIGURE 5.20 Text wrap options built into an object style.

SUBTLE DROP SHADOWS

The easier drop shadows are to create—and InDesign makes them very easy— the more they're overused. Unfortunately, InDesign's default settings create pretty ugly drop shadows. They're too dark, too big, and not at all natural looking. Those defaults can't be redefined, but an object style that applies *only* a drop shadow—built to your taste—can make the difference between an eyesore and a subtle, tasteful effect. And it can do it with one click.

To quickly apply a more desirable set of drop shadow attributes, create a new object style, deselect all attribute categories in the top pane and only turn on Drop Shadow in the lower pane. Click Drop Shadow to access the object-level drop shadow settings and adjust the settings accordingly. My personal

TIP
When building drop shadow object styles with a rich black, create two versions using two different rich black swatches: one "cool" rich black (C=60,M=60,Y=40,K=100) and one "warm" rich black (C=40, M=60, Y=60, K=100). You'll then have drop shadows that blend more effectively against warm backgrounds (reds, yellows, oranges) or cool ones (blues and greens). After creating the first "warm" object style, create a new style based on it, and switch only the drop shadow color to the "cool" version.

preference is a drop shadow of about 30% opacity using a "rich black" swatch (a combination of 100% black and percentages of cyan, magenta, and yellow). I like it to be relatively close to the object (offset about 4 to 6 points). I tend to keep its size only slightly greater than the offset (6 to 8 points), and I *always* add 2% noise to my drop shadows to add a bit of grain that makes the drop shadow look less machine perfect (FIGURE 5.21).

FIGURE 5.21 Drop shadow settings in the Object Style Options dialog.

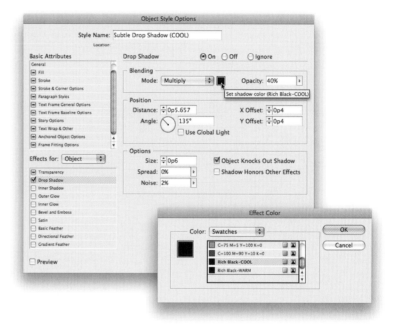

An object style with *only* its drop shadow settings switched on and all other attributes ignored can be applied to many objects, each with dramatically different formatting (FIGURE 5.22).

FIGURE 5.22 One drop shadow object style adds a consistent (and tasteful) drop shadow setting to a transparent object, placed image, text frame, and drawn shape.

PRE-ANCHORED ANCHORED OBJECTS

Anchored Objects—especially the Custom variety—is a great feature made difficult only by its many (and somewhat unintuitive) options. Besides picking what
point on the object will be the basis for all location settings, you must indicate
what part of the frame it's anchored to relative to that reference point on both
the X and Y axes (FIGURE 5.23). Once you figure it out and get it right, you don't
want to repeat those steps for all similar objects.

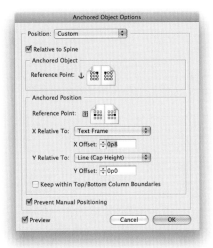

FIGURE 5.23 Custom
Anchored Object settings
specific to the top anchored
object in Figure 5.24.

Even if you set up one custom anchored object precisely the way you want, everything you've done gets wiped out when you copy the object and paste it into
another frame or paragraph. The copied object reverts from Custom to Inline,
using that anchored object type's default settings (FIGURE 5.24).

The only way to preserve all your hard work is to save the settings to an object
style after the object has been anchored at its desired position. An object style
also affords another otherwise impossible option: applying Anchored Object
settings to an object that's not anchored. The Anchored Object Options menu
item is unavailable for any object that isn't pasted into a text frame. However,
that feature's options *are* available in the Object Style Options dialog whether or
not the object is currently anchored.

FIGURE 5.24 A custom anchored object (top image) reverts back to an inline anchored object when copied and pasted.

Jane Doe, President & CEO Ehendiam, quodist etur audit et fugia velleni mpossuntur? Te volest, to tem sin nos earumquo ipsum faceptat harumqu asperspis eresto te landa estet, esequam simus, explique officat emporentur? Feriatu restrum fuga. Nam dunti alignis pore nem serum vollore peliatum vel- prer issitio. Ehenim et lit que ducimol corum resti quas consed eum, saerum est volor.

John Smith, CFO litas molo voloribusa velecul parumquas molupta sitibusda vo- luptibusa num qui comnimustia dolorep udionsequo im quatur ad ute res et velis et ipsam con poriat quis quiatus sus parchit quo quid quis dolorentum essimet

CONVERTING FLEXIBLE OBJECT STYLES

Because the unique attributes in the examples discussed in this chapter aren't included in the "flexible" object style's definition, you can't use the Redefine Style command unless you change some aspect of the attribute that *is* defined. The good thing about that is you can't *accidentally* redefine the style, which might cause many different objects to adopt an unwanted appearance.

After you've applied one of these styles to take advantage of its specific format- ting, you may want to add other attributes and define a new, more highly de- fined style with the original attribute *and* your modifications. To do this, select the modified object and choose New Object Style from the Object Style panel menu or the Object Style icon in the Control panel. The only attribute that does not automatically get added from the selection is the paragraph style used in the frame (see "Combining Paragraph Styles and Object Styles" earlier in this chapter), so remember to select it if you need a paragraph style included.

If you keep the new style's Based On definition set to the flexible style you first applied, any changes to that parent style will be passed down to this new style. Choose Based On: None if you want to permanently break any association with the flexible style you started out with, so the new style will not inherit any later changes made to the original.

CHAPTER 6

Table and Cell Styles

A KEY COMPONENT OF DESIGN is the process of organizing information in a clear and compelling way, and nothing is better at presenting complex information than a well-designed table. Other applications offer table-creation capabilities, but none compare with InDesign in terms of features, flexibility, and ease of use.

Tables can get pretty complex. It can take a long time to format a single table, and even longer to format several, even if they are similar. Yet the ability to capture table formatting in styles only became available in InDesign CS3. Styling tables—which involves table styles and cell styles—follows many of the conventions used by other styles in InDesign but adds its own unique features (and some challenges) to bring order to all those cells, rows, and columns.

Table Styling

Like paragraph, character, and object styles, InDesign's table and cell styles can be defined by either specifying attributes directly in the Table Style Options or Cell Style Options dialogs, or (with some limitations) by formatting a table or cell to your satisfaction and then creating a new style based on that formatting.

Other style behaviors are similar, too. For example, as with text and object styles, if you override a table style's or cell style's formatting, the overrides are displayed as a tooltip when you mouse over the style name. You can incorporate those overrides into the style by choosing Redefine Style from the Table Styles or Cell Styles panel menu. You can also load table or cell styles from another document by choosing Load Styles from the Table Styles or Cell Styles panel menu.

Like text and object styling, table styling can be an enormous time-saver and greatly increase the efficiency, accuracy, and flexibility of your designs. But whereas styling for text and objects can fully automate formatting, there are some limitations to the extent of automation possible with table styling. Understanding what styling tables *can't* do is as important as understanding the remarkable power they provide. For fast formatting of multiple tables that have the same structure and appearance, table and cell styles are essential. They're also the *only* way to maintain links to Excel spreadsheets and preserve table formatting applied in InDesign. Table styles can be complex. They're not as intuitive as other kinds of styles and may require a little more setup time, but the rewards can be huge.

Table and cell styles also exist in perfect harmony with InDesign's other styles. The text frame in which a styled table exists can have an object style applied to it, and styled objects can be anchored in table cells. All paragraph and character style features—including Nested Styles and GREP styles—are supported within any styled cell (FIGURE 6.1).

Table Styles vs. Cell Styles

When designing and formatting any table, it's important to understand the distinction between table-level formatting and cell-level formatting, which is akin to the difference between paragraph-level attributes and character-level attributes, as described in Chapter 1, "The Fundamentals: Paragraph and Character Styles." Table attributes are modified in two dialogs: Table Options and Cell Options, and the division of attributes between those dialogs is consistent with the available settings for a table style or cell style, respectively. However, the Table Style Options dialog is not identical to the Table Options dialog, nor is the Cell Style Options dialog exactly the same as the Cell Options dialog. Some options are added and some options are missing, as you'll see further on.

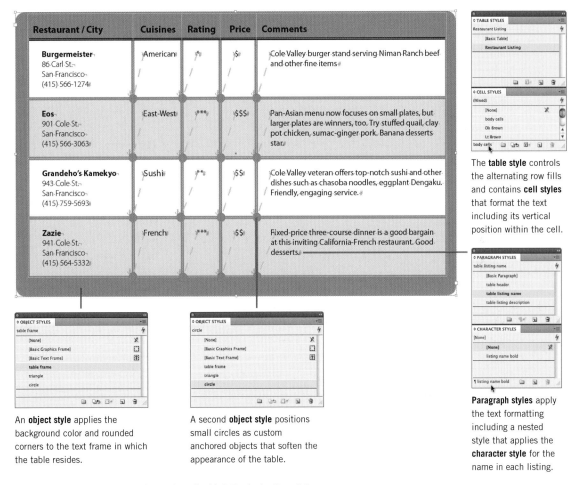

The **table style** controls the alternating row fills and contains **cell styles** that format the text including its vertical position within the cell.

Paragraph styles apply the text formatting including a nested style that applies the **character style** for the name in each listing.

An **object style** applies the background color and rounded corners to the text frame in which the table resides.

A second **object style** positions small circles as custom anchored objects that soften the appearance of the table.

FIGURE 6.1 Table and cell styles work well with InDesign's other styles.

Table-level formatting affects the *entire* table and includes controls for tasks like drawing a border around the entire table (using its outside strokes), controlling the space before or after the table in the text flow, and establishing alternating fills or strokes for rows or columns.

Cell-level formatting, on the other hand, is much more granular and can be applied to an individual cell or group of cells, up to *every* cell in a table, if desired. Cell-level formatting controls tasks like the vertical alignment of text within a cell and the cell's text insets as well as its fill and stroke settings. Where styling tables is concerned, it's best to start with cell styles, and then build your way up to table styles.

CELL STYLES

Cell styles can be applied directly to cells in your table. They can also be built into a table style, much like character styles can be nested within a paragraph style. It's quite easy to design a table that's too complex to be *fully* defined by a table style, but cell styles can still speed up the formatting process. Many tables can be most efficiently formatted using only cell styles.

TIP
If you want to create a cell style based on the attributes of only one cell, you can simply click anywhere in the cell with the Text tool. You don't need to select the entire cell.

If you define a cell style by uniformly formatting a number of cells first, and then create a new style based on that formatting, InDesign will pick up formatting only from the *first* cell selected, ignoring all others.

Cell styles share certain characteristics with character styles. Like character style attributes, the attributes in a cell style are initially set to a "neutral" state; they are not defined by default. Attributes you specifically define *are* considered part of the style; all other attributes are not. This means if you select cells to which a cell style has been applied and then change an attribute that isn't defined in the style, the local formatting change will *not* be recognized as an override (FIGURE 6.2), and you can't use it to modify the style with the Redefine Style command in the Cell Styles panel menu. Instead, you must set the new attribute by editing the style from the Cell Style Options dialog.

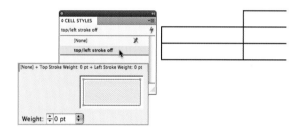
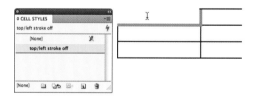

FIGURE 6.2 The top and left stroke are part of the style definition. Changes to the bottom and right stroke are not recognized as overrides and can only be added to the cell style by editing the style directly.

The attributes you can define in the Cell Styles dialog are for the most part the same as those in the Cell Options dialog used to manually format cells (FIGURE 6.3), but with one very significant exception. You can't define row height or column width in a cell style. The Cell Style Options dialog is missing a tab for rows and columns, which is where row height and column width are controlled. So if you're using cell styles to format cells directly or build cell styles into a table style, you will *always* have to format the row heights or column widths manually.

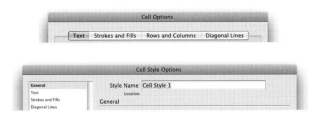

FIGURE 6.3 Tabs in the Cell
Options dialog (top) and the
categories in the Cell Style
Options dialog (bottom).

The Cell Style Options dialog is composed of four panes on the left side: General, Text, Strokes and Fills, and Diagonal Lines.

Cell Style General options

The General pane of the Cell Style Options dialog (FIGURE 6.4) contains settings similar to those found in the General pane of other InDesign style dialogs.

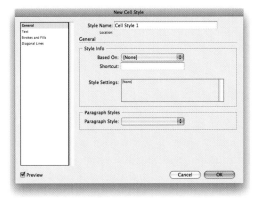

FIGURE 6.4 The General
pane of the Cell Style
Options dialog.

Style Info. Like paragraph and character styles, cell styles can be based on other cell styles for greater "trickle-down" formatting efficiency. As with the Based On behavior described in Chapter 2, "Nesting and Sequencing Styles," changes to the parent cell style are automatically passed down to the child cell style.

Paragraph Styles. This powerful feature lets you assign a paragraph style to format the text within the styled cell. It doesn't include the handy Apply Next Style option found in the Object Style Options dialog, but it fully supports all other paragraph style settings like Nested Styles, Nested Line Styles, and GREP styles.

Cell Style Text options

The Text pane of the Cell Style Options dialog (FIGURE 6.5) contains settings identical to those found in the Text tab of the Cell Options dialog, including text inset, vertical alignment, and the position of the first baseline.

NOTE
Unfortunately, the paragraph style used in a selected cell *will not* automatically get picked up when you create a new cell style based on that selected cell. Paragraph styles must be specifically chosen in the Cell Style Options dialog.

FIGURE 6.5 The Text pane
of the Cell Style Options
dialog.

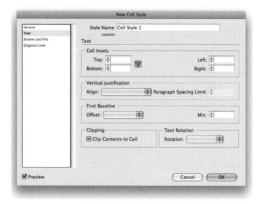

Cell Insets. Cell insets push text away from the inner edges of a table cell. You can set different insets for the top, bottom, left, or right edge of a cell, or make them all the same by clicking the Link icon to a locked position and then inputting a value in any one of the fields.

Vertical Justification. In any cell, you can control the vertical alignment of text within the cell. The default setting is that text is Top aligned. Options include Align Top, Align Bottom, Align Center, Justify Vertically, and (Ignore). The Ignore option is not found in the Cell Options dialog. In a cell style, anything set to Ignore will disregard that attribute and instead honor existing local formatting.

When text is set to Justify Vertically, the lines of text will be evenly distributed from the top to the bottom of the cell. If the cell contains multiple paragraphs of text, you can control the amount of space between paragraphs using the Paragraph Spacing Limit.

First Baseline. This setting allows you to control the position of the first line of text in a cell. The default setting for the Offset is Ascent, which causes the top of the ascenders to fall at the top of the cell. As with vertical justification, you can use the Ignore option to leave this setting unchanged in the cell to which the style is applied.

You can further control the distance of the first baseline from the top cell edge with the Min field. For example, you can set a specific distance by choosing Fixed in the pull-down menu and then inputting a value.

Clipping. Clipping is generally used for table cells that contain images. It allows you to crop an image so that it doesn't extend beyond the edge of the cell. The exact behavior that results from this setting depends on other attributes of the cell, including whether or not row height is set to be a fixed amount, the cell's vertical alignment setting, and insets.

Text Rotation. Text within a cell can be set to rotate at 90° angles. The default setting is 0° but can be set to 90°, 180°, or 270°.

Cell Style Stroke and Fill options

The Strokes and Fills pane of the Cell Style Options dialog (FIGURE 6.6) contains controls for the appearance of the strokes around a cell and the fill background of a cell.

Cell Stroke. The controls for cell stroke are identical to those found in the Cell Options dialog. You first set up the proxy to represent the strokes you want to format. This can be somewhat counterintuitive, because you click to deselect the strokes in the proxy that you *don't* want to format, leaving selected the strokes you *do* want to format. After setting up the stroke proxy, you can then set the stroke's Weight, Type (of line style, such as solid or dashed), Color (from the document's swatches list), and Tint. All line styles, except for a solid line, can have a Gap Color and Tint applied, and both the stroke and gap color can be set to overprint.

Cell Fill. You can select a fill color and tint for a cell by clicking the Color pull-down menu and choosing from the list of the swatches in your document. You can also set a Tint value for the color and specify if the fill should overprint.

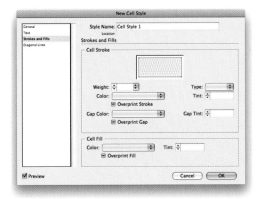

FIGURE 6.6 The Strokes and Fills pane of the Cell Style Options dialog.

Cell Style Diagonal Line options

The controls for setting diagonal lines in cells are the same as in the Cell Options dialog (FIGURE 6.7). The icons at the top of the dialog let you set a single diagonal stroke—drawn from the upper-left to the lower-right or from the upper-right to the lower-left—or let you set crossed lines creating an "x."

Line Stroke. These controls are identical to those found in other dialogs where lines strokes are controlled, including Weight, Type (of line style, such as solid or dashed), Color (from the document's swatches list), and Tint. By clicking the Draw pull-down menu, you can set whether the diagonal line strokes are on top of or behind the cell's contents.

FIGURE 6.7 The Diagonal Lines pane of the Cell Style Options dialog.

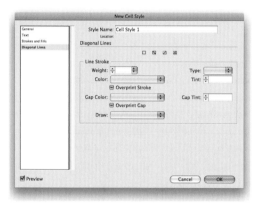

TABLE STYLES

In the strictest sense, table styles can be defined using the same technique as other styles, either by specifying style attributes directly in the Table Style Options dialog or by formatting a table first and then creating a new style based on that formatting (or a combination of the two techniques). However, practically speaking, it is usually not possible to define a table style without first defining a cell style or two—or three or four—and these cell styles must be entered directly into the Table Style Options dialog.

In theory, if you design a table by setting only the attributes found in the Table Options dialog, you could then define a table style easily by simply selecting the formatted table and creating a new table style. But for most tables you design, you'll need to define cell-level attributes as well, like setting text insets, setting the vertical alignment of the text within a cell, or changing the fill or stroke of some cells to differentiate them from others in the table. In that case, you must include cell styles when defining the attributes for your table style.

Overall, the attributes you can set in the Table Style Options dialog are similar to those found in the Table Options dialog (FIGURE 6.8).

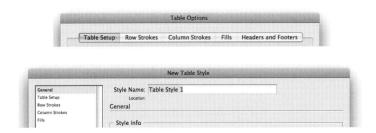

FIGURE 6.8 Tabs in the Table Options dialog (top) and the categories in the Table Style Options dialog (bottom).

But as with cell styles, there is one important exception: You cannot specify header and footer rows in table styles. This has some important implications when you are trying to format a table automatically using table styles. It means that you must always manually select and specify the rows to be designated as header and footer rows, either by using the Convert Rows command or by using the Table Options dialog.

The real key to successfully setting up table styles goes back to understanding the difference between table-level formatting and cell-level formatting. For example, the border or stroke around the entire table is controlled by table-level settings. This means that for cells in the left-most column of the table, the stroke on the left side of those cells is controlled by the table-level attribute, not at the cell level, whereas all the other strokes of the first-column cells are set by cell-level attributes. As you'll see, table styles often work best when correctly formatted cell styles are referenced as part of the table style.

Basic Table style

As with text, there is a built-in default table style called Basic Table. Similarly to the way the Basic Paragraph style affects text, the Basic Table style is applied to all tables that are created in InDesign, including those created by converting tabbed text to a table. The Basic Table style is also applied to any imported table. But if the imported table has formatting applied, that formatting will be treated as a local override to the Basic Table style.

The Basic Table style references an *implied* basic cell style; there is no basic cell style that can be modified. This implied cell styling includes the application of the Basic Paragraph style to the text along with 4-point text insets, top vertical alignment, a 1-point stroke around all cells, and no fill pattern.

Table Style General options

The General pane of the Table Style Options dialog (FIGURE 6.9) contains options similar to other style dialogs, including those found in the Cell Style Options dialog.

FIGURE 6.9 The General pane of the Table Style Options dialog.

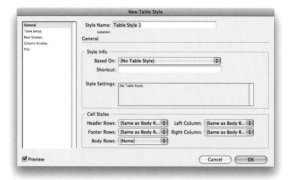

Style Info. Using the Based On pull-down menu, you can base one table style on another, and as is the case with other based-on style relationships, when you change the style named in Based On, the table style will update the shared attributes that have been modified.

You can assign a keyboard shortcut that can be used when applying the table style by typing it in the Shortcut field. Like other style keyboard shortcuts, you are limited to using the keys on the numeric keypad with various modifier keys, such as Shift, Option or Command (Mac)/Alt or Ctrl (Windows).

Style Settings summarizes all the formatting attributes that have been set for the table style.

Cell Styles. Setting up this part of the style definition correctly can be one of the most critical steps in creating an effective table style, and one of the most confusing.

Cell styles can be set for five categories of table cells: those for the Header Rows and Footer Rows, those for all the cells in the Left Column or the Right Column of the table, and using the Body Rows pull-down menu, all the other cells in the table. This can seem confusing at first, but many tables contain formatting that requires the ability to define each of these areas separately. One example is pictured in FIGURE 6.10. The table is not particularly complicated, but it does require different cell styles for four different areas.

TIP
You cannot select a table that contains cell styles and then define the table based on your selection and have it pick up the cell styles automatically. You must assign the cell styles manually by choosing them from the pull-down menus in the Cell Styles section of the dialog.

The table style sets the alternating row fill pattern and specifies cell styles for various parts of the table, including styles for the header row, the body cells, and the left- and right-column body cells.

The cell style for the header row specifies the text insets, the vertical text alignment, a paragraph style to format the text, and the cell fill color.

COMPANY	LENGTH	TYPE	YARD NO.
ASTILTEROS TALLALA SA	28.3m/93'	MY	XED094267
AZALEA MARINIST	28.3m/93'	SY	Hull 140
AZENCIALACA	34.15m/112'	MY	XXD112328
BANCO DE FRANCO	35.36m/116'	MY	XXD116279
FITTIPALDI YACHTS	33m/110'	MY	FP X1W
INACELLALAPA	27.43m/90'	EY	RG588
OCEANFEST	48m/157'	MY	418169
WALLALA YACHTS	26.5m/87'	MY	876615

The cell style for the left column is based on the Bodycells cell style but applies a different paragraph style to make the text in this column bold. It also turns off the stroke on the left side of these cells.

Most of the cells in the table are formatted by the Bodycells cell style, which specifies the text insets, the vertical text alignment, and the paragraph style applied to the text, and sets up the vertical strokes.

The cell style for the right column is based on the Bodycells cell style but turns off the stroke on the right side of the cells in this column.

FIGURE 6.10 Cell styles play an important role in setting up effective table styles.

Table Style Table Setup options

The table setup options in the Table Style Options dialog (FIGURE 6.11) are similar to those found in the Table Setup pane of the Table Options dialog but are missing controls for setting table dimensions, such as the number of body rows and columns and header rows and footer rows. These settings cannot be contained as part of the table style. As mentioned, the fact that you cannot assign header or footer rows in the style means that you have to select and use the Convert Rows command each time you apply the style to a table or in any way update a table.

FIGURE 6.11 The Table Setup pane of the Table Style Options dialog.

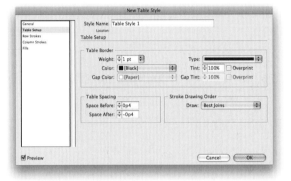

Table Border. The table border is essentially the stroke around all four sides of the table. The standard line style settings—for Weight, Type (of line style), Color, and so forth—cannot be applied to just one side of the table. It's all the way around or not at all.

Table Spacing. Table spacing refers to the vertical space above or below the entire table. Tables are, after all, anchored within text frames and can sit in between two paragraphs of text. This control lets you adjust the vertical spacing above or below the table within a text flow, much as Space Before or Space After paragraph attributes can be applied.

Stroke Drawing Order. The stroke drawing order essentially lets you control whether row strokes or column strokes draw on top. If you apply row and column strokes using alternating strokes in the Table Styles dialog or by setting strokes in the Cell Options dialog, the default is that row strokes will be drawn on top of column strokes. You can reverse this order using the Stroke Drawing Order pull-down menu (FIGURE 6.12). If, however, you set up the table's row and column strokes outside of a table style by using the Stroke panel and the Swatches panel, they will be drawn in the order in which you set them up in those panels, and this command will not reverse them.

FIGURE 6.12 Row strokes will appear on top of column strokes unless you switch them with the Stroke Drawing Order command.

Table Style Row and Column Stroke options

Unlike stroke option settings for cell-level formatting, the Row Strokes pane (FIGURE 6.13) and the Column Strokes pane (FIGURE 6.14) allow you to set *alternating* row or column stroke attributes and affect all row or all column strokes in the entire table.

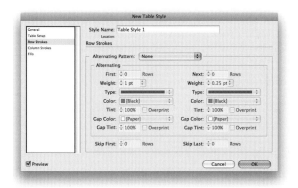

FIGURE 6.13 The Row Strokes pane of the Table Style Options dialog.

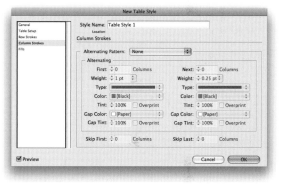

FIGURE 6.14 The Column Strokes pane of the Table Style Options dialog.

Alternating Pattern. The pull-down menus (FIGURE 6.15) let you choose from alternating patterns for row strokes or column strokes, skipping one or more rows. This menu is followed by standard controls for setting strokes, including Weight, Color, and Style (line style of stroke).

FIGURE 6.15
The Alternating Pattern pull-down menus let you set different patterns for row strokes (left) or column strokes (right).

Skip First/Last. This setting lets you control how many body rows down or how many columns over the alternating stroke pattern will begin.

Table Style Fill options

Like the Row Strokes and Column Strokes panes, the Fills pane of the Table Style Options dialog (FIGURE 6.16) lets you set alternating fill patterns for all the rows or all the columns in the table. And, like the controls for strokes, these settings affect the entire table body, not including header and footer rows.

FIGURE 6.16 The Fills pane of the Table Style Options dialog.

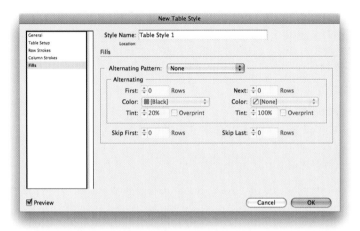

Alternating Pattern. The pull-down menu (FIGURE 6.17) for alternating patterns allows you to set different alternating fill patterns for either rows or columns. After you choose the pattern, you can use standard controls for setting the fills using colors from the swatches in your document.

FIGURE 6.17 Alternating patterns that can be set for table fills.

Skip First/Last. This option is the same as the option for alternating row and column strokes, allowing you to exclude body rows and columns from the alternating fill coverage.

Working with Table Style Limitations

As mentioned at the beginning of this chapter, with all the power of table and cell styles it is important to understand not only how they work and what they can do for you, but also to understand their limitations.

Two formatting features missing in table and cell styles have already been discussed: You will *always* have to set the column width and row height of cells when applying a table style for the first time, and you will *always* have to convert body rows to header and/or footer rows every time you apply a table style for the first time or update the table's data. There's no way around these limitations in the current iteration of the feature.

But there's another kind of limitation that's important to keep in mind as you are designing tables: It is very easy to design a table that cannot be completely defined by a table style. In many cases, you'll need to define an extra cell style or two that lets you complete the formatting. Following are just a few examples:

Header (or footer) rows that require different formatting for the leftmost or rightmost cell. There are many situations where the header or footer row might need different styling on the left or right. The simplest case is where there are strokes between all the heading columns but no table border (FIGURE 6.18). In this situation, you must set up a vertical stroke on the left or right side of the header's cell style, but on one side or the other of the table you'll end up with an extra stroke. You can create a cell style that will clear out the stroke and apply it to the cell after applying the table style.

Location	by	LOW	HIGH		Location	by	LOW	HIGH
Edisto Beach, Edisto Island	JCB	-0:31	-0:25		Edisto Beach, Edisto Island	JCB	-0:31	-0:25
Edisto Marina, Big Bay Creek entrance	DAP	-0:14	-0:11		Edisto Marina, Big Bay Creek entrance	DAP	-0:14	-0:11
Carters Dock, Big Bay Creek	JCB	-0:09	+0:04		Carters Dock, Big Bay Creek	JCB	-0:09	+0:04

FIGURE 6.18 The table style's header row sets a stroke on the right side of each cell, resulting in the final cell having an extra stroke that needs to be removed.

Irregularly repeating pattern of cell fills or other formatting. Any time a cell, row, or column needs to be differentiated from others and is not part of a regular pattern, you'll need to do some formatting outside the table style. A classic example would be where there are subheads within a table (FIGURE 6.19). In this case, you can apply the overall formatting with a table cell, and then create and apply a separate cell style that formats the subhead rows.

FIGURE 6.19 Irregularly repeating heading rows within a table cannot be handled within the table style and require applying a separate cell style to each row as needed.

Project Name	Builder	Type	Code
AUSTRALIA			
JACKSONVILLE	Aribian	Residential	AWX-YZB12
SOUTH TAHIBA	Lewhawken	Mixed Use	
CANADA			
VICTORIA II	Beckingham	Residential	FRONT123
KLEPPINGTON	Vladdnost	Commerical	W3W5H-B12
SHENANDOAH	Murphy	Mixed Use	
HACKNEYED	Becker	Mixed Use	
IRELAND			
LUCKY CHARMS	Shannon	Commercial	98UIY-YZB11
VANDYHAM	Lichtner	Commerical	
HANNENSTEDTS	Vorctner	Residential	XXH-18504

Alternating row and column fills in the same table. While InDesign does a great job of applying alternating fills to columns *or* rows, you can't *automatically* format both within the same table (FIGURE 6.20). It would be nice if you could, but it's a little more complicated than you might think, because you have to figure out what intersecting cell colors should be. Until InDesign provides this capability, you have to format as much of the table as possible with a table style, and then use cell styles to do the rest.

Restaurant / City	Cuisines	Rating	Price	Comments
Burgermeister 86 Carl St. San Francisco (415) 566-1274	American	*	$	Cole Valley burger stand serving Niman Ranch beef and other fine items
Eos 901 Cole St. San Francisco (415) 566-3063	East-West	***	$$$	Pan-Asian menu now focuses on small plates, but larger plates are winners, too. Try stuffed quail, clay pot chicken, sumac-ginger pork. Banana desserts star.
Grandeho's Kamekyo 943 Cole St. San Francisco (415) 759-5693	Sushi	**	$$	Cole Valley veteran offers top-notch sushi and other dishes such as chasoba noodles, eggplant Dengaku. Friendly, engaging service.
Zazie 941 Cole St. San Francisco (415) 564-5332	French	***	$$	Fixed-price three-course dinner is a good bargain at this inviting California-French restaurant. Good desserts.

FIGURE 6.20 The table style applies an alternating row pattern. But the columns have an alternating pattern also, which must be formatted with two different cell styles.

Maintaining Links and Updating Tables

As discussed earlier, table and cell styles help automate the process of applying the same formatting attributes to a series of different tables. Once this job is done, it would be nice if the information inside those tables never changed, but that is often not the case. When it comes to *updating* the content of tables, styles become indispensable.

The most efficient way to update table content is to create links between your InDesign table and an external Excel spreadsheet. As discussed in Chapter 4, "Auto-styling Imported Word and Excel Files," you can create links to an Excel file by turning on the Create Links When Placing Text and Spreadsheet Files option in InDesign's preferences (Preferences > File Handling).

When updating linked Excel files, table styles are essential. If you format your imported Excel data using a table style, the format of the table will for the most part remain intact. If you simply format the table directly without using table or cell styles, all the formatting will be lost when you update the linked file.

You can also create links to Word documents containing tables, but as discussed in Chapter 4, all formatting—including that applied via styles—is lost, so it's hardly worth the effort. Another way to update tables is to copy and paste new data into an existing table, and if styles are used, this can be a viable alternative to linking to Excel spreadsheets.

IMPORTING EXCEL SPREADSHEETS

Regardless of whether your Excel spreadsheet file is formatted or unformatted, you'll generally want to import it as an unformatted table, which is not the default setting. Change this setting in the Import Options dialog. You can access the Microsoft Excel Import Options dialog by selecting Show Import Options in the Place dialog or by holding down the Shift key as you double-click on the filename when placing. Set the formatting to Unformatted Table, and if you've already set up a table style, choose it from the Table Style pull-down menu.

Whether you apply the table style on import or import the table and then apply the style, the table is likely not yet complete. Because cell styles cannot adjust row height or column width, you'll need to set those manually using the Cell Options dialog or the Control panel. If the table and the table style call for a header or footer row, you'll also have to manually select the appropriate rows in the table, and then use the Convert Rows command to convert those body rows to header or footer rows (FIGURE 6.21).

Donor Country	Location	Ref No.	Material
Italy	Murano or possibly northern Europe, 1550 - 1570	1879-11-A, 1879-12-AB	Free-blown colorless (slightly gray) glass with opaque white (lattimo) canes and applied decoration
Austria	Hall, 1534 - 1536	2479-99-AG	Free-blown and mold-blown colorless (slightly gray) glass with gilding and cold-painted decoration
Greece	Ionia, about 625 B.C	3579-65-G, 3579-66-H	Terracotta
France	Paris, about 1550	2873-21-A	Lead-glazed earthenware
Bulgaria	Sophia, about 1710 - 1715	4462-53-L, 4465-53-L	Oak veneered with satiné (bloodwood); gilt bronze mounts

FIGURE 6.21 A newly imported spreadsheet with a table style applied (left) requires manual adjustment of the row heights and column widths, and setting of the table header/footer rows (right).

Updating the linked file

After you've formatted an Excel spreadsheet using table and cell styles, it can be relatively painless to import new data. When the original Excel spreadsheet has been updated, the filename in the Links panel will show a warning icon. To update the link and bring in the new data, choose Update Link from the Links panel menu or click the Update icon at the bottom of the Links panel. A warning dialog (FIGURE 6.22) indicates that all table formatting that is not applied via table styles or cell styles will be lost!

FIGURE 6.22 A warning dialog appears when you update an Excel spreadsheet link.

When the table data has been updated, all formatting applied via the table style will be intact. And fortunately, column widths and row heights—which initially had to be formatted manually outside the table and cell styles—are still set correctly when the linked file is updated. For many tables, the only modification you will need to make when updating is to set the header and/or footer rows. Simply select the appropriate rows and use the Convert Rows command. The table style's setting for Header Row and/or Footer Row kicks in based on the cell style assigned to it, and the table is complete (FIGURE 6.23).

Merge Cells		
Unmerge Cells		
Split Cell Horizontally		
Split Cell Vertically		
Convert Rows ▸	To Header	
	To Body	
Distribute Rows Evenly	To Footer	
Distribute Columns Evenly		
Go to Row...		
Edit Header		
Edit Footer		

Country	Location	Ref No.
Japan	Nara or East Kyoto, 697-782	2039-41-A,
China	Siberia, 1250-1390	2479-99-AG, 5436-70-B
Korea	Seoul, about 625 B.C.	4279-65-G, 4579-66-L
Vietnam	Hanoi plain, about 1550	2873-21-A
Thailand	Phuket, 1810 - 1815	4462-53-L, 4465-53-L

Donor Country	Location
Japan	Nara or East Kyoto, 697-782
China	Siberia, 1250-1390
Korea	Seoul, about 625 B.C.
Vietnam	Hanoi plain, about 1550
Thailand	Phuket, 1810 - 1815

FIGURE 6.23 Complete the formatting of an updated linked Excel spreadsheet by converting the header and footer rows (left). Then the cell styles set in the table style will be applied (right).

COPYING AND PASTING NEW TABLE DATA

You often can't control the source of data that you receive. So when you can't use a nice, neat Excel file for updating table data, there is another alternative that works well. Since InDesign CS3, designers have had the ability to update tables with the contents of the clipboard, meaning you can cut or copy and paste new data into existing tables. Table styles don't make the process perfectly automatic, but they help smooth the process.

The new data that you want to use must be in a tab-delimited format with paragraph returns at the end of each line. The number of entries in the data should correlate with the number of cells in your InDesign table, with corresponding rows and columns. You can also confine the newly pasted text to one section of the table by highlighting the cells where you want to paste the new data, but it's often just as easy to update the entire table.

When you have new data for a table, it's best to use a two-stage process to prepare the information for a smooth transfer into the table. Start by choosing File > Place to temporarily place the text on the pasteboard using the Import Options dialog to strip out any formatting. Highlight all the new text with the Type tool, and then copy or cut it into the clipboard (FIGURE 6.24).

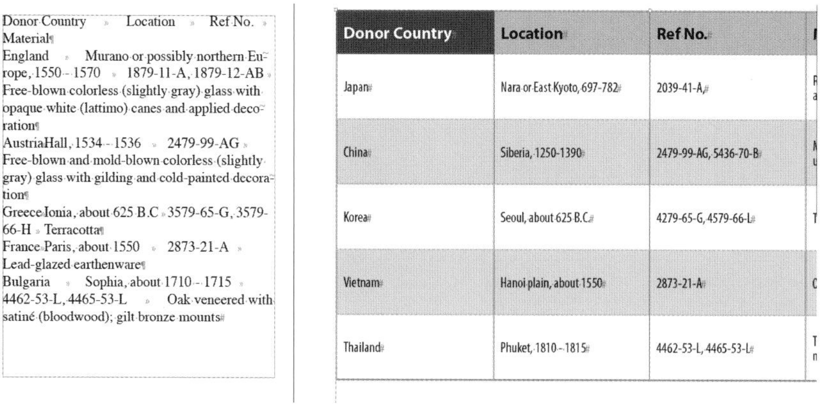

FIGURE 6.24 Place the new text for the table on the pasteboard, use the Type tool to select all the text, and then cut or copy into the clipboard.

To paste the text into the table, you need to select the first cell (pressing the Esc key is the easiest way). You cannot simply click in the cell or all the text will be pasted into the first cell only. With the first cell selected, paste the text into the table.

When you paste the new data, there will be local overrides present, so the cell styles within the table style will not be applied. Click the Clear Overrides icon at the bottom of the Cell Styles panel, and your table is complete. You do not have to respecify the header or footer rows, nor adjust the column widths or row heights (FIGURE 6.25) if you have set the rows to a fixed height.

It may not be as smooth as linking to an Excel spreadsheet, but the ability to copy and paste new data into an existing table can be a tremendous time-saver.

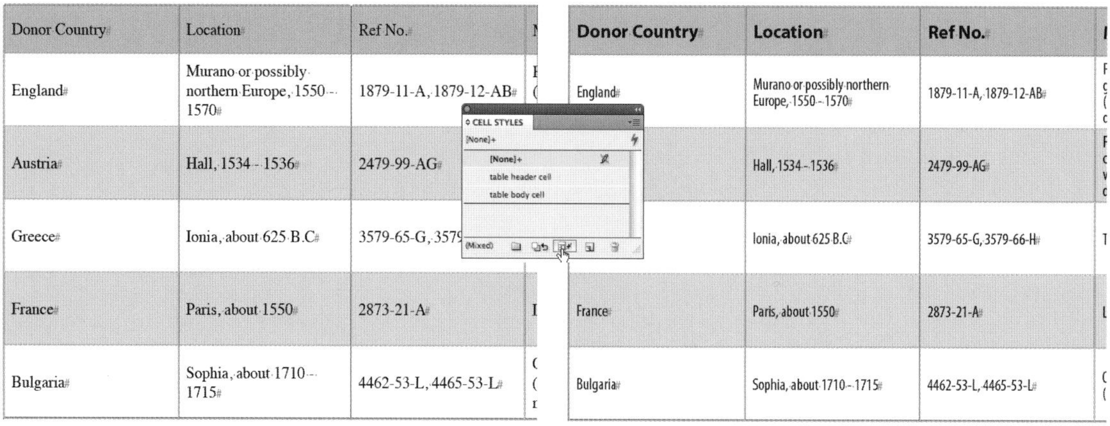

FIGURE 6.25 After pasting the new text (left), click the Clear Overrides icon at the bottom of the Cell Styles panel to complete the Table Style formatting (right).

CHAPTER 7

Drop Caps, Bullets, and Numbering

MANY INDESIGN FEATURES are not actual styles, but they incorporate style choices into their settings to increase formatting options and add efficiency. Among the most common are drop caps and automatically generated bulleted or numbered lists. Of course, you *can* use these features without saving them in a paragraph style or calling on any character styles, but to do so is to invite additional work for yourself.

Styles eliminate multiple steps required to create truly great-looking drop caps. They're the *only* way to attach custom formatting to the bullets in a bulleted list, and they're an *essential* list management tool when you work with numbered lists, especially as those lists get more

Drop Caps

Drop caps are a great typographic convention for starting off an article, document section, or book chapter, and their most basic implementation in InDesign is nearly a push-button process. With the text cursor in any paragraph, simply enter the number of lines the drop cap should span in the Drop Cap Number of Lines field in either the Control panel (FIGURE 7.1) or the Paragraph panel (FIGURE 7.2). A single-character drop cap is established automatically.

FIGURE 7.1 Drop Cap fields for Number of Lines and Number of Characters in the Control panel.

FIGURE 7.2 Drop Cap fields for Number of Lines and Number of Characters in the Character panel.

TIP
Because drop caps are dynamic, mathematically enlarged characters, they won't indicate that they're a different point size from the other text in the paragraph when selected. If the paragraph text is 9 points, the drop cap will always show as 9 points in the Character panel or Control panel regardless of how large it appears to be.

Drop caps are created by a mathematical algorithm. When you enter a number of lines for a drop cap, InDesign looks at the typeface and leading used, and then calculates the proper size at which to present the drop cap so that it fully spans the desired number of lines. If the font size or leading of the paragraph increases or decreases, the size of the drop cap is adjusted accordingly.

As effortless as this functionality is, it almost always results in a rather artless drop cap. FIGURE 7.3 shows a drop cap created in this bare-bones manner, and it exhibits a number of inherent problems. The most obvious problem is that the top arm of the drop cap F collides with the letter that follows it in the paragraph. That can be fixed with tracking, but it adds a step. A more subtle problem is that the drop cap doesn't align properly with the left edge of the column. That can also be fixed (as you'll see shortly), but it also adds another step. On a purely subjective note, it's a pretty dull drop cap. It's the same typeface and weight as the body copy, so there's no typographic interest created, and it's the same color as the rest of the text, so there's no contrast. Both problems can be fixed by changing the attributes of the drop cap, but that requires two more steps. That brings the number of steps required to create a *good-looking* drop cap to a minimum of five.

For several days after leaving Nantucket, nothing above hatches was seen of Captain Ahab. The mates regularly relieved each other at the watches, and for aught that could be seen to the contrary, they seemed to be the only commanders of the ship; only they sometimes issued from the cabin with orders so sudden and peremptory, that after all it was plain they but commanded vicariously.

FIGURE 7.3 A drop cap using only the default settings typically suffers from spacing and alignment problems, as well as a lack of visual appeal.

The drop cap shown in FIGURE 7.4 is spiced up quite a bit, producing a much more interesting and pleasing result. However, getting it to look like this required *many* additional steps, including:

- Adjusting the tracking of the drop cap character to properly modify the space between it and the text that follows

- Changing the typeface, point size, and color

- Adding a custom underline

- Adding a hair space before and after the drop cap character to complete the "box" effect created by the custom underline

- Changing the number of characters in the drop cap from 1 to 3 so that the two hair spaces would be included

For several days after leaving Nantucket, nothing above hatches was seen of Captain Ahab. The mates regularly relieved each other at the watches, and for aught that could be seen to the contrary, they seemed to be the only commanders of the ship; only they sometimes issued from the cabin with orders so sudden and peremptory, that after all it was plain they but commanded vicariously.

FIGURE 7.4 A highly customized drop cap using a character style that changes typeface, size, and color; adjusts tracking; and adds a custom underline.

Wherever else this drop cap needs to be applied, each of these repetitive steps is an obstacle to productivity and consistency. It's essential to use styles to minimize this kind of effort whenever possible.

DROP CAP OPTIONS

The Control panel and Character panel offer only two of five possible drop cap settings. The rest reside in the Drop Caps and Nested Styles dialog (Command-Option-R/Ctrl-Alt-R) or in the Drop Caps and Nested Styles area of the Paragraph Style Options dialog (FIGURE 7.5). Let's explore *all* options for a drop cap and how they can be streamlined for speed to produce better-looking results.

FIGURE 7.5 The Drop Caps
and Nested Styles options
in the Paragraph Style
Options dialog.

Lines [   ]. The value you enter here determines the number of lines the drop cap will span. If there aren't enough lines in the current paragraph to accommodate the number of lines entered here, the drop cap will extend as far as necessary into the *next* paragraph (FIGURE 7.6).

FIGURE 7.6 If necessary,
a drop cap will span multiple
paragraphs.

I was so tired that even my fears were not able to keep me awake long.

When I next came to myself, I seemed to have been asleep a very long time. My first thought was, "Well, what an astonishing dream I've had!"

Characters [   ]. A drop cap can span more than one character. If, for example, a paragraph starts with a quote, setting this value to 2 will format the opening quotation mark and the first character that follows it as the drop cap. Spaces and tabs also count as characters. The drop cap in Figure 7.4 is surrounded on either side by thin space characters, so it's set up as a three-character drop cap with only one of those three being a visible letter.

Character Style. Assigning a character style to a drop cap is the best way to quickly apply a drop cap that stands out from the rest of your text with variations in typeface, weight, and color. The drop cap in Figure 7.4 uses a character style that changes the size, color, and typeface of the drop cap; applies a custom underline; and baseline shifts the drop cap for optimal positioning, effectively eliminating several formatting steps every time the drop cap style is applied.

All existing character styles in your document are available here, and you can create a new style by selecting New Character Style at the bottom of the menu. Choosing [None] leaves the drop cap formatting identical to the rest of the text in the paragraph, just bigger.

Even if you *want* a drop cap that's the same font, weight, and color as your body copy, it's still a good idea to create a drop cap character style. As shown in Figure 7.3, drop caps are often uncomfortably close to the text that wraps around them. A character style with a positive tracking value built into it can effectively push away the text in the paragraph and create a comfortable buffer around the right side of the drop cap character.

Align Left Edge. Until InDesign CS3, drop caps had always been positioned out of alignment with the left edge of a column (FIGURE 7.7). This was especially noticeable in sans-serif type on letters with an entirely vertical left edge (B, F, M, etc.), but round characters didn't fare much better. Ironically, the very thing that keeps drop caps flexible and simple to implement is what creates this problem. InDesign doesn't actually *change* the point size of the drop cap character, so all spacing decisions made by the type engine are based on a character of a much smaller size regardless of how it appears on the page. As a result, the spacing around the drop cap character is not properly adjusted. The Align Left Edge option was added to the Drop Cap options in InDesign CS3 and later to correct this (FIGURE 7.8).

TIP
How Align Left Edge affects a drop cap's position depends on the typeface, the specific letter, and whether or not Optical Margin Alignment is turned on. To allow for the best drop cap positioning in any situation, make one paragraph style with Align Left Edge turned on and a second style *based on the first one* with Align Left Edge turned off, and apply the appropriate style as needed.

But as for Queequeg—why, Queequeg sat there among them—at the head of the table, too, it so chanced; as cool as an icicle. To be sure I cannot say much for his breeding. His greatest admirer could not have cordially justified his bringing his harpoon into breakfast with him, and using it there without

FIGURE 7.7 Align Left Edge turned off.

But as for Queequeg—why, Queequeg sat there among them—at the head of the table, too, it so chanced; as cool as an icicle. To be sure I cannot say much for his breeding. His greatest admirer could not have cordially justified his bringing his harpoon into breakfast with him, and using it there without

FIGURE 7.8 Align Left Edge turned on.

Scale for Descenders. Another drop cap problem affects characters with descenders (Q and J, for example) that dip into the body copy (FIGURE 7.9), requiring a baseline shift or point size reduction to position them properly. The Scale for Descenders option, when its check box is selected, looks at the optical body of the character and automatically resizes it so that the descender does not extend into the paragraph (FIGURE 7.10). Letters that don't require this adjustment won't be affected by this setting.

TIP
Characters with greatly exaggerated descenders (the Q in Trajan Pro, for example) *will be* adjusted by the Scale for Descenders option but probably not enough to clear the text in the rest of the paragraph.

Queequeg and I had just left the Pequod, and were sauntering away from the water, for the moment each occupied with his own thoughts, when the above words were put to us by a stranger, who, pausing before us, levelled his massive forefinger at the vessel in question.

FIGURE 7.9 Scale for Descenders turned off.

Queequeg and I had just left the Pequod, and were sauntering away from the water, for the moment each occupied with his own thoughts, when the above words were put to us by a stranger, who, pausing before us, levelled his massive forefinger at the vessel in question.

FIGURE 7.10 Scale for Descenders turned on.

Boxing Off a Drop Cap

A custom underline (see Chapter 1, "The Fundamentals: Paragraph and Character Styles") built into the character style used by a drop cap can create the illusion of a box behind the individual letter, but that box is restricted to the exact width of the letterform. Making that underline look like a box—with some extra space on either side of the letter—requires a three-letter drop cap, where the letter is surrounded on either side by a hair space (**FIGURE 7.11**).

Adding that hair space is the one part of this look that *can't* be built into the style or drop cap settings. However, there is a way to speed up the additional step of inserting hair spaces around the letter, and styles play a key role in that automation process, too.

Using the GREP features in Find/Change, you can search for any single character that appears at the beginning of a paragraph (^(.)) and limit that search to only text formatted with your drop cap paragraph style by selecting that paragraph style in the Find Format Options. Then, in the Change to field, replace that with a hair space, whatever the first character found was, and another hair space (~I$1~I). Combined with a three-letter drop cap setting and a character style with a custom underline, this creates a fully editable "boxed" drop cap.

The background for this technique (and the meaning of the metacharacters required to implement it) can be found in the "Metacharacters" section in Chapter 3, "Automatic Styling with GREP," and in Chapter 8, "Advanced Find/Change with Styles." See those chapters for more in-depth coverage of these settings.

It's a simple but effective visual cheat, so don't shy away from using it just because you think adding all those hair spaces is a tedious task. It doesn't have to be.

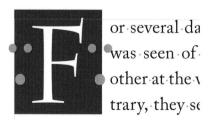

FIGURE 7.11
Hair spaces and underlining create a "box" for drop caps.

Locking these settings into a paragraph style makes short work of drop cap application, allowing you to simultaneously add a drop cap to the paragraph and a character style to that drop cap with a single click.

Bullets and Numbering

Like drop caps, bulleted and numbered lists also have their own push-button implementation methods available in the Control panel (in paragraph mode): the Bulleted List and Numbered List buttons (FIGURE 7.12). Clicking the corresponding button converts any selected text to a bulleted list or numbered list using InDesign's defaults. Option-clicking/Alt-clicking either button opens the Bullets and Numbering dialog, which is mirrored in its entirety in the Bullets and Numbering area of the Paragraph Style Options dialog (FIGURE 7.13).

FIGURE 7.12 Default bullets and numbering can be applied with one click from the Control panel (in paragraph mode) using the Bulleted List and Numbered List buttons.

FIGURE 7.13 The Bullets and Numbering area in the Paragraph Style Options dialog.

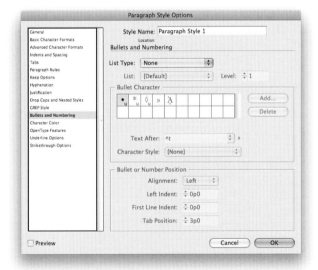

BULLETED LISTS

The default List Type setting for any paragraph or a new paragraph style is None. When Bullets is selected from the List Type menu, the bullet-related options in the dialog become available.

Bullet character

The grid of available bullet characters (FIGURE 7.14) contains a few preset options. Bullets can be font specific (e.g., a square bullet specific to Zapf Dingbats or an ornamental bullet specific to Garamond Premier Pro), or they can be generic. The latter is appropriate when using characters that are common across many typefaces (e.g., the Option-8 default bullet on the Mac or the Alt-8 default bullet in Windows). Bullet characters that are *not* associated with a specific font appear in the Bullet Character grid with a small "u" in the lower-right corner, indicating that the bullet is determined by its Unicode value rather than by a specific typeface.

FIGURE 7.14 The bullet grid can contain up to 20 entries for quick access to your favorite bullet characters.

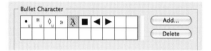

Add button. The Add button opens the Add Bullets dialog, where you can choose any active typeface with the Font Family and Style menus, and then click any glyph in the resulting grid to select it as a bullet (FIGURE 7.15). If your bullet *must* be associated with a specific font (Zapf Dingbats or Wingdings, for example), be sure to select the Remember Font with Bullet check box at the bottom of the dialog.

FIGURE 7.15 The Add Bullets dialog.

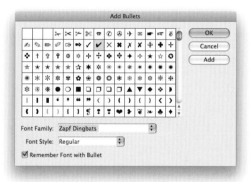

Delete button. Click the Delete button to remove any selected glyph from the Bullet Character grid. All but the first bullet in the grid (•) can be deleted.

Text After. InDesign automatically generates not only the bullet, but whatever character(s) you want to follow it, such as a space or tab. If the character you want can't be typed in the dialog (a tab, for example), the flyout menu at the end of this field includes a number of likely options. You can also type the appropriate metacharacter here if you know what it is.

Character Style. You can assign any character style to the bullet to give it a different appearance. This is the *only* way to influence the formatting of the bullet beyond associating it with a particular typeface. By default, the bullet selected will be the same size and color as the text of the paragraph to which it's assigned (FIGURE 7.16). Changes in the size, fill, stroke, baseline shift, or any other attribute can only be achieved by assigning a character style in the Bullets and Numbering dialog. This is because bullets in a bulleted list (and numbers in a numbered list) technically don't exist on the page. You can *see* them, but you can't select them (FIGURE 7.17). They're automatically generated characters that exist beyond the reach of the Text tool in a layout. If you want a red bullet, you need to create a character style with red chosen for the character color.

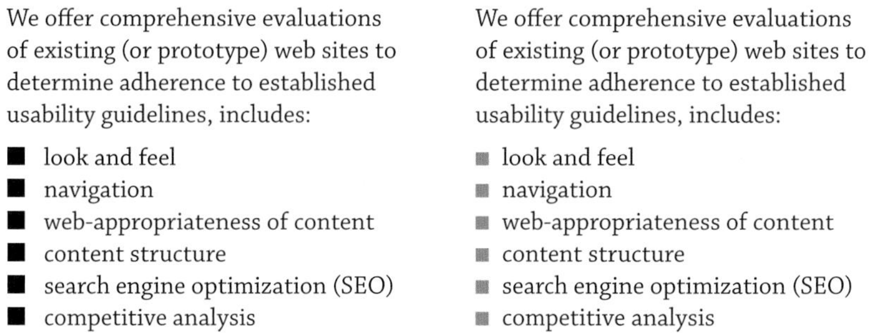

We offer comprehensive evaluations of existing (or prototype) web sites to determine adherence to established usability guidelines, includes:

- look and feel
- navigation
- web-appropriateness of content
- content structure
- search engine optimization (SEO)
- competitive analysis

We offer comprehensive evaluations of existing (or prototype) web sites to determine adherence to established usability guidelines, includes:

- look and feel
- navigation
- web-appropriateness of content
- content structure
- search engine optimization (SEO)
- competitive analysis

FIGURE 7.16 Bullets with no character style assigned (left) versus bullets using a character style that changes the type size and color (right).

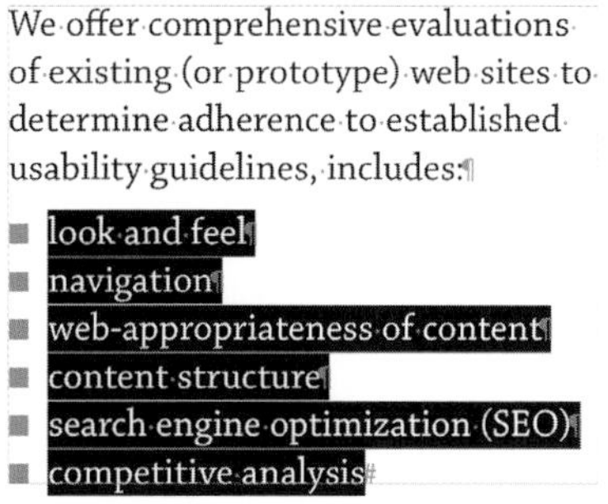

We·offer·comprehensive·evaluations· of·existing·(or·prototype)·web·sites·to· determine·adherence·to·established· usability·guidelines,·includes:¶

- look·and·feel¶
- navigation¶
- web-appropriateness·of·content¶
- content·structure¶
- search·engine·optimization·(SEO)¶
- competitive·analysis¶

FIGURE 7.17 Since bullets can't be selected, formatting can only be applied by designating a character style in the Bullets and Numbering dialog.

When Bullet Styles Collide

Font-specific bullets (those defined with the Remember Font with Bullet option selected) supersede any conflicting font in the character style assigned to them. In other words, if a square bullet specific to Zapf Dingbats is selected for a bulleted list, but the character style assigned to the bullet has Newspaper Pi defined as its typeface, the character style's typeface is ignored. However, all other attributes of the character style—size, color, baseline shift, and so on—*will* be applied to the bullet.

Aligning Bullets

The options in the Bullet or Number Position area control the position of the bullet (or number) and the text that follows it. From here, the bullet can be indented or set to "hang" by adjusting the left indent and first line indents. For the most part, these settings work like normal paragraph indentation settings but with a list-specific twist. The peculiarities of this group of options are best demonstrated in the context of a numbered list, so a full explanation of these settings is found in the "Bullet or Number Position" section later in this chapter.

NUMBERED LISTS

InDesign's numbered lists provide very powerful and sophisticated options, but implementing them is not an exercise for the timid. Everything gets far more complicated and cryptic once you choose Numbers from the List Type menu, which completely changes the dialog to reveal the options for numbered list formatting (FIGURE 7.18).

FIGURE 7.18 Numbering options displayed when Numbers is selected from the List Type menu.

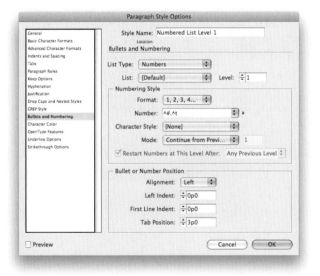

Defining a numbered list

InDesign can handle very complex, hierarchical lists, and a single document can contain many different lists running concurrently, each with their own unique numbering. Numbered lists can be interrupted by nonnumbered paragraphs and be continued later in the document, even if the list is not in the same story or if the list continues across multiple documents managed by the Book panel. These discontinuous lists are called "running lists."

To establish a running or multilevel list, the list must first be *defined* so that In-Design can track its numbering throughout a document or across several documents. When a defined list is built into a paragraph style (which is the only way to work with this feature *and* stay sane), the list's formatting and its connection to the defined list are preserved and applied with a single click of the style name in the Paragraph Style panel.

The defined list is like an invisible thread, connecting any paragraphs associated with it anywhere in your document (or documents, if the list runs through several files in an InDesign book). Their association with the list establishes a relationship between every numbered paragraph so that the numbering sequence can be maintained even when those numbered paragraphs are non-consecutive. Defining multiple lists creates multiple threads, each of which maintains its unique sequential numbering that doesn't interfere with other defined lists. For instance, one defined list can be used to handle all standard numbered lists within a document's body copy, whereas another could be used to auto-number all figure captions in the same document.

To define a list, choose New List from the List menu. In the New List dialog (FIGURE 7.19), name the list and select either (or both) of the options that apply to your list. Continue Numbers across Stories enables numbering that continues in separate, unthreaded text frames; Continue Numbers from Previous Document in Book extends that functionality to multiple documents provided they're part of a book managed by the Book panel.

FIGURE 7.19 The New List dialog is displayed when New List is selected from the Bullets and Numbering dialog.

Lists can also be defined from the Type menu. You can choose Bulleted & Numbered Lists > Define Lists, which opens a dialog where you can define new lists. The Define Lists dialog is also the only place where you can rename, delete, or load lists from other InDesign documents (FIGURE 7.20).

FIGURE 7.20 The Define Lists dialog centralizes control over the creation, deletion, renaming, and loading of lists.

Multilevel lists

When a list is defined, it's assigned a level of 1 in the Level field (FIGURE 7.21). Any defined list can have many levels. For hierarchical lists (e.g., 3.1, 3.2, 3.2a, 3.2b), there's no need to define a new list for each level. The levels of a multilevel list should all be associated with *one* list, but each should have a different level number assigned to it.

FIGURE 7.21 All new lists start at Level 1.

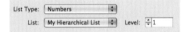

Once a level of 2 or greater is selected in the Level field, the Restart Numbers at This Level After option (located at the bottom of the Numbering Style area) becomes available (FIGURE 7.22). When activated, the default setting for this option is Any Previous Level. This allows the numbering at the current level to automatically start from 1 again when a paragraph at the *current* level imme-diately follows a paragraph assigned to a higher (meaning a lower-numbered) level. Deselecting this check box continues sequential numbering from section to section. FIGURE 7.23 compares a multilevel list where the Level 2 and Level 3 items use the Restart Numbers at This Level After Any Previous Level to the same list where that option is turned off. In the left example, each Level 2 item that appears after a Level 1 item starts numbering from (a) again, and each Level 3 item that appears after a Level 2 item starts numbering from 1 again. In the right example, numbering of Level 2 and 3 items continues to increase regardless of the level that precedes them.

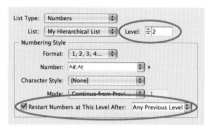

FIGURE 7.22 Adding a level to a list activates the Restart Numbers at This Level After option.

I. This is a Level 1 item.

    (a) This is a Level 2 item.

        1. This is a Level 3 item.

        2. This is a Level 3 item.

        3. This is a Level 3 item.

    (b) This is a Level 2 item.

    (c) This is a Level 2 item.

II. This is a Level 1 item.

    (a) This is a Level 2 item.

        1. This is a Level 3 item.

        2. This is a Level 3 item.

    (b) This is a Level 2 item.

        1. This is a Level 3 item.

        2. This is a Level 3 item.

    (c) This is a Level 2 item.

    (d) This is a Level 2 item.

I. This is a Level 1 item.

    (a) This is a Level 2 item.

        1. This is a Level 3 item.

        2. This is a Level 3 item.

        3. This is a Level 3 item.

    (b) This is a Level 2 item.

    (c) This is a Level 2 item.

II. This is a Level 1 item.

    (d) This is a Level 2 item.

        4. This is a Level 3 item.

        5. This is a Level 3 item.

    (e) This is a Level 2 item.

        6. This is a Level 3 item.

        7. This is a Level 3 item.

    (f) This is a Level 2 item.

    (g) This is a Level 2 item.

FIGURE 7.23 Restart Numbers at This Level After Any Previous Level turned on in a list (left) and turned off (right).

While each level of a hierarchical list calls on the *same* defined list, each of those levels requires *its own paragraph style* to handle the numbering format, its presentation, and any renumbering instructions. FIGURE 7.24 diagrams the relationships between lists, levels, and styles in InDesign.

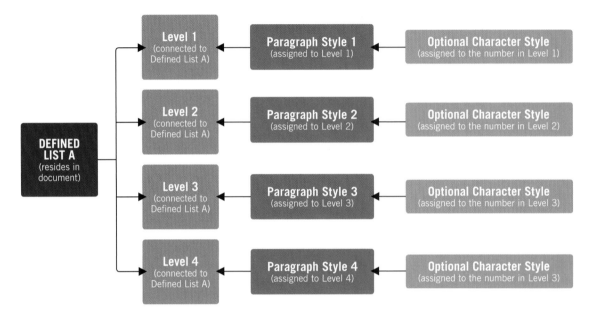

FIGURE 7.24 Levels are connected to an individual list, and styles are associated with each level. Optionally, character styles for numbers can be built into those paragraph styles.

Numbering Style options

The options in the Numbering Style area handle the presentation of the numbers InDesign generates, from the numbering system used to the character style applied to that number and any static text, spacing, or punctuation that must surround it.

Format. Numbered lists can use Arabic numerals (1, 2, 3, 4) with or without leading zeros (for numbers up to four digits), uppercase or lowercase Roman numerals (i, ii, iii or I, II, III), or alphabetical characters from A to Z. In multilevel lists, this is the setting most likely to change from level to level.

Number. The expression in this field (a combination of characters and metacharacters) determines how the number InDesign generates will appear and what characters will automatically precede or follow it.

The default expression for numbered lists is ^#.^t: The ^# represents the number that will automatically be generated; the period is a literal period that will appear after that number; and the ^t represents a tab following that period. Any number placeholder can be combined with literal text and/or other metacharacters to produce highly customized auto numbering. Placeholders can refer back to other levels in a list or call on a document's chapter number, if used.

There's a very specific limitation to what can precede the number InDesign generates. If you want to right-align the numbers in a list so that double- and single-digit numbers line up properly, you might think that setting a right-indent tab in the ruler for the paragraph and then including a tab metacharacter *before* the number placeholder in your numbering expression would accomplish this. Unfortunately, a tab cannot exist anywhere but at the very end of a numbering expression (FIGURE 7.25). You *can* right-align numbers in a numbered list, but it has to be done in the Bullet and Number Position area of the dialog. This is yet another counterintuitive process that is covered later in this chapter.

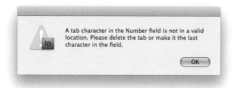

FIGURE 7.25 Tabs are only accepted at the end of a numbering expression.

Other number placeholders include Level 1 through Level 9 for hierarchical, nested lists (1.1, 1.2, 1.3, etc.) and a Chapter Number placeholder that calls on any chapter numbering established for the document in the Numbering & Section Options dialog. TABLE 7.1 lists all number placeholder metacharacters and the numbers they produce.

TABLE 7.1 **Number Placeholders for Numbered Lists**

Placeholder Metacharacter	Number Inserted
^#	Current Level (more precisely, the current *number* at this level)
^1	Level 1 (reports back the number as defined for Level 1 of the current list but not any static text defined for that level's number such as tabs, periods, parentheses, etc.)
^2 thru ^9	Level 2 thru Level 9 (behaves exactly like the ^1 metacharacter but reports back the appropriate number for the appropriate level, up to a maximum of 9 levels)
^H	Chapter Number (reports back the chapter number established in the document's Numbering & Section Options dialog)

TIP

If you find you *do* need to restart numbering from a specific number, it's best to make that change locally. To do this, insert the text cursor in the paragraph where the numbering change should occur, Control-click/right-click, and then choose Restart Numbering. You can accomplish the same thing from the Type menu (Type > Bullets and Numbering > Restart Numbering).

Character Style. You can assign any existing character style to the numbers generated by InDesign (including all the surrounding text you may have built into your expression in the Number field), which gives them a different appearance from the other text in the paragraph.

Mode. When defining numbering options in a paragraph style, use the Continue from Previous Number default option, which numbers all items in the list consecutively. The other option in this menu—Start At—activates the field next to it, where a specific number can be entered. However, if Start At is built into the paragraph style, *every* paragraph in the numbered list will use the number entered here. So, for example, this would create a list where every paragraph is numbered 4 if that's the value entered for Start At—this is not very useful. Start At should be used for local overrides, where numbering needs to be restarted from a specific number.

Bullet or Number Position

One of the most puzzling aspects of the Bullets and Numbering feature is how the options for aligning numbers work. At first glance, the alignment options are similar to standard paragraph indentation options, but there are some very unusual and significant differences specific to bulleted and numbered lists.

The behavior of the Alignment menu options differ from InDesign's normal alignment options. This setting has nothing to do with the alignment of the paragraph. Rather, it designates the alignment of the bullet or number *and* establishes the left side, center point, or right side of that bullet or number as the reference point for the first line indent.

Left alignment. When the alignment for the bullet or number is set to Left (the default), the value entered in the Left Indent field sets the position of *the leftmost edge* of the bullet or number. When Left alignment is chosen, the Left Indent and First Line Indent options behave just like their counterparts in the Indents and Spacing options for a paragraph. As with paragraphs that are *not* bulleted or numbered, a negative first line indent will create a "hanging" indent (FIGURE 7.26).

- look and feel
- navigation
- web-appropriateness of content
- content structure
- search engine optimization (SEO)
- competitive analysis

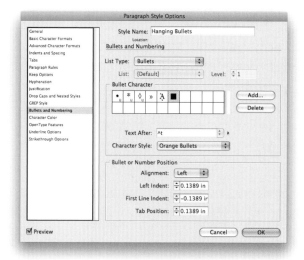

FIGURE 7.26 A left indent combined with a negative first line indent creates a "hanging" bullet.

Right alignment. When a numbered list has more than nine items in it—or any time Roman numerals are used—it's preferable to choose Right from the Alignment menu so that the single- and double-digit numbers in the list (and the periods that follow them) line up properly. However, things get more confusing as soon as you choose either Right or Center. With Right alignment selected, the first line indent positions *the rightmost edge of the number* relative to the left indent. For instance, if the left indent of a right-aligned numbered list is set to 1 pica, 8 points (1p8), a first line indent of -0p6 positions the right side of the period after the number 6 points away from the left indent position (FIGURE 7.27), not from the left edge of the column or frame.

Because of this behavior, a bit of trial and error is required to properly position right-aligned numbers so that the left side of the number is also where you'd like it to be. When right-aligning numbers, it's best to make sure the Preview check box is selected so you can see how your number position is affected by your left and first line indent settings. Also, establish your alignment based on the longest possible number that will appear in the list.

Center alignment. Center alignment follows the same logic (or lack thereof). For instance, when center-aligning a bullet (a more likely candidate for this alignment choice than a number), the first line indent value defines the *middle* of that bullet so that half of the bullet will fall to the left of that position, and the other half will fall to the right of it.

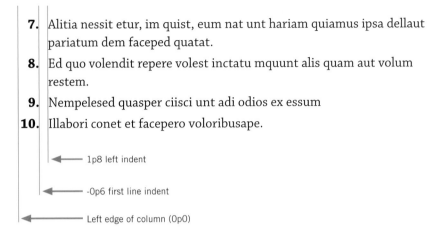

7. Alitia nessit etur, im quist, eum nat unt hariam quiamus ipsa dellaut pariatum dem faceped quatat.

8. Ed quo volendit repere volest inctatu mquunt alis quam aut volum restem.

9. Nempelesed quasper ciisci unt adi odios ex essum

10. Illabori conet et facepero voloribusape.

1p8 left indent

-0p6 first line indent

Left edge of column (0p0)

Tab Position. The Tab Position behavior can also seem confusing. By default, the tab position for a list is set to 3 picas. If the left indent exceeds 3 picas, the tab will automatically be reset to 6 picas or whatever the next highest 3-pica increment is. This is actually the same way standard InDesign tabs behave if no tab positions are specifically set. However, there's nowhere else in the application where you literally *see* these 3-pica jumps occurring as you work. You can manually fine-tune the tab position in the Tab field, but this reactive behavior, if triggered, will always supersede your custom settings.

Numbering across stories and documents

The figure captions in *this* book are part of a numbered list that spans multiple stories and multiple documents in an InDesign book, so let's use the figures you see in this and every other chapter as an example. They demonstrate many of InDesign's advanced numbering options, including insertion of static text (the word Figure and a space) and the current chapter number.

All the figure captions are numbered with the *x.x* format, where the number before the decimal point is the current book chapter, and the number after the decimal sequentially numbers each figure in the chapter. The chapter number is established in the Numbering & Section Options (Layout > Numbering & Section Options) dialog. Every chapter is a stand-alone InDesign document, but all of those individual documents (and their sequential chapter numbering) are managed by the Book panel.

The paragraph style used for the figure captions is associated with a list that continues across all the documents in the InDesign book. The number expression used by that paragraph style is Figure ^H.^#.^>. The word "Figure" and the space that follows it are both literal text. The metacharacter ^H is the chapter number placeholder, which is followed by a literal period, then the metacharacter ^# for the current number, followed by an en space, which is represented by the ^> metacharacter (FIGURE 7.28). Everything generated by that expression is styled with an all caps, bold character style that also uses a different color.

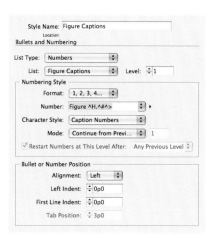

Although each figure number exists in its own text frame and those frames are not threaded as part of a continuous story, the numbering continues throughout the document (and through all other documents managed by the Book panel) because each caption uses the same paragraph style, and that style is tied to a defined list.

Styles as list managers

With all the potential levels and attributes that can be attached to a numbered list and the instructions for handling numbering level by level, *list management* quickly becomes an important consideration. Assigning a paragraph style to a numbered list is the easiest, most efficient way to manage and apply that list once all of its attributes have been defined. It also helps you avoid repeated trips to this very intimidating dialog of options.

Styles are designed to store attributes that will be applied multiple times, and very few InDesign features have more complex attributes than numbered lists. Consider the relationships being maintained in a multilevel list: a list is defined; multiple levels are associated with that list; each level looks to what precedes it to start renumbering sequences; number placeholders refer back to other levels in the list; and character styles are assigned to format those numbers. If the sum of these tasks isn't an argument for paragraph styles as list managers, I don't know what is.

NOTE

One *very* important detail is that numbering across multiple, nonthreaded text frames is based on the order in which those text frames were *created*, not the order in which they *appear* in the layout. If you're taking advantage of this feature and move the caption (by dragging the frame) for "Figure 1.12" back three pages in the document so it appears between figures 1.4 and 1.5, it will still be numbered Figure 1.12. No renumbering occurs when frames are physically moved around the document.

CHAPTER 8

Advanced Find/ Change with Styles

ONE OF THE CHALLENGES designers and long document producers face once they know how to build smart, efficient styles is how to *apply* those styles with equal intelligence and efficiency. Selecting dozens—or possibly hundreds—of paragraphs and clicking style names in the panels for each is not only repetitive, it's unreliable. People, especially *busy* people, miss things, but computers are far less likely to. The whole point with styles is to reduce tedious work and improve consistency. All machine-based tasks *should be* exploited to speed up this type of work, and InDesign's Find/Change feature is a style-savvy powerhouse that can reduce time and errors when formatting large amounts of text.

Don't discount Find/Change as a mere editing tool. Throughout many versions, InDesign's text-based Find/Change has been completely "wired in" to InDesign's text styles, allowing search and replace for formatting as well as text. Any character or paragraph style—indeed, *any* text attribute—can act as search criteria or be applied as change criteria in a replace instruction.

InDesign CS3 added Glyph, GREP, and Object searching; the latter two increased the power of Find/Change exponentially. GREP, as covered in Chapter 3, "Automatic Styling with GREP," allows text to be described in the abstract, found based on its location, or subject to specific matching conditions. Object Find/Change takes search-and-replace functionality beyond text, enabling you to find any *object* attribute or object style and replace it with any other.

In addition, the engineers added a means to save queries for future use and increased the number of ways by which searches can be either limited or expanded—all very valuable tools for a busy InDesign user.

Throughout this chapter, the terms search, replace, find, change, and query will be used a lot. Just to avoid confusion, search and find mean *exactly* the same thing and are used interchangeably. The same applies to replace and change. Query, on the other hand, refers to the entire Find/Change operation, including what's being searched for, what's being replaced, all limiting factors (Whole Word, Case Sensitive, Include or Exclude Master Pages, etc.), and any formatting specified in either the find or change part of the query.

Finding and Changing Text Styles

In both text and GREP searches, a query can be limited by (or expanded to, depending on your point of view) a number of criteria. Text searches include the Whole Word and Case-sensitive options designers are used to from search-and-replace tools in older InDesign versions and other applications, but those options don't apply to GREP searches. Both search types, however, include the limiting criteria that have been part of InDesign's Find/Change operation from the very start: All Documents, Document, Story, To End of Story, and Selection (FIGURE 8.1).

FIGURE 8.1 What you choose in the Search menu determines whether InDesign searches only the selected text, within the current story, from the cursor location to the end of the current story, the entire document, or all open documents.

In addition, you can structure text and GREP queries so that the search (not the replace) includes or excludes any of the following:

- Locked Layers (off by default)
- Locked Stories (off by default)
- Hidden Layers (off by default)
- Master Pages (off by default)
- Footnotes (on by default)

These options are toggled on or off using the row of icons below the Change to field (FIGURE 8.2), and they offer very versatile and powerful search-and-replace functionality. For instance, if you use layers meticulously in your document and keep all your photo captions on their own layer, you could lock all other layers except the caption layer to limit your query to your captions.

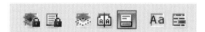

FIGURE 8.2 Search-limiting icons in the Text Find/ Change dialog (left to right): Locked Layers (Find only), Locked Stories (Find only), Hidden Layers, Master Pages, Footnotes, Case Sensitive, and Whole Word.

Let's face it; most designers are not as meticulous with layers as they should be. But by now you should be convinced that being meticulous with *styles* is a new way of life for you. If all your captions use a specific caption style, both text and GREP searches allow you to include that style as part of the search criteria. To exploit this benefit, you should always click the More Options button (FIGURE 8.3). In fact, *wherever* you see a More Options button in InDesign, you should click it to discover all the options available to you.

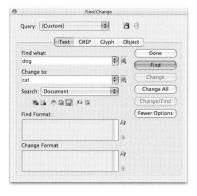

FIGURE 8.3 More options revealed in the Find/Change dialog.

The first of the two boxes revealed when More Options is clicked—Find Format—enables you to select a character style, paragraph style, or a wide range of individual text attributes as limiting criteria for a search. The second—Change Format—lets you specify styles and attributes as modifications to be made in the change portion of a query.

INCLUDING STYLES IN FIND/CHANGE QUERIES

In the previously mentioned example where the goal is to search for text only within captions and the captions are in multiple text frames throughout a document, you would take the following steps:

1. Specify the text you're looking for in the Find what field.

2. Specify the text you want to replace it with in the Change to field.

3. Choose Document from the Search menu.

4. Click the Specify Attributes for Search icon 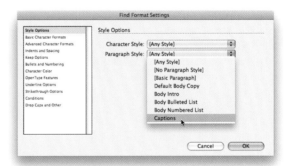 to the right of the Find Format box.

5. In the Find Format Settings dialog, choose your desired paragraph style from the list of existing document styles in the Paragraph Style menu (**FIGURE 8.4**). If you're limiting your search to a character style, make your selection from the Character Style menu.

6. Click OK to close the Find Format Settings dialog.

7. Click Find to start the search.

FIGURE 8.4 A paragraph style selected as a search criteria.

Once formatting of any kind has been included as part of the search criteria, a warning icon ❶ appears above the Find what field, indicating that formatting is part of the search. Also, the name of the selected style appears in the Find Format box. You can also use standard limiting criteria, such as Case Sensitivity and Whole Word, in combination with this or any other style search attributes.

The principles for attaching formatting to the *replace* portion of a Find/Change query are essentially the same as those just described for searching. Any text found by a search can have its formatting modified whether or not the text is changing. To apply a style or other formatting when changing text:

1. Establish your Find what and Change to criteria in the appropriate fields. If desired, set any other limiting criteria using either the Search menu or the icons below it.

2. Click the Specify Attributes for Search icon to the right of the Change Format box.

3. In the Change Format Settings dialog, select the desired character style or paragraph style.

4. Click OK.

5. Click Find to start the search.

One feature that is unique to the Change to part of a query bears mentioning. When you're searching for a style, you can only search for existing styles, but when you're using a style as replace criteria, you can create a completely new style by choosing New Paragraph Style or New Character Style from the respective menus in the Change Format Settings dialog.

Beware of Sticky Formatting Criteria

When you add formatting attributes to either the find or change portion of a query, they become "sticky," meaning they'll still be defined as attributes for the next search you perform, just as the last words you used in a query still appear in the Find what and Change to fields. This is why the warning icon appears above those fields. Unfortunately, the warning icon in CS3 that replaced the more prominent yellow caution triangle in CS2 is much easier to overlook. Many times I've run a Find/Change query only to discover that my text also changed to italic, bold, or some other formatting left over from a previous search.

To clear out any formatting that lingers from a previous query, click the Clear Specified Attributes icon [image] to the right of the Find Format or Change Format boxes, whichever is appropriate. Unless *you* clear out the formatting or modify it, the attributes will remain until you quit and relaunch InDesign.

These Find/Change formatting settings are specific to the type of search you performed last, so the formatting you included as part of a Text query will *not* be included if you switch to the GREP tab. Each of the four Find/Change types is self-contained. Information from one is not passed to another.

HOW STYLE ATTRIBUTES AFFECT FIND/CHANGE BEHAVIOR

It's important to note that as soon as a style or any other formatting attribute is included as part of either the search or replace portions of a query, the behavior of the Find what and Change to fields changes significantly. Under normal circumstances, if you search for a word and leave the Change to field blank, you effectively delete all instances of that word. A blank Change to field means "replace with nothing," and you can't even initiate a Find/Change query if the Find what field is blank. The Find button is grayed out.

However, if a style or formatting attribute is defined for a search, the Find button becomes active, even with no text entered in the Find what field (FIGURE 8.5). The meaning of that blank field becomes "any text to which this formatting is applied." Similarly, when a style or formatting attribute is defined for the change portion of a query, the blank Change to field no longer means "replace with nothing." Instead, it means "leave the found text unchanged and just apply the selected formatting."

FIGURE 8.5 Formatting attributes allow searches, even with a blank Find what field.

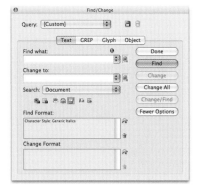

So, for example, if you typed Super Widget in the Find what field and left the Change to field blank but specified a bold character style in the Change Format Settings dialog, all instances of Super Widget would be preserved but would have the bold character style applied.

GREP Find/Change vs. GREP Styles

There's no disputing the geeky awesomeness of GREP styles. Their singular advantage over GREP in Find/Change is that they work continuously, parsing your paragraphs for patterns so you don't have to run GREP Find/Change queries over and over as content in a document is updated.

GREP styles, however, lack half of what GREP was initially intended to do. They find patterns, but other than applying formatting, they can't change those patterns or modify the text found.

The same GREP expression that sniffs out patterns automatically in a GREP style will work the same way in Find/Change, but that pattern can then be rearranged; have certain parts of it removed while others are retained; add text before, after, or within the pattern; and more. The Change portion of a GREP query in Find/Change can also refer back to certain parts of the pattern and reuse them, no matter how unique the found text may be.

Chapter 3 mentioned that subexpressions (parts of a GREP expression enclosed in parentheses) play a key role in GREP-based Find/Change operations that they don't in a GREP style. Recall the following GREP expression that defines any variation of a U.S. phone number:

```
1?[-.\s]?\(?\d{3}\)?[-.\s]?\d{3}[-.]?\d{4}
```

The GREP style could only *format* those phone numbers. It could not remove the number one before an area code, remove the parentheses around the area code, or uniformly present all the numbers so that they used periods instead of dashes. To accomplish this with Find/Change, the parts of the phone number that *must* be preserved—the ten digits—can be retained and reinserted when you mark them as a subexpression. This is as simple as wrapping the reference to the area code (\d{3}), the first three digits of the number (\d{3}), and the last four digits (\d{4}) within parentheses. The pattern would then look like this:

```
1?[-.\s]?\(?(\d{3})\)?[-.\s]?(\d{3})[-.]?(\d{4})
```

The area code is the *first* of three subexpressions in the overall expression. The first three digits of the phone number are the second subexpression, and the last four digits are the third. Each can be "referred to" in the Change portion of the query as Found Text: listed as Found 1 ($1), Found 2 ($2), and Found 3 ($3), respectively. These Found Text metacharacters are available in the Special Characters for Replace menu at the end of the Change to field (FIGURE 8.6).

FIGURE 8.6 Marking subexpressions are recalled using the Found Text metacharacters available in the Special Characters for Replace menu.

TIP

You can quickly toggle between any of the Text modes in the Find/Change dialog using the keyboard shortcuts Command/Ctrl-1, 2, or 3 for Text, GREP, or Glyph modes, respectively. Pressing Command/Ctrl-4 jumps to the Object search options, and the previous keyboard shortcuts stop working. The shortcuts revert to how they'd behave if you *weren't* in the Find/Change dialog, which is to change the zoom view of the layout.

With this ability to recall portions of a GREP search query, you can reformat phone numbers so that dashes appear between the different parts of the number instead of periods, and eliminate all extraneous formatting elements (the 1 before the area code, any unwanted dashes, periods, or parentheses, etc.) using this simple expression in the Change to field:

$1-$2-$3

In metacharacter terms, this expression recalls the Found Text as Found 1, a dash, then Found 2, a dash, and Found 3, but in plain English it means *put back* only *the numbers of the phone number using dashes to separate each part.* If, at the same time, you want to apply a character style to the reformatted phone numbers, that's also an option.

GREP styles and GREP Find/Change each has its specific strengths and weaknesses. Knowing what those are will help you plan which is best to use for a given situation.

Saving Queries

TIP

You can also use a saved query to clear out any "sticky" formatting or limiting criteria from a previous search. If you save a Text query with both the Find what and Change to fields blank, clear out any formatting that may be present, reset the limiting icons to their defaults (search footnotes on but all others off), and name the query something like Reset Text Search, you can quickly start over with a blank slate in the dialog by selecting that saved query from the Query menu.

You can save and recall any query type—Text, GREP, Glyph, or Object—at any time for future use. Historically, the last 15 search and replace criteria used were stored and available from the drop-down menus at the end of the Find what and Change to fields, but this was a temporary storage method only. After a sixteenth search was run, the oldest of the previous criteria was cleared out. Another significant drawback was that there was no link between the previous search criteria and the previous change criteria. Remembering which one went with which was entirely up to you.

But InDesign CS3 changed that by adding a Save Query function for all four Find/Change types. Saved queries remember the find and change parts of a query. They also store all formatting attributes attached to the query and all limiting criteria such as Whole Word or Include Master Pages. The only thing *not* saved in a query is the range of the search defined by the Search menu (Document, Selection, Story, etc.).

To save any type of Find/Change query, click the Save Query icon 💾. In the Save Query dialog, name the query and click OK (FIGURE 8.7). The Query menu at the top of the Find/Change dialog contains all saved queries, which are grouped together by type, top to bottom.

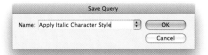

FIGURE 8.7 Saving a Find/Change query.

Saved queries save time—especially when using GREP queries, which can be long and complex. Queries are stored as XML files in the InDesign application folder under Presets\Find-Change Queries (Windows) or Presets/Find-Change Queries (Mac) in individual folders for each query type, and they can be shared with other users. As long as the XML file is placed in the right folder in that path, it is *instantly* available from the menu without having to relaunch the application or even close the current document.

Advanced Style-based Search Techniques

With styles and Find/Change working together, local overrides can be found and formatted with proper character styles. Combined with GREP, Find/Change can detect manual numbered lists and convert them to InDesign's automatic numbering. A handful of strategic Find/Change queries that include formatting can reduce hours of work to mere minutes. Once created, these queries can be saved, recalled at any time, and shared with other people in your workgroup.

SEARCHING FOR PARAGRAPH AND CHARACTER STYLES SIMULTANEOUSLY

You can specify paragraph and character styles at the same time in the Find Format Settings dialog, allowing you to search for an instance of a specific character style *only* if it's applied to text that's already using a specific paragraph style. If you're using a flexible character style like Generic Italics, as described in Chapter 2, "Nesting and Sequencing Styles," you may have applied it locally to text formatted with any number of paragraph styles. If you want to find all text that uses that italic character style but only in your bulleted lists, select the italic character style and the bulleted list paragraph style from their respective menus (FIGURE 8.8). If your goal is to change all those italicized instances to something like bold or small caps, simply define either of those character styles as part of the Change to criteria in the Change Format Settings dialog.

TIP

The Find/Change dialog is one of a very few "non-modal" dialogs in the application, meaning it does not have to be closed before you can resume work in the document.

TIP

Only one of each style type can be applied at any given time using Find/Change. Although the Next Style setting is honored when you apply formatting to multiple paragraphs on the page or select the Apply Next Style check box in an object style, the same is not true when a Find/Change query spans multiple paragraphs.

FIGURE 8.8 Character and paragraph styles selected simultaneously as search criteria.

FIGURE 8.9 Formatting on a much more granular level can be included as part of search-and-replace criteria.

STYLE CLEANUP

The Find Format Settings dialog contains not only the character style and paragraph style options, but a menu of other formatting attributes that can be attached to a style (FIGURE 8.9). This menu is not quite as robust as the similar one found in the Paragraph Style Options dialog (paragraph rules, hyphenation, and tabs, among others, are noticeably absent), but is also not nearly as limited as the one found in the Character Style Options dialog.

These individual formatting attributes can be combined with styles in the search or replace portions of a query. They're "tacked on" to the selected style, so that choosing a body copy style and adding the small caps attribute from the Basic Character Formats options means, "find any small caps applied within the body copy paragraph style." These additional attributes are reiterated in either the Find Format or Change Format boxes (FIGURE 8.10), similar to the way a paragraph style's attributes are listed in the General area of the Paragraph Style Options dialog.

FIGURE 8.10 A paragraph style combined with another formatting attribute (all caps) as displayed in the Find Format box. The Change Format box presents information the same way.

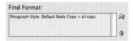

This is especially helpful when performing style cleanup in a document. If italics, bolds, all caps, or other common attributes have been applied manually throughout a document, you may want to replace those local overrides with proper italic, bold, or small cap character styles.

This level of style fussiness may seem over the top, but it can prove invaluable for certain workflows. When using the Export for Dreamweaver feature, for example, manually applied attributes like bold, italic, and all caps are not recognized or tagged. All that formatting is lost in the resulting HTML file. Any such text styled with a character style, however, gets wrapped in a SPAN tag, eliminating duplicative reformatting for the Web of text that's already been formatted for print.

UNNESTING NESTED STYLES

A variation on the style cleanup technique described in the previous section can help overcome a related shortcoming mentioned in Chapter 2. One of the only drawbacks of Nested Styles is that the character styles used in them are "invisible" to the Export for Dreamweaver function. Your carefully structured "this style through 1 whatever, then that style up to..." formatting amounts to nothing in the exported HTML file. None of those nested character styles are tagged in the text.

Using one or more clever GREP queries via Find/Change can find the nested formatting and manually apply the appropriate character style. The query won't remove the nesting instructions. It will just manually apply the appropriate character style *on top* of that. This is best left until the end of the proofing process on a project, and even then it's best to use a copy of the original file (just in case). Every nesting scenario is different, so let's look at a simple example. The bulleted list style used in FIGURE 8.11 includes a nested bold character style through one colon and then reverts to the paragraph's default appearance. When exported for Dreamweaver, the bulleted list will be converted to an unordered list (FIGURE 8.12), but the bold lead-in text won't be tagged as bold.

■ **Revolutionary New Design:** The 2009 Super Widget X1 has been redesigned from the ground up with state of the art technology and materials.

■ **Guaranteed Quality:** We back every Super Widget we ship with an unconditional lifetime money-back guarantee—no questions asked!

FIGURE 8.11 A bulleted list with a nested style through one colon.

```
<ul>
        <li class="body-bullet-list-with-bold-lead-in">Revolutionary New Design:
The 2009 SuperWidget X1 has been redesigned from the ground up with state of the art
technology and materials.</li>
                <li class="body-bullet-list-with-bold-lead-in">Guaranteed Quality: We
back every SuperWidget we ship with an unconditional lifetime money-back guarantee—
no questions asked! </li>
        </ul>
```

FIGURE 8.12 The same list exported for Dreamweaver. Note that the appropriate UL tags are present, but the bold formatting is lost.

To prep this list for proper HTML tagging, you can use GREP in Find/Change to look for *any text followed by a colon that appears at the beginning of a line that uses the Body Bulleted List With Bold Lead In paragraph style*. To tell InDesign how to locate this, do the following:

1. Switch to the GREP area of the Find/Change dialog.

2. In the Find what field, type ^(.+:)?. This translates to *the beginning of a line followed by any one or more characters followed by a colon, shortest match*.

3. Click the Select Attributes to Find icon.

4. In the Find Format Settings dialog, choose the appropriate paragraph style (in this example, it's Body Bulleted List With Bold Lead In).

5. Click OK.

The Change to portion of this query is actually quite simple. Since the text is not changing to anything, your change instruction will amount to *leave the found text there, but apply the Generic Bold character style to it*. Here's how that's done:

1. Leave the Change to field blank. You're not replacing the text with anything, just changing its formatting. Also, since this is a GREP search, it will find different text at the start of each bullet point. Anything typed in the Change to field would replace all of that unique text.

2. Click the Select Attributes to Change icon.

3. In the Change Format Settings dialog, choose the appropriate character style (in this example, it's Generic Bold).

4. Click OK.

FIGURE 8.13 shows what the Find/Change dialog looks like with this GREP search and all the style criteria defined. When Change All is clicked, there should be no visual change to the bulleted list since the character style being applied is the same character style nested in the list already. However, when *this* list is exported to Dreamweaver, the bold text through the colon is wrapped in a SPAN tag (FIGURE 8.14).

FIGURE 8.13 A GREP search tied to formatting and a replace for formatting only.

FIGURE 8.14 Unlike nested character styles, applied character styles are tagged properly in an exported HTML document.

```
<ul>
    <li class="body-bullet-list-with-bold-lead-in">
<span class="generic-bold">Revolutionary New Design: </span>
The 2009 Super Widget X1 has been redesigned from the ground
up with state of the art technology and materials.</li>
    <li class="body-bullet-list-with-bold-lead-in">
<span class="generic-bold">Guaranteed Quality: </span> We back
every Super Widget we ship with an unconditional lifetime money-
back guarantee—no questions asked! </li>
</ul>
```

INSERTING ANCHORED OBJECTS WITH FIND/CHANGE

Anchored Objects are a fantastic InDesign feature, but to position them properly, you'll need to spend a lot of time modifying the settings in the Custom Anchored Object Options dialog. Its myriad options—including two reference point proxies, X and Y relative to menus and offset fields—are neither user friendly nor terribly intuitive to the uninitiated. Even if you're familiar with the workings of Anchored Objects, there are probably better things you could be doing with your time than applying these settings one anchored object at a time.

As you learned in Chapter 5, "Object Styles," assigning an object style to an object can eliminate having to keep coming back to this dialog. But quickly assigning Anchored Object settings via an object style is one thing; inserting that object many times in specific locations in a document is quite another.

There are a number of reasons you might need to insert an anchored object in many different places in a document in one fell swoop. In a directory, you may need graphic frames for photos inserted at the beginning of every line that uses a particular paragraph style. In a table, you may want to cheat the appearance of irregularly shaped cells by anchoring a shape at the beginning of each cell. Or, you may simply want to insert a graphic "story stopper" at the end of each story in a newsletter.

For the directory example—inserting anchored image frames at the beginning of a line to which a specific paragraph style is applied—styles, GREP, and a little-known Find/Change feature combined can make short work of an otherwise tedious task. Although Find/Change is, strictly speaking, a text-related function, there *is* a way to make almost any object part of the change instruction.

GREP can handle the first part of this task with the beginning of line metacharacter (^) in the Find what field. To ensure that only the beginning of a line styled with a specific paragraph style is matched, click the Select Attributes to Find icon and select the desired paragraph style in the Find Format Settings dialog. This will successfully find that location, but a location can't be changed. The beginning of a line is and always will be the beginning of a line, whether or not any text exists on that line.

To overcome this obstacle, you must instead search for *any character at the beginning of a line* using the desired paragraph style and enclose that any character metacharacter (.) in parentheses, making it a marking subexpression, like this:

^(.)

It's important that the search be set up this way, because the characters at the beginning of each line must be retained so they can be reinserted during the change portion of the query.

TIP
Formatted clipboard items—whether they're text, objects, or a combination of both—retain all their original attributes when they are inserted with Find/Change. When Clipboard Contents, Unformatted is used, text in the clipboard will pick up the attributes of the text it's inserted into, but *objects* in the clipboard still retain all their formatting.

Before setting up the change instruction for this query, the anchored object you want to insert needs to be copied to the clipboard. Ideally, this copied object would already have an object style applied to it that includes the necessary Anchored Object settings to position it properly. After the styled object is copied, you can return to the Find/Change dialog and build the replace pattern.

From the Special Characters for Replace menu at the end of the Change to field, go to the Other submenu and choose Clipboard Contents, Formatted (FIGURE 8.15). This is how any object in the clipboard—a shape, stroke, placed image, group, and so on—can be part of a Find/Change operation. The ~c metacharacter is put in to represent the formatted contents of the clipboard. Next, the first character from the beginning of the line that was matched in the search must be reinserted using the Found Text 1 metacharacter ($1). The Change to field would look like this:

~c$1

Clicking Change All at this point will replace the first character at the beginning of any line using the selected paragraph style with the object copied to the clipboard followed by the first character found on each line, whatever that character may be.

TIP

Clipboard Contents, Formatted and Clipboard Contents, Unformatted can also be part of the Change to instructions of a Text search and replace. The two options are *not* exclusive to GREP. In a Text Find/Change query, however, the metacharacters would be ^c and ^C.

FIGURE 8.15 Anything in the clipboard can be recalled in the Change to field with the Clipboard Contents, Formatted (or Unformatted) metacharacters.

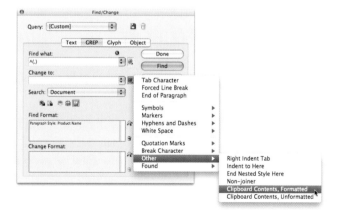

Find/Change for Objects

An object-based Find/Change operation has nothing whatsoever to do with text. The options in the Object area of the Find/Change dialog (FIGURE 8.16) are *only* for formatting attributes for objects—frames, shapes, lines, and so on—and for object styles. When you click the Specify Attributes to Find icon in the Object area of the Find/Change dialog, notice that the Find Object Format

Options dialog that opens up looks remarkably like the Object Style Options dialog (FIGURE 8.17). In fact, they're identical with only one exception. The Paragraph Style options for an Object Style are not present for Object Find/Change operations, because searching for a paragraph style can be accomplished by both Text and GREP Find/Change queries.

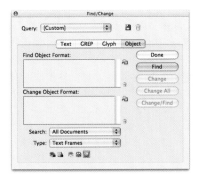

FIGURE 8.16 The Object area of the Find/Change dialog.

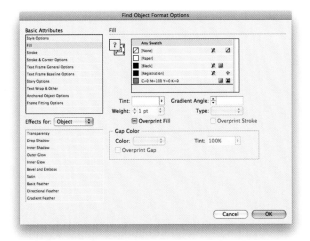

FIGURE 8.17 The Find Object Format Options and Change Object Format Options dialogs are nearly identical to the Object Styles dialog.

The behavior described in this chapter for text-based formatting searches also applies to object searches. Any object style or individual formatting attribute can be selected as search criteria as well as replace criteria. Additional attributes can be "tacked on" to an object style, and any found object style can be replaced by any other object style.

The narrowing criteria for Object queries are slightly different, however. In addition to the Search menu, there's also a Type menu from which you can limit a search to only Text Frames, Graphic Frames, or Unassigned Frames, or expand it to include All Frames.

TIP
The All Frames option is the only way to include drawn lines in an Object query.

TIP
When deleting an object style, you're asked to select a style to replace it with. This has been a tried-and-true method of changing all objects formatted with a specific style to a different style. But sometimes you may not *want* to delete the existing style. Using Find/Change to replace one object style with another is an excellent way to replace all instances of an applied object style without deleting that style.

Another small difference between the Object Style dialog and the Find Object Format Options dialog is that when searching for swatch-related attributes like Fill and Stroke, only colors that are applied to objects in the document are available, regardless of how many swatches actually exist in the document.

However, the Change Object Format Options dialog presents all possible swatch options. If the document uses colors created with the Color panel rather than as swatches, each color appears in the Find Object Format Options and Change Format Options dialogs as [Unnamed Color], even though they have not been saved as swatches.

CHAPTER 9

Generating Dynamic Content with Styles

STYLES DON'T JUST FORMAT TEXT; they can also *generate* text for other InDesign features. Tables of Contents, for example, rely entirely on paragraph styles to work. Styles are required to generate running header text variables, and the new cross-reference feature in InDesign CS4— while not *entirely* style-dependent—can produce cross-references directly from instances of styled text.

These three features have their own specific—and distinctly different—work area and implementation process; each of which you'll explore in this chapter. At their core, however, they all do the same thing: find text that uses a particular style, collect that text, and then serve it up elsewhere in a document. They also maintain a link between the styled text and the table of contents, running header, or cross-reference that either updates any time the source text is updated or is refreshed by a simple update process.

Tables of Contents

Although tables of contents (TOCs) are typically discussed in conjunction with the Book panel as part of InDesign's "long document" features, any InDesign document can be used to generate an automatic TOC. Whether it's being used for one document or many, the feature won't work unless paragraph styles are used in a precise and organized way. The TOC feature seeks out all instances of the paragraph styles you specify, collects all the text they're applied to (along with the page number on which that text appears), and delivers it back to you for placement on the page. If your paragraph styles aren't used consistently, your TOC will be equally inconsistent. TOCs cannot be generated from character styles.

PLANNING A TABLE OF CONTENTS

NOTE
There is a 256-character limit for any TOC entry. For chapter and section names, this is usually sufficient, but if you want your TOC to include a chapter's introductory paragraph or other lengthy descriptive text, this limitation could result in truncated TOC text.

To prepare for a TOC, you must designate one or more paragraph styles as the source text from which it will be built. In a book, this could be the style used for each chapter name. If that chapter has sections within it, the section name style could also be included in the TOC (FIGURE 9.1). In a catalog, the paragraph style applied to each product category might be called on as TOC text.

It's crucial that these "source styles" be applied *only* to text that you want to appear in your TOC, because every instance of text using these styles (even those with many overrides applied) will be collected and included in the TOC.

CREATING A TABLE OF CONTENTS

To create a TOC, you must first determine where the TOC will be placed. In a single document, this would most likely be on one of the first few pages in the file. For multiple documents managed by the Book panel, it could be in a separate document. It helps to be on the page where the TOC will be placed before you start the TOC creation process, because after you've confirmed all your options, you'll get a loaded text cursor with the TOC text ready to be placed.

Open the Table of Contents dialog (Layout > Table of Contents) and click the More Options button to reveal all settings (FIGURE 9.2). These options allow you to more specifically format your TOC, gather styled text from all the documents in an InDesign Book, use the TOC to generate PDF bookmarks, and more.

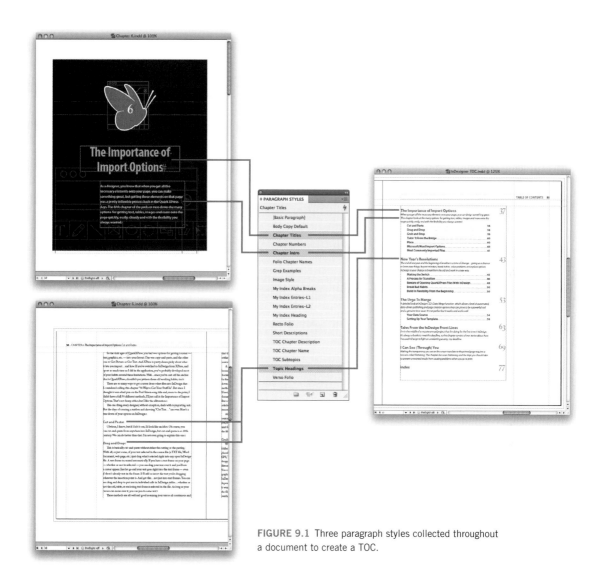

FIGURE 9.1 Three paragraph styles collected throughout a document to create a TOC.

FIGURE 9.2 The Table of
Contents dialog with all
options displayed.

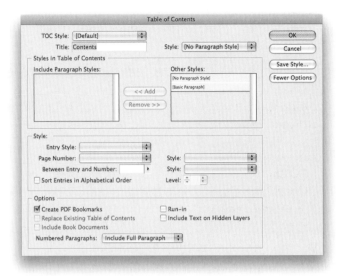

The heart of the TOC feature is in the Styles in Table of Contents area, where
styles in the document(s) are selected from the Other Styles list on the right and
added to the Include Paragraph Styles list on the left by clicking the Add button
(FIGURE 9.3). Once a style is added to *this* list, it's removed from the Other Styles
list. No paragraph style can be included twice in a TOC. If you inadvertently add
an unwanted paragraph style, select it and click the Remove button to return it
to the Other Styles list.

FIGURE 9.3 Available
document styles selected for
inclusion in a TOC.

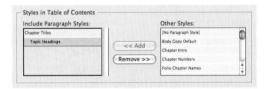

Each item added to the Include Paragraph Styles list is called an entry, and the
order in which the entries appear in the list is the order in which they'll appear
in the TOC. You can change that order by selecting a style name in the Include
Paragraph Styles list and dragging it above or below any other style name.

InDesign examines the entire document to find each instance of text to which
the desired styles are applied and notes the page number for each. Each time a
new instance of the first style in the list is encountered, InDesign seeks out the
second style. This is repeated as often as necessary, in page order, until no more
styled text is found. FIGURE 9.4 shows chapter names (in purple) and subtopics

(in black) gathered from styled text and delivered as a TOC in page order. The third entry in the figure has no subtopics beneath it because the subtopic style was not used in that chapter.

Introduction 1

- My History With InDesign 2
- The InDesigner's Audience 4

Learning How To Learn 7

- Free Stuff 8
- Cheap Stuff 9
- Moderately Priced Options 10
- Deep Pocket Options 11

If You (Re)build It, You Will Learn 15

Four To Be Thankful For 21

- Formatting Unselected Text 22
- InDesign Does Math 23
- Better Bolds and Italics 24
- Keyboard Navigation Through Dialog Boxes 24

FIGURE 9.4 Gathered text from styles in a TOC.

STYLING TOC ENTRIES

The association of document styles with TOC entries is all that's absolutely *required* to create a TOC, but the dialog offers other options—many of them style-related—for formatting and organizing the TOC.

Any text entered in the Title field of the TOC dialog will be added as a heading at the beginning of the TOC, and a paragraph style can be assigned to it from the adjacent Style menu.

When any entry is selected in the Include Paragraph Styles list, you can assign paragraph styles to it from the Style area of the Table of Contents dialog. Click the More Options button to reveal all the Style area controls. If a style called Chapter Titles is selected, the Style area reflects that by changing its heading to Style: Chapter Titles. All settings made here are specific to *that* entry. Clicking any other entry name in the Include Paragraph Styles list resets the Style area so that a new set of entry-specific styling can be established.

Entry Style. By default, Same Style—meaning the same style currently selected in the Include Paragraph Styles list—is preselected as the entry's paragraph style

FIGURE 9.5 Page numbers generated for the TOC can have a character style assigned to them in the TOC Style settings.

in the Entry Style menu. To assign a different style to the entry, select any existing paragraph style (or create a new one by choosing New Paragraph Style) from the Entry Style menu.

Page Number. An InDesign TOC tracks the location of the styles used to create it and reports back the appropriate page number. From the Page Number menu, you decide whether that number appears before the text of the entry, after it, or is entirely omitted.

Between Entry and Number. If you choose to include page numbers either before or after the entry, you can instruct InDesign to insert a tab, em space, or other separator text between the entry and the number. Tabs and other special characters must be represented by metacharacters in this field (^t for a standard tab and ^y for a right-align tab, for example). You can also add actual text such as "pg." and a space so that page numbers are presented as "pg. 12," for example.

Styling the entry components. You can assign a character style to the page number as well as to whatever appears *between* the entry and the number (FIGURE 9.5), which is often an alignment character like a tab or right-align tab. If the tab includes leader dots and the entry font is bold, the leader dots will also be bold. Assigning a character style with a lighter, smaller font to the tab between the entry and number creates more subtle leader dots (FIGURE 9.6).

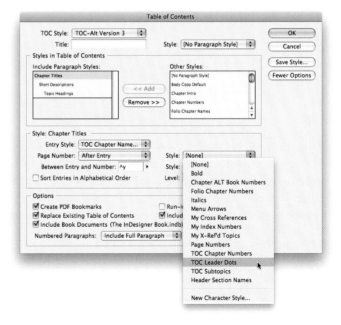

Free Stuff 8
Cheap Stuff 9
Moderately Priced Options 10
Deep Pocket Options 11

Free Stuff...8
Cheap Stuff.. 9
Moderately Priced Options...................... 10
Deep Pocket Options............................. 11

FIGURE 9.6 Tab leader dots with no character style applied (top) and with a character style applied that adjusts the font size and weight (bottom).

MODIFYING A TABLE OF CONTENTS

To modify a TOC's settings, choose Table of Contents from the Layout menu and make the required changes in the Table of Contents dialog. When changing any setting for a TOC other than its TOC Style (see the sidebar "TOC Styles: The Style Within a Style-driven Feature"), you only need to select the Replace Existing Table of Contents check box (FIGURE 9.7) and click OK. The existing version of the TOC is replaced in its entirety.

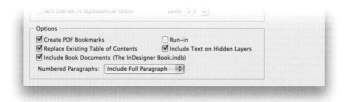

FIGURE 9.7 Select Replace Existing Table of Contents to refresh an existing TOC after editing its settings.

UPDATING A TABLE OF CONTENTS

Text changes to the generated TOC text should never be made on the page. The purpose of a TOC is to maintain a link between it and the styled text in the document. If the text or its location changes, the TOC can be updated to reflect the most current text and page numbers. When that update occurs, any text edits or formatting changes you've made to the previous version will be entirely replaced.

When changes have been made to text in your document(s) that uses your source styles or the location of any of that text changes, place your cursor in the text frame containing your TOC and choose Update Table of Contents from the Layout menu. All text in the frame is replaced by up-to-date TOC entries. Updating a TOC should always be one of the very last steps taken before printing, exporting, or packaging a project for output.

TOC Styles: The Style Within a Style-driven Feature

Once established, you can save all your TOC settings as yet another kind of style: the TOC Style.

If you're still deciding how your TOC should look and want to experiment with different appearances, you can "test-run" a version, save it as a TOC Style, and then change the settings and save *those* as another TOC Style. For example, if you set up a TOC in which page numbers follow the entry text and would like to try an alternate version where the page numbers precede the entry, save the first version as a TOC Style with the name of your choice. Then modify the Page Number placement (and any other) setting as needed and save those settings as another TOC Style with a different name (**FIGURE 9.8**). Each saved TOC Style is added to the TOC Style menu at the top of the dialog.

You'll need to generate a new TOC for each style you choose to try out. Any time you switch a TOC style, InDesign treats it as the start of a new TOC and gives you a new loaded text cursor, even if another TOC already exists.

To delete a TOC Style or load one from another document, choose TOC Styles from the Layout menu and select the appropriate option in the resulting dialog. If you choose to edit a TOC Style starting from this dialog, only its *settings* are changed. Any TOC already generated and placed on the page will not reflect those changes until you run the Update Table of Contents command.

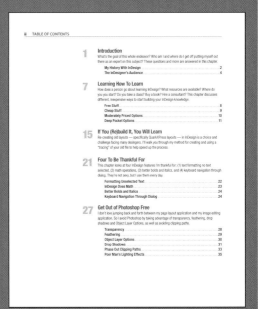

FIGURE 9.8 Two TOCs generated from the same paragraph styles, but each uses its own TOC Style.

Running Header Text Variables

The text variables feature introduced in CS3 can generate and insert text wherever a variable *placeholder* is inserted. Most text variables are generated from information about the actual document, like the file's name, creation date, and modification date. The running header variable, however, is entirely style-driven.

Like TOCs, running header text variables track the text in a document that uses a particular style, collect that text, and deliver it elsewhere. Their behavior *differs* from TOCs in three distinct ways:

- Running headers can be generated from both paragraph and character styles.

- Multiple running header text variables can exist in a document. Typically, they're set up on master pages and can potentially appear on every page in a file.

- The text generated by a running header text variable changes based on the variable's location relative to the styled text it tracks. In other words, a variable that appears at the top of page 4 only looks for styles used on page 4.

The most basic example of a running header is a dictionary or glossary, where the header helps readers quickly determine how close they are to the word they're looking for. The page headers reflect the first word defined on the left page and the last word defined on the right page (FIGURE 9.9).

In the example in FIGURE 9.10, each definition has a bold character style called "Term" applied to the term being defined. The document's left and right master pages have text variables inserted in the page header (FIGURE 9.11). Each variable "watches" the text that flows through the document pages for specific occurrences of the "Term" character style applied in each definition. The variable in the left page header watches for the *first* instance of the character style on the left page, and the variable in the right page header watches for the last instance of the character style on the right page. The text found with that style in those locations is used to populate the variable in the respective page's header (FIGURE 9.12).

As additions, deletions, or other changes reflow the text in the document, the variables in the header automatically update to present the *current* first and last instances on the spread.

TIP
Text variables update instantaneously when the text that "feeds" them is changed, but you won't *see* those updates without some form of screen refresh like zooming in or out, or turning guides on or off. The fastest way to see a variable updated is with the keyboard shortcut Shift-F5, which invokes the little-known Force Redraw command.

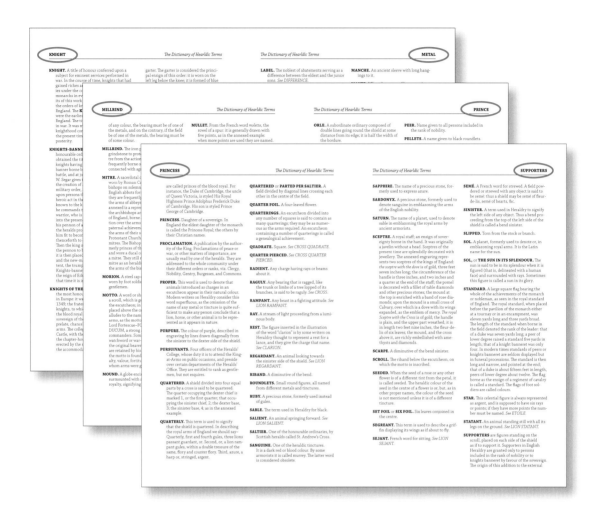

FIGURE 9.9 Dictionary page headers establish the range of words defined on a given spread.

FIGURE 9.10 A character style applied to the dictionary term.

MILLRIND. The iron placed in the centre of a grindstone to protect the hole in the centre from the action of the axis; it is a charge frequently borne on escutcheons of persons connected with agriculture.

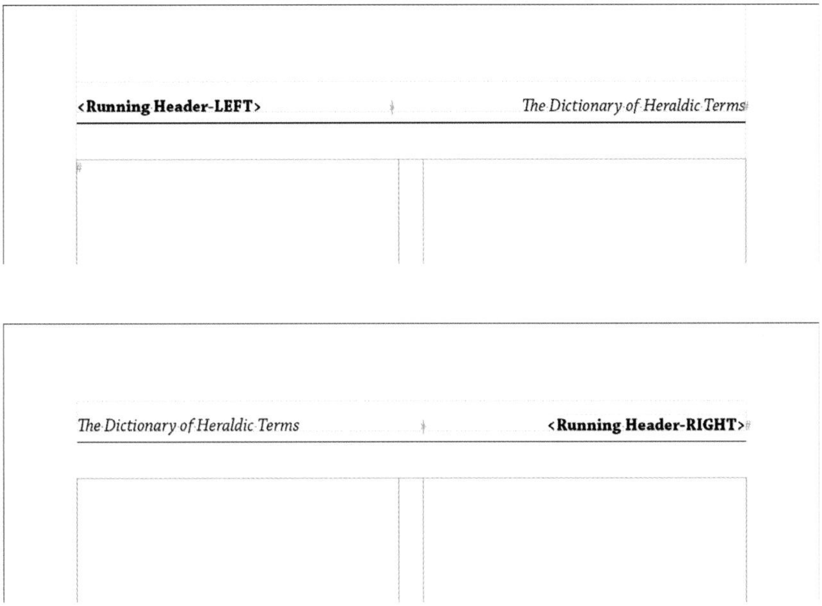

FIGURE 9.11
The dictionary's left and right master pages with variable placeholders.

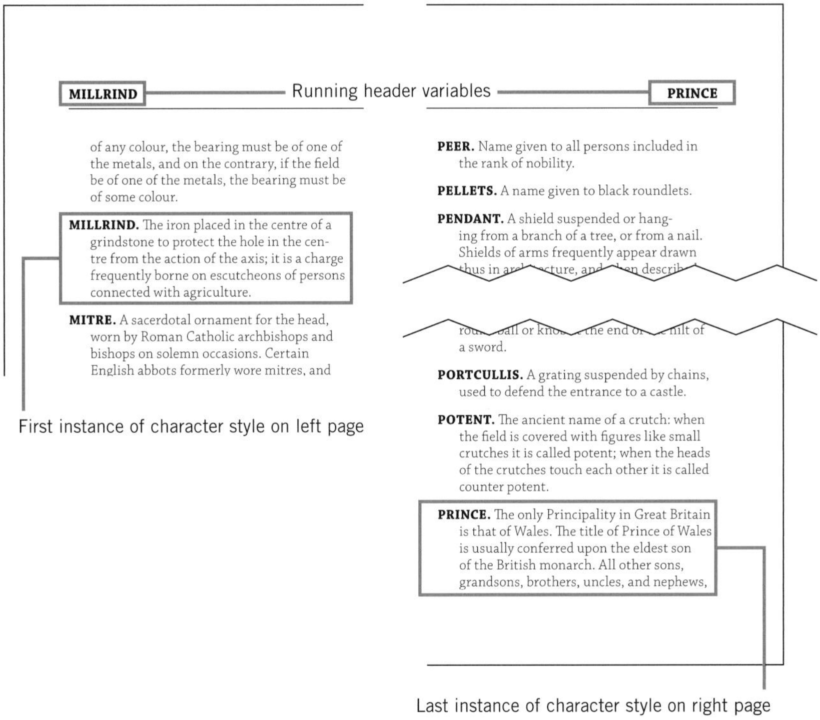

<Running Header-LEFT>   The Dictionary of Heraldic Terms

The Dictionary of Heraldic Terms   <Running Header-RIGHT>

FIGURE 9.12 Styled text detected on the page and "reported back" by the variable.

MILLRIND ——— Running header variables ——— PRINCE

of any colour, the bearing must be of one of the metals, and on the contrary, if the field be of one of the metals, the bearing must be of some colour.

MILLRIND. The iron placed in the centre of a grindstone to protect the hole in the centre from the action of the axis; it is a charge frequently borne on escutcheons of persons connected with agriculture.

MITRE. A sacerdotal ornament for the head, worn by Roman Catholic archbishops and bishops on solemn occasions. Certain English abbots formerly wore mitres, and

First instance of character style on left page

PEER. Name given to all persons included in the rank of nobility.

PELLETS. A name given to black roundlets.

PENDANT. A shield suspended or hanging from a branch of a tree, or from a nail. Shields of arms frequently appear drawn thus in architecture, and often describ

round ball or knob at the end of the hilt of a sword.

PORTCULLIS. A grating suspended by chains, used to defend the entrance to a castle.

POTENT. The ancient name of a crutch: when the field is covered with figures like small crutches it is called potent; when the heads of the crutches touch each other it is called counter potent.

PRINCE. The only Principality in Great Britain is that of Wales. The title of Prince of Wales is usually conferred upon the eldest son of the British monarch. All other sons, grandsons, brothers, uncles, and nephews,

Last instance of character style on right page

CREATING RUNNING HEADER VARIABLES

To add a variable to a page, you must first define the variable. InDesign has nine different variable types, but this section exclusively discusses the two style-related variables: Running Header (Character Style) and Running Header (Paragraph Style). As their names suggest, the former is generated from text to which a particular character style is applied, and the latter is generated from text styled by a paragraph style.

Continuing with the example in Figures 9.9 through 9.12, here are the steps for creating the dictionary's left page running header:

1. From the Type menu, choose Text Variables > Define to access the Text Variables dialog (FIGURE 9.13).

FIGURE 9.13 Text variables are added to or removed from a document from the Text Variables dialog.

NOTE
The Running Header (Character Style) variable will only find a character style that has been applied manually or is part of a standard nested style. It will not detect character styles that are part of a nested line style, GREP style, or any character style used to style the numbers in a numbered list.

2. Click the New button to access the New Text Variable dialog.

3. Choose Running Header (Character Style) from the Type pull-down menu. The dialog changes to reflect options specific to this kind of variable (FIGURE 9.14).

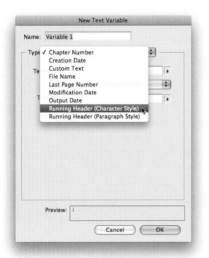

FIGURE 9.14 Option for a Running Header (Character Style) variable.

4. Select the character style to be used by the variable from the Style menu, which includes all available character styles in the document. You can also create a new character style by choosing New Character Style at the bottom of the list.

5. From the Use menu, select either First on Page or Last on Page (FIGURE 9.15). For this example, First on Page is the appropriate option for the header on the left page.

6. To wrap "static" text around the variable, enter text in the Text Before or Text After fields; each of which has a pull-down menu of special characters available to it. This is similar to how specific text is included before the number in a numbered list (see Chapter 7, "Drop Caps, Bullets, and Numbering"). In this example, neither is necessary.

FIGURE 9.15 Select which instance of the character style to assign to the variable.

Suppressing Static Text

It's best to include any static text *within* the variable rather than typing it outside of the variable placeholder as "live" text in the header. Let's assume your variable is tied to a subtopic paragraph style and the header follows the format "Chapter Name: <Subtopic>." You'll want to build the colon and the space that follow the chapter name into the Text Before field of the variable. That way, if *no* subtopic style is used (and therefore no variable is generated), there won't be a trailing colon after "Chapter Name" on any page header. If a variable is not generated on a given page, neither is any static text in the Text Before and Text After fields.

7. In the Options area, fine-tune the presentation of your running header in two additional ways:

   - **Delete End Punctuation.** You can delete any ending punctuation in the text to which the selected character style is applied by selecting Delete End Punctuation (FIGURE 9.16). In this dictionary example, each definition term is followed by a period, which also has the "Term" character style applied to it. With Delete End Punctuation selected, that period does not get included in the header.

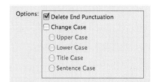

FIGURE 9.16 Punctuation and case-changing options.

   - **Change Case.** Optionally, you can choose Change Case to change the case in which the variable presents the text. This is not the same as choosing between normal and all caps as a character-level formatting option, which can't lowercase text that's specifically *typed* as uppercase. The options here actually change the case of the text regardless of how it's typed. Text Variables is the only InDesign feature that supports these case-changing options in a dynamic way.

8. Name the style, click OK in the New Text Variable dialog to close it, and then click Done in the Text Variables dialog.

The right header variable would be created in the same way except you would choose Last on Page in step 5 instead of First on Page.

Beware of Long Variables

The dictionary example uses a running header variable driven by a character style, but the same principles and behavior apply to a running header variable driven by a paragraph style. In that instance, the text of the entire *paragraph* would populate the variable. This brings up an important caution about text variables in general: The text that populates a variable will *never* wrap onto another line (or lines). Whatever text is collected by the variable is considered a single, nonbreaking entity. Therefore, the text frame into which you've inserted a variable placeholder must be large enough to fit the largest possible amount of text it may find on a single line. When a variable's text exceeds that length, it won't create overset text. Instead, the text will be jammed together into a sequence of overlapping characters to force all the text onto a single line in the text frame containing the variable.

For this reason, the Running Header (Paragraph Style) variable typically calls on styles for category headings and section breaks, not body text.

INSERTING A RUNNING HEADER TEXT VARIABLE

After your variable's parameters have been defined, you need to insert a placeholder for what will populate that variable. Running headers are so named because they typically appear on the page header and run through the entire document. This makes a document's master page(s) the most likely place for the variable to be inserted.

To insert a running header text variable, place your text cursor in a frame at the position where the variable should be inserted and choose Text Variables > Insert Variable > *Your Variable Name* from the Type menu (FIGURE 9.17).

FIGURE 9.17 Inserting a text variable.

A variable inserted on a master page will appear as the "pure form" of the placeholder, which is the variable name enclosed in angle brackets (

Header-LEFT>, for example). Variables inserted on a document page show up already populated by the text to which the nearest instance of the targeted style has been applied.

Regardless of how many letters and words make up the variable's name, the variable placeholder is a single character. No portion of it can be selected, only the entire variable. You'll also notice, on close inspection, that it's surrounded by a hairline box the same color as the guides of the layer where the variable exists (FIGURE 9.18).

FIGURE 9.18 A thin outline box indicating a variable on a master page.

‹Running·Header-LEFT›

If the style designated to populate a variable is not applied to any text in the document, the variable on the document page will be an empty zero-width character (FIGURE 9.19). If the style is not used on the current page, the variable will search backward as far as it needs to go until it finds the nearest *prior* instance of that style in the document. In that event, the text that's found—however many pages back it may be—will populate the variables on all page headers until the style is encountered again later in the document.

FIGURE 9.19
An unpopulated variable with hidden characters showing.

FORMATTING A VARIABLE

Any paragraph or character style can be applied to a variable. However, since a variable is a single character, regardless of how many words populate it, the formatting will apply to the whole variable. Nesting and other sophisticated style options are not supported within the variable.

Cross-references

Cross-references have been a highly requested feature for almost as long as InDesign has been on the market. Now that cross-references have been added in CS4 it's curious that the feature doesn't seem to warrant its own dedicated panel in the application. Cross-references share space at the bottom of the Hyperlinks panel (Window > Interactive > Hyperlinks or Window > Text & Tables > Cross-References), even though the two features are entirely separate. For your convenience as well as mine, I'll use the term "Cross-References panel" throughout this section, rather than "the Cross-References area at the bottom of the Hyperlinks panel."

WHAT MAKES UP A CROSS-REFERENCE?

At a minimum, each InDesign cross-reference consists of two parts: a source and a destination. The source is the reference *to* something ("See such and such on page x," for example), which can include pieces of referenced text, a page number, and static text (FIGURE 9.20). The destination is the text being *referred to* (FIGURE 9.21), which is tracked by the source for both its content and location in the document.

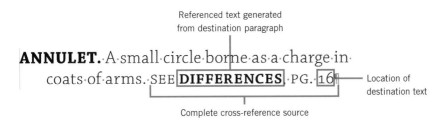

Referenced text generated
from destination paragraph

Location of
destination text

Complete cross-reference source

FIGURE 9.20
The individual components
of a cross-reference source.

FIGURE 9.21 A cross-
reference destination (the
entire paragraph) indicated
by the cross-reference
marker when Show Hidden
Characters is turned on.

A cross-reference tracks text and its location (the destination), and generates a reference to it (the source) that can include the destination's full text, a specific portion of it, and optionally, the page number on which it appears. As with TOCs and running header variables, a cross-reference reacts to changes to the text and location of its destination. When the *location* of the text being referenced changes, the cross-reference updates automatically. When the *text* being referenced changes, however, the reference appears in the Cross-References panel as modified, requiring an update. In this way, the Cross-References panel serves a similar function as the Links panel (FIGURE 9.22).

TIP

When you print a document
or export it to PDF, a warning message will alert you
to the presence of any missing or out-of-date cross-
references.

FIGURE 9.22 The status of different cross-references indicated in the Cross-References panel.

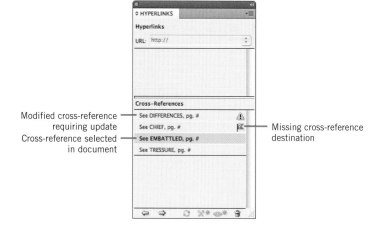

Modified cross-reference requiring update

Cross-reference selected in document

Missing cross-reference destination

CROSS-REFERENCES AND STYLES

Unlike TOCs and running header text variables, which track specific styles wherever they appear in a document or InDesign book, each cross-reference tracks only one specific paragraph. Although paragraph styles are not *required* to create a cross-reference, they make working with the feature faster and more manageable. A cross-reference can also track a specific text anchor or any paragraph of unstyled text. But since this is a style-centric book, the focus will be on how the cross-references feature is integrated with styles at its core and how you can capitalize on that.

The ideal workflow for effective, efficient cross-reference creation is to assign a specific paragraph style to any paragraph to which you intend to refer via a cross-reference. The cross-reference doesn't track the style, it tracks *one paragraph* (that you specify) to which that style is applied. The style just helps you quickly drill down to the paragraph you want to reference, which can be very beneficial in a long document. Cross-references cannot, however, use a character style as a narrowing criterion.

For maximum formatting flexibility, cross-references can have a character style preassigned to them, so you won't need to style them once they're generated. You can also specify additional character styles to be applied to specific *portions* of the reference in addition to the style assigned to the reference as a whole. Paragraph styles cannot be assigned in the cross-reference's formatting options.

CREATING A CROSS-REFERENCE

The process for cross-referencing starts at the source, meaning *where* you want the reference to appear.

1. With your text cursor in the desired location, create a new cross-reference from the Cross-References panel by either clicking the Create Cross-Reference icon  at the bottom of the panel or choosing Insert Cross-Reference from the panel menu. The New Cross-Reference dialog opens (FIGURE 9.23).

FIGURE 9.23 The New Cross-Reference dialog.

The dialog in Figure 9.23 displays the options available when creating cross-references in the same dictionary document used to demonstrate running header text variables earlier in this chapter. Some of the definitions in this dictionary need to reference other terms ("See Embattled " or "See Helmet," for example). They can also reference the page on which that other term appears ("See Embattled on page 17" or "See Helmet on page 19"). While an alphabetically organized dictionary may not require those page numbers, I'll include them in this process just to show what *can* be done.

2. At the top of the dialog, choose whether the cross-reference links to a text anchor or a paragraph. In this instance, let's leave this set to the default of Paragraph. The specific paragraph to which a cross-reference will point is selected in the Destination area of the dialog. The left pane displays all paragraph styles in the current document, starting with [All Paragraphs], [No Paragraph Style], and [Basic Paragraph], followed by all other styles in the document, listed alphabetically.

TIP

To reference text in a *different* InDesign document, select Browse from the Document menu in the New Cross-Reference (or Edit Cross-Reference) dialog, and then choose the other document. Its styles will populate the list on the left.

If you choose [All Paragraphs], you'll quickly realize why working with specific styles is best. All Paragraphs means just that—every paragraph in your document will be listed in the right pane of the dialog (FIGURE 9.24). A snippet of the text that starts each paragraph helps you identify the paragraph you want to reference, but in a long document (precisely the type of project cross-referencing is ideal for), this list could contain hundreds of paragraphs. You'll have to scroll through *all* of them; there are no shortcuts to move through the list, and you can't make the pane any bigger.

FIGURE 9.24 All documents in a paragraph displayed in the Destination area of the New Cross-Reference dialog.

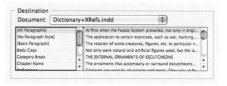

FIGURE 9.25 Paragraphs filtered according to the paragraph style applied to them.

3. Pare down your choices to specific paragraphs by selecting a paragraph style to filter that list down to a much more manageable length. The cross-references I want to add in this dictionary all refer to other definitions, all of which are styled with the Definitions style. Selecting the Definitions paragraph style in the left pane (FIGURE 9.25) eliminates all extraneous paragraphs from the list on the right, making it easier and faster to get to the destination for the cross-reference.

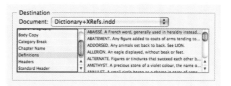

4. Reset the cross-reference's appearance options at the bottom of the dialog. The default is the same as those for hyperlinks—a black rectangle drawn around the cross-reference. This is an unappealing setting for hyperlinks, and it makes even less sense for cross-references. Change these settings to Invisible Rectangle with a highlight of None (FIGURE 9.26). You may want your cross-references to be visibly different, but you can accomplish that with far greater control and subtlety by assigning a character style to them.

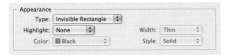

FIGURE 9.26 Invisible Rectangle and None are preferable to InDesign's default appearance settings for cross-references.

FORMATTING A CROSS-REFERENCE

After the destination paragraph for a cross-reference is selected, InDesign offers a number of options for the format of that cross-reference. Note that format in this context does not refer to the cross-reference's typeface, size, or color. A cross-reference's format is its structure: what pieces of the paragraph are used, whether or not a page number is included, and what static text appears around the cross-reference. It's similar to the expressions used to define the presentation of a number in a numbered list (see Chapter 7) or the Text Before and Text After options for a running header variable described earlier in this chapter.

The New Cross-Reference dialog's Cross-Reference Format menu contains a number of common format choices (FIGURE 9.27). You can opt to include the full text of the paragraph (good for section and category headings) with or without a page number, or to include only the page number and none of the paragraph text (e.g., "See page 29"). If the selected paragraph is part of a numbered list, you can exclude the number (Paragraph Text) or show *only* the number and none of the text (Paragraph Number).

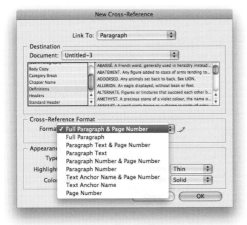

FIGURE 9.27 Default cross-reference format options.

In a catalog where a product category heading like "Accent Tables" might be the full text of a paragraph, you could choose the Full Paragraph & Page Number format, which generates *"Accent Tables" on page 8* as a reference (including the quotation marks). Choosing Full Paragraph would give you, simply, "Accent

Tables" (also including the quotation marks). But neither of these includes the word "See" before the referenced text. You could type the word right before the cross-reference's insertion point in the text, but it would not be part of the cross-reference. That defeats the purpose of a completely dynamic cross-reference feature.

Fortunately, these formats are fully editable. You can either modify the existing formats to suit your needs or create your own cross-reference formats to add to this list by clicking the Create or Edit Cross-Reference Formats icon to the right of the Format menu. This opens the Cross-Reference Formats dialog (FIGURE 9.28).

FIGURE 9.28 The Cross-Reference Formats dialog.

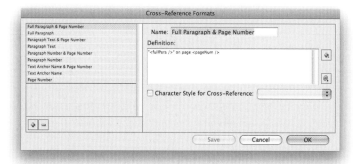

The list in the left pane of the dialog contains all the formats listed in the Format menu in the New Cross-Reference dialog and any custom formats you add. The plus and minus buttons at the bottom of that pane add or delete, respectively, formats from the list.

BUILDING A CUSTOM CROSS-REFERENCE FORMAT

All cross-reference formats are constructed from a handful of specific building blocks (TABLE 9.1), and you can use those building blocks to construct your own formats. For example, to make your own version of the Full Paragraph & Page Number format that begins with the word See and doesn't wrap the referenced text in quotes, select Full Paragraph & Page Number from the list of formats on the left and click the Add button to create a duplicate of that format.

When any new format is added, it picks up the settings of whatever format is currently selected in the list, which is helpful if you want to build a custom format that branches off from what's already established in an existing one. The new format name is the same as the original but with a number in parentheses at the end.

TABLE 9.1 **Cross-reference Building Blocks**

Building Block	Reference Text Generated
<pageNum/>	The page number where the referenced text exists.
<paraNum/>	The automatic number of a paragraph in a numbered list, but none of the paragraph text.
<paraText/>	The text of a paragraph in a numbered list, but not the number.
<fullPara/>	All text in the paragraph.
<fullPara delim="*delimiter*" includeDelim="false"/> OR <fullPara delim="*delimiter*" includeDelim="true"/>	A portion of text starting at the beginning of a paragraph up to a specific delimiter character that you specify (a period, colon, or em dash, for example). The true or false statements determine whether or not the text in the cross-reference includes that delimiter character. This is listed in the building blocks menu as Partial Paragraph.
<txtAnchrName/>	The name of the text anchor designated as the cross-reference destination.
<chapNum/>	The chapter number as set in the Numbering & Section options of the destination's document.
<fileName/>	The name of the file (including its .indd extension) containing the reference.
<cs name="*StyleName*">*Text of Reference*</cs>	This pair of building blocks brackets some part of the format to apply a character style to that portion of the cross-reference. You must type the name of the character style within the quotation marks in the opening part of the building block. If the style has not yet been created, a warning message will notify you that the style doesn't exist, but you can still save the format and add the character style to the document afterward. The style name is also case sensitive.

Cross-reference formats are customized in the Definition field of the dialog, where building blocks and static text are combined to create a pattern for the format. For example, the format for Full Paragraph & Page Number is

"<fullPara/>" on page

TIP

Use the Load Cross-Reference Formats option from the Cross-References panel menu to import existing formats from another file.

A modified version of that format that includes the word "See" at the beginning, removes the quotes around the destination paragraph text, and finishes the reference off with a period would be

See <fullPara/> on page <pageNum/>.

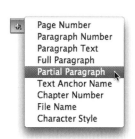

FIGURE 9.29 The cross-reference building block menu.

None of these predefined formats suit my needs for the cross-references I want to add to my dictionary definitions. Each dictionary term is within the same paragraph as the full definition, but <fullPara/> would include the *entire* definition in the cross-reference. My cross-references should only include the term being defined, not the definition. For that I need to use the Partial Paragraph building block (<fullPara delim="" includeDelim="false"/>), which can be inserted using the building block menu (FIGURE 9.29) or by typing in the proper syntax.

To generate a partial paragraph cross-reference, InDesign needs to know where to *stop* including text from the destination paragraph. A delimiter character is required to mark that cut-off point, just as a delimiter is used to end a nested style instruction (see Chapter 2, "Nesting and Sequencing Styles"). Since each term in the dictionary is followed by a period, that can act as the delimiter. Type the delimiter (a period in this example) between the quotes in the delim="" part of the Definition. The Partial Paragraph building block's default condition of "false" is appropriate to keep that period from being included in the cross-reference. Therefore, the customized building block would be

<fullPara delim="." includeDelim="false"/>

STYLING A CROSS-REFERENCE

Below the Definition pane is a Character Style for Cross-Reference check box and menu from which you can select a character style to assign to the entire cross-reference. However, I want the term in the cross-reference to have another character style applied to it other than the character style I'll eventually apply to the entire reference. I can accomplish that by enclosing the Partial Paragraph building block in the Character Style building block and customizing it with the name of the desired character style, as shown here:

<cs name="*Cross-reference Terms*"><fullPara delim="." includeDelim="false"/></cs>

Everything else in this cross-reference format is static text: the word "See," a comma after the referenced text, a space, the abbreviation "pg.," and the period after the page number. The static text combined with the different building blocks completes the cross-reference format, as shown here:

See <cs name="*Cross-reference Terms*"><fullPara delim="." includeDelim="false"/></cs>, pg. <pageNum/>.

After you've finalized all format settings, click OK in the Cross-Reference Formats dialog, and then click OK in the New Cross-Reference dialog. FIGURE 9.30 shows how the complete, customized cross-reference, as defined in the previous steps, appears at the end of a definition.

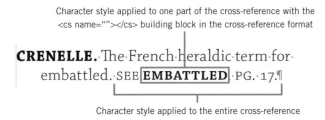

Character style applied to one part of the cross-reference with the <cs name=""></cs> building block in the cross-reference format

Character style applied to the entire cross-reference

FIGURE 9.30 A completed cross-reference with a custom format, an overall character style, and a second character style applied just to the referenced text.

Any change to a cross-reference format will affect existing cross-references that use that format, much the same way that changing a paragraph or character style definition changes all text to which those styles are applied.

INSERTING ADDITIONAL CROSS-REFERENCES

After you've established the desired format, it's available from the Format menu in the New Cross-Reference dialog for all references created in the document. Creating additional references with the same format does not require a trip to the Edit Cross-Reference dialog. You can define each new cross-reference—and select its custom format—from the New Cross-Reference dialog. However, you must add each reference one at a time, because each has a one-to-one association between the source and a specific destination paragraph.

TIPS FOR WORKING WITH CROSS-REFERENCES

A cross-reference destination is marked with a zero-width character at the beginning of the paragraph, and only a faint hairline around the page number (if included) in the source indicates that the text is a live cross-reference. Both of these indicators are only visible when Show Hidden Characters is turned on (Type > Show Hidden Characters). Without hidden characters showing, there's no way to differentiate a cross-reference source or its destination from any other text in the document. When working with cross-references, it's a good idea to keep Show Hidden Characters turned on.

Cross-reference sources and destinations also stand out more prominently in the Story Editor (Edit > Edit in Story Editor or Command/Ctrl-Y), where the source is enclosed within blue markers (FIGURE 9.31) and the destination is preceded by a marker character [⊛].

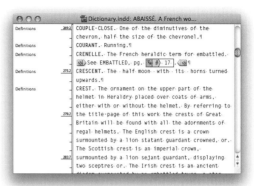

When your text cursor is within a cross-reference source, that cross-reference is highlighted in the Cross-References panel. Double-clicking the cross-reference name opens the Edit Cross-Reference dialog, where you can make changes to the destination paragraph and cross-reference format. Cross-references appear in the panel in the order in which they were added to the document, but you can sort them by name or by type from the Sort submenu in the panel menu.

If you delete a cross-reference destination—or just its invisible marker character—a missing reference icon ![icon] appears alongside the reference name in the panel. If you change the text used by the reference, a modified reference icon ![icon] appears alongside the reference name.

If a cross-reference's destination is in a separate document and you move that document to a location that InDesign can't find, you can reestablish the link between the source and the destination by choosing Relink Cross-Reference from the Cross-References panel menu.

CHAPTER 10

Styles, CSS, and XML

IN THE PAST, a discussion of Web applications for InDesign documents would have been limited to an overview of the program's PDF or JPEG export features. InDesign was originally built to create print-based documents, pure and simple. But things change. The ability to export and import XML was added in InDesign CS. The ability to export XHTML (see the sidebar "What's XHTML?") was added in CS3.

The ability to move content from print documents to the Web has advanced well beyond simple copy and paste. But before you get too excited, it doesn't mean that doing so is either easy or foolproof. And, as you've probably already guessed, InDesign styles are a crucial component of this capability.

> ### What's XHTML?
>
> While you may be familiar with HTML, InDesign exports only XHTML. So, what's the difference? XHTML (Extensible Hypertext Markup Language) offers all the capabilities of HTML but follows the stricter syntax rules of XML (Extensible Markup Language). In other words, the main difference between a Web page written in HTML and one written in XHTML is that the XHTML page will feature clean, properly structured code elements. In fact, sloppy, improperly structured code that would still function as an HTML page will often cease to work in a browser expecting to see "strict" XHTML. Visit www.w3schools.com/xhtml to learn more about XHTML.

Before discussing the methods for exporting content to XHTML and XML, let's first address any expectations you have of these features. If you're expecting In-Design to create a replica of your print document for the Web, you'll be heartily disappointed. If you need a re-creation of your layout, stick to the PDF and JPEG export filters.

Export for Dreamweaver

You'll find the Export for Dreamweaver command in the File menu. Although it would be more accurate to call it "Export to XHTML," in a way, this feature is aptly named because it identifies the crucial role Adobe Dreamweaver plays in the process. To achieve a truly usable result from this feature requires the able assistance of Dreamweaver or some other HTML editor. This section focuses primarily on items within this feature that relate to styling and formatting. For a complete description of the Export for Dreamweaver capabilities, see InDesign's Help file.

TIP

A word of advice to non-Web designers: Keep HTML filenames short and exclude spaces and punctuation marks other than hyphens (-) and underscores (_).

Choose File > Export for Dreamweaver to begin the process of exporting to XHTML. In the Save As dialog, which opens after you select the command, name the file and click Save.

InDesign adds an extension (.html) to the file automatically. Feel free to change the extension in the dialog to suit your own needs. InDesign will honor any manual alteration and then remember your preferred extension during subsequent export operations.

After saving the file, the XHTML Export Options dialog opens (FIGURE 10.1). Within the dialog are three categories—General, Images, and Advanced; each offers options to help specify the kind of XHTML to create, but the amount of tweaking you can do is not extensive.

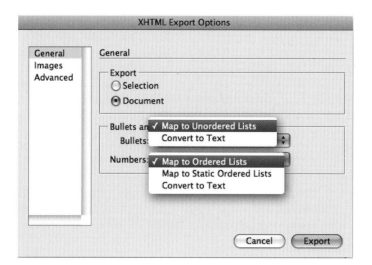

FIGURE 10.1 The options listed within this dialog help create the desired XHTML structure and formatting.

GENERAL OPTIONS

In the General section of the XHTML Export Options dialog, you can control which parts of the file are exported and how bulleted and numbered lists are mapped or converted.

Export. Choose Document or Selection to export an entire document or merely items selected within the document. Items can be chosen with either the Selection or Text tools. If nothing is selected when the command is activated, the Selection option is grayed out and the entire contents of the document are exported by default.

Using the Text tool you can target specific paragraphs, words, or even characters that you want to export. It can export only one story, or a portion of story, at a time.

Use the Selection tool to select multiple text and graphic frames. It's important to know that InDesign exports all the contents of a selected text frame, including text in threaded frames on other pages.

When graphics are selected, or are anchored in selected text frames, InDesign exports them along with the text. Unfortunately, this doesn't include graphics or graphical objects created within the program or pasted into the layout from other programs. Only graphics listed in the Links panel can be exported to XHTML.

Be cautious when you choose to export the entire document, because the option does export almost everything in the file—often in a jumbled mess that may be more trouble than it's worth.

Bullets and Numbers. As every Web designer knows, HTML can generate bulleted and numbered lists automatically. InDesign can format lists with bullets and numbers, too. The export filter allows you to map the InDesign-based formatting to the method used in HTML.

- **Bullets.** Choose Map to Unordered Lists from the drop-down menu when the bullets are in consecutive paragraphs. Bullets formatted with special glyphs or custom fonts will be replaced by standard HTML bullets.

  Choose Convert to Text when the bullets in the document are scattered in nonconsecutive paragraphs. This option converts the bullets to actual characters in the text. However, use this option with care. If you've chosen custom bullet characters, like ☺☻★, there's no telling how they will be converted. When in doubt, it's best to use the unordered list option.

- **Numbers.** Choose Map to Ordered Lists from the drop-down menu when your numbered paragraphs are consecutive. Like InDesign, HTML lists will update automatically when you add or delete list items.

  Choose Map to Static Ordered Lists when the numbers are scattered through the document or when the paragraphs are consecutive but you want to freeze the numbering as is. This option generates class and value attributes to specify what number to use for each paragraph. In this case, numbers will not update automatically when you add or delete items from the list.

  Choose Convert to Text when you want the actual numbers inserted in each paragraph.

IMAGE OPTIONS

As described earlier, InDesign can export linked graphics. The Images category of the dialog (FIGURE 10.2) provides options for exporting graphics and images. It basically does so by converting InDesign-based link information to be compatible with HTML. It can also create Web-compatible (GIF and JPEG) versions of each graphic when you select Optimized from the Copy Images drop-down menu. If you allow InDesign to handle the image conversion for the Web, there are two main concerns pertaining to styling:

NOTE

When it comes to elaborate numbering schemes employing indentation and mixtures of Roman, Arabic, and alpha characters, there is good news and bad news. The Ordered and Static Ordered options will preserve the indentation of such lists but display all numbering in Arabic characters by default. On the other hand, Convert to Text preserves the numbering scheme exactly as it appears in InDesign but drops the indentation. Fortunately, you can use Cascading Style Sheets (CSS) to address both issues (see the sidebar "The ABCs of CSS").

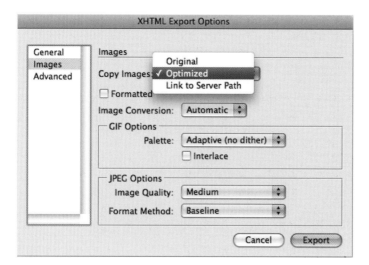

FIGURE 10.2 Select the Formatted check box if you want to include cropping and other effects, like drop shadows, too.

- On export, InDesign converts the object style name to a CSS class attribute and assigns it to the <div> element containing the HTML graphic reference. It happens automatically when a style is used, and the only way to prevent it from happening is to remove the object style from the frame before exporting. The class will also be added to the CSS declarations if you choose to export them as described in the following "Advanced Options" section. The class attribute that is created may come in handy for formatting the images for the Web.

- Whenever the Optimized option is selected from the drop-down menu, you'll notice that the Formatted check box will become selectable. Choose this option whenever you want to preserve the cropping or other effects applied to linked images within InDesign.

Although the ability to export linked graphics is handy at times, you may find that you end up creating most of the Web graphics manually outside of InDesign. If this is the case in your workflow, be sure to select Link to Server Path in the drop-down menu so that InDesign inserts an HTML-compatible reference to the image in the code.

ADVANCED OPTIONS

The heavy lifting (styling) happens in the Advanced category of the XHTML Export Options dialog (FIGURE 10.3). Choose Empty CSS Declarations to convert the text and object styles to CSS-based classes. No CSS does exactly what it says: nothing. Choose External CSS if you have an existing CSS file, and enter the name and path in the available field.

FIGURE 10.3 The Advanced options in the XHTML Export Options dialog.

CSS Options

NOTE
While most Web designers prefer to use external CSS files, you can save a lot of time by first choosing the Empty CSS Declaration option. InDesign will create the rule list for you. Then it's an easy matter in Dreamweaver to move the entire list to an external file.

Choose Empty CSS Declarations or External CSS to make InDesign convert and export all paragraph, character, table, cell, and object styles as CSS classes (see the sidebar "The ABCs of CSS"). If you select the option Empty CSS Declarations, corresponding CSS rules will be generated (without any styling information) and inserted automatically within the <head> region of the XHTML file. Select External CSS and InDesign exports the content but only links the XHTML to an external CSS file. You are responsible for creating the CSS file and the necessary CSS rules.

Choose No CSS when you want to create your own formatting based on criterion other than styling. Text will be exported using plain <p> tags, and any references to style names from InDesign will be discarded. If you don't use paragraph, character, table, cell, or object styles at all, just choose No CSS, because there's nothing to export anyway.

The JavaScript Options don't involve styles so we'll skip it.

A simple flyer demonstrates the potential results of exporting from a document that doesn't use styles but has all formatting applied manually. The formatting and positioning are not retained. The options used to export the XHTML are shown in FIGURE 10.4.

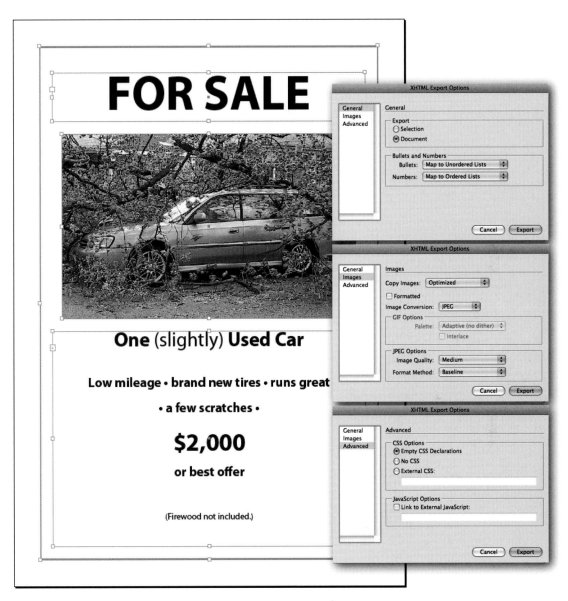

FIGURE 10.4 XHTML export options (right) cannot fix this layout for the Web.

The results of exporting an unstyled InDesign layout as XHTML are far from impressive. In Dreamweaver's Design view, the text shows no formatting whatsoever, and the picture has been moved to the bottom of the layout (FIGURE 10.5).

FIGURE 10.5 Unformatted text and incorrect picture position are possible results of exporting an unstyled layout.

In Code view, you can see how the <div> elements correspond to various text and graphic frames from the InDesign file (FIGURE 10.6). Being able to switch from design to code quickly in one program demonstrates vividly why Dreamweaver is an essential part of your workflow. You could easily fix the code problems in Dreamweaver, but it's more effective to create layouts in InDesign that are compatible to the requirements of the Web from the beginning.

FIGURE 10.6 Styled text and picture frames from the InDesign file correspond to **<div>** elements in the exported code.

```
1    <!DOCTYPE html PUBLIC "-//W3C//DTD XHTML 1.0 Strict//EN"
     "http://www.w3.org/TR/xhtml1/DTD/xhtml1-strict.dtd">
2    <html xmlns="http://www.w3.org/1999/xhtml">
3        <head>
4            <meta http-equiv="content-type" content="text/html;charset=utf-8" />
5            <title>online-Ad</title>
6            <style type="text/css" media="screen"><!--
7                div.image {}
8                div.story {}
9            --></style>
10       </head>
11       <body>
12           <div id="online-ad">
13               <div class="story">
14                   <p>FOR SALE</p>
15                   <p>One (slightly) Used Car</p>
16                   <p>Low mileage • brand new tires • runs great </p>
17                   <p>• a few scratches • <br />$2,000 </p>
18                   <p>or best offer</p>
19                   <p>(Firewood not included.)</p>
20               </div>
21               <div class="image">
22                   <img src="online-Ad-web-images/forsale_opt.jpeg" alt="forsale.tif" />
23               </div>
24           </div>
25       </body>
26   </html>
```

The ABCs of CSS

InDesign users have a full toolbox of paragraph, character, table, cell, and object styling to format almost everything within a document. Web designers have only Cascading Style Sheets (CSS).

But don't feel bad for the Web designer. CSS features all the power of paragraph, character, table, cell, and object styles combined, and more! CSS also offers *contextual formatting*, which InDesign can't (yet). This means you can insert a paragraph element in the header section, and it's automatically formatted with the header settings. Then you can insert the same paragraph in the footer section, and it reformats to the entirely different footer settings—all without changing anything other than its location in the layout.

HTML and XHTML consist of fewer than 100 code elements. These elements are responsible for creating Web page structures and for rudimentary formatting of text and objects. To accomplish this, each element comes with a built-in collection of default formats and settings.

For example, the `<p>` code element creates the structure of a paragraph and formats it automatically with font settings, color, alignment, and so on. In most browsers the text will be black, aligned to the left, and probably formatted to be Times or Times New Roman, 12pt.

The power of CSS is its ability to redefine the default settings and even add some of your own. Let's say you wanted to make all the paragraphs in a Web page display in red. The CSS rule would look like this:

```
p {
color: red;
}
```

Then you decide that some paragraphs should display in blue but only those that appear in tables. No problem; simply create a compound CSS rule like this:

```
table p {
color: blue;
}
```

There are situations where compounds won't be enough, so CSS allows you to add exceptions to each element and compound with the use of attributes called "ids" and "classes." An id is a unique identifier that should be used only once per page, whereas classes are like categories that can be used multiple times on each page, like styles in InDesign. These attributes can be applied directly to the element, such as `<p class="sidebar">`, or more commonly to the containing `<div>` element, such as `<div class="sidebar"><p></p></div>`.

continues on next page

The ABCs of CSS (continued)

You identify an id modifier in CSS rules by using a hash mark (#) and a class modifier with a period (.), such as:

```
#header p {
color: green;
}

.sidebar p {
color: orange;
}
```

With these four simple rules, one tag has been formatted in four completely different ways, yet there's no modification made to the `<p>` element used in the code. Simply insert the paragraph into the location context defined by the rule, and the color will change based on whether it is in body text, a table tag, header id, or sidebar class.

Considering there are dozens of books of more than 200+ pages describing all the capabilities of CSS, this humble sidebar can't do the subject justice. So check out www.w3schools.com/css for a quick tutorial on CSS.

Here are some reference books on the subject:

- *Stylin' with CSS: A Designer's Guide* (2nd Edition) by Charles Wyke-Smith (New Riders Press, 2007)

- *CSS Web Site Design: Hands-On Training* by Eric Meyer (Peachpit, 2006)

- *Bulletproof Web Design: Improving flexibility and protecting against worst-case scenarios with XHTML and CSS* (2nd Edition) by Dan Cederholm (New Riders Press, 2007)

- *CSS: The Missing Manual* by David McFarland (Pogue Press, 2006)

- *The Zen of CSS Design: Visual Enlightenment for the Web* by Dave Shea and Molly E. Holzschlag (Peachpit, 2005)

- *Transcending CSS: The Fine Art of Web Design* by Andy Clarke (New Riders Press, 2006)

CREATING WEB-AWARE LAYOUTS

A close look at the exported code in the preceding section tells you a lot about how InDesign creates XHTML (see Figure 10.6). Basically, it starts at the top of the layout and works toward the bottom of each page, working from left to right. Frames (text and graphic) are converted to <div> elements, and their entire contents are exported before it deals with the next element. Graphics that are not inserted (inline or anchored) in the text are exported separately and may end up anywhere in the code. If an InDesign document isn't structured from the beginning to be "Web-aware," all the CSS in the world won't be able to help it. On the other hand, a few minutes in InDesign can save you hours of work in Dreamweaver.

To create a more Web-aware layout, a bit of modification to the original design is required:

- Wherever possible, link text frames together to create a single text flow. Connect any free-floating heading frames to their stories, and daisy-chain stories together if they relate to a single topic or will be sharing space in the final Web page.

- Don't embed graphics or create essential illustrations within InDesign that you want in the XHTML. Create them in other programs and save them as independent graphics first, and then place them into InDesign as links.

- Insert all Web-bound graphics inline or anchored at the appropriate position in the text so they are part of the text flow.

- Preserve the existing styling; format text and graphics by using paragraph, character, table, cell, and object styles.

These simple procedures will pay dividends in the long run by creating more effective XHTML structures, achieving much better code, and saving you time in Dreamweaver (FIGURE 10.7). For future projects, incorporate these techniques during document production. So when you've finished the layout, the document will be ready for XHTML as is.

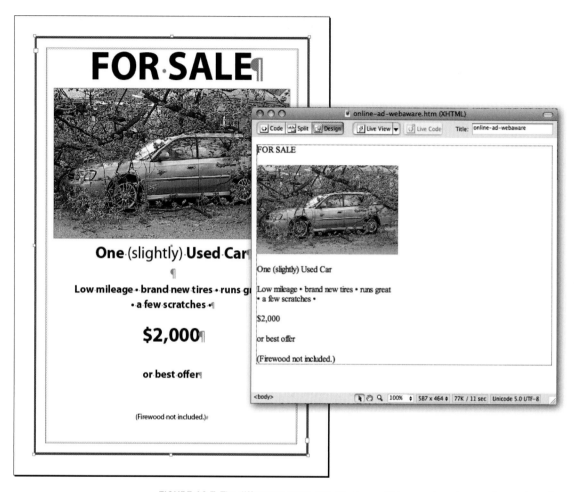

FIGURE 10.7 The differences when exporting from a Web-aware layout versus its counterpart are obvious. This exported XHTML page is ready to be formatted by CSS.

DEFINING CSS RULES

When XHTML is created from a styled document and you choose to export Empty CSS Declarations, all the text-based styles as well as object styles are converted to CSS classes and inserted as a block within the <head> element. To comply with Web standards, the style names are reformatted in lowercase and spaces are replaced with hyphens (FIGURE 10.8).

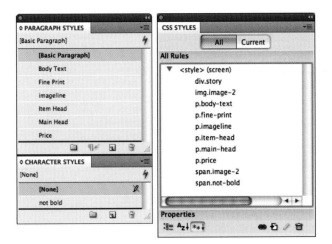

FIGURE 10.8 InDesign converts paragraph and character styles (left) into properly structured but empty CSS rule elements in Dreamweaver (right).

To edit the CSS rules, double-click on the one you want to change. When the CSS Rule Definition dialog opens, select the options you want to apply. But don't be fooled by all the empty fields in the dialog (FIGURE 10.9). An empty field doesn't mean there isn't a setting. Most HTML elements come with a full set of built-in formats, or default specifications.

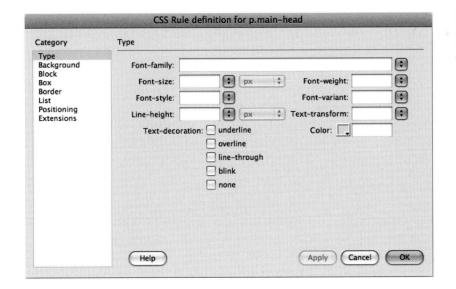

FIGURE 10.9 Dreamweaver's CSS Rule Definition dialog allows you to create and edit CSS rules.

While it may seem at first an inconvenience to build Web-aware layouts, it only takes a few minutes at most and it really doesn't affect your design options or what you can achieve. The combination of a Web-aware layout in InDesign and a set of well-defined CSS rules can produce far more desirable results more quickly (FIGURE 10.10).

FIGURE 10.10 The resulting XHTML layout viewed in Dreamweaver.

Creating and editing the CSS rules in your XHTML file can be fun as you experiment with different settings. But here's a warning to the novice Web designers: You'll discover that what looks fine in one browser can look horrible in another! Sometimes the variations between browsers are dramatic, even unsettling.

Print designers are accustomed to text and objects remaining where they put them and how they formatted them. On the Web, all bets are off. Until you're more familiar with CSS, a guiding principle for Web design is to *keep it simple*.

GLASS CEILINGS AND BRICK WALLS

For the near future, using InDesign to create usable Web pages is more of a parlor trick than a true workflow. While it's relatively easy to obtain usable results from one- or two-page documents, attempting to export an entire newsletter of three or more pages all at once is an exercise in aggravation. This is especially true for multipage and intricately designed documents, because you may find yourself spending too much time in Dreamweaver cleaning up the results.

A better process is to export one page, or spread, at a time to create individual, self-contained Web pages. Be aware of stories that continue on other pages (FIGURE 10.11) and confirm that all linked text flows are exported completely.

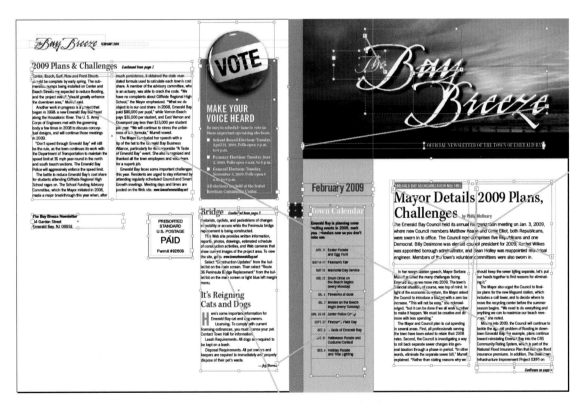

FIGURE 10.11 Multipage documents may have text links that need careful attention on export.

There are simply too many impediments to using this basic export process for professional, high-end workflows. Some of the limitations revolve around InDesign's inability to adapt content to any HTML elements other than <p>, <div>, and <span>, as well as its dependence on formatting based on ids and classes. Besides being limiting, it doesn't conform to current best practices for the Web.

Yet with two improvements, the Export to Dreamweaver feature could provide real productivity gains. An interface that would let users choose how styles are mapped to HTML elements *and* the ability to manipulate the XHTML structure before it's exported would be ideal. You can, however, already do that in InDesign with XML.

Styles and XML

Until Adobe provides better XHTML mapping capabilities, you can always use XML. XML is a way to identify data based on the type of information it represents. Out of the box, InDesign is second only to Adobe Framemaker in the breadth and depth of its capabilities for importing and exporting XML for print-based documents (FIGURE 10.12). For example, XML can help automate publishing data from spreadsheets and databases; it can dynamically generate documents—like business cards, price lists, and catalogs—much faster than you can by hand; and it can move content quickly and efficiently from one document to another, or even to and from the Web. And best of all, it's tightly integrated with InDesign's text-based styles.

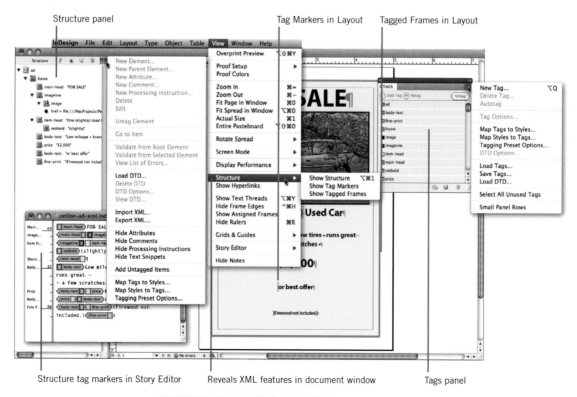

FIGURE 10.12 Most of InDesign's XML features and interface are hidden when you start the program and must be turned on or made visible.

EXPORTING XML

Successfully exporting XML from InDesign requires a multistep process.

Optimize the layout. The first step is to create a fully styled and completely threaded document similar to the Web-aware layout described earlier in the chapter (see Figure 10.7). This is not only useful for Web-based workflows, it's effective for almost any kind of XML application, because logical and well-organized document structures result in logical and well-organized data structures. The car flyer is already converted, so it's an ideal test case for the process of exporting XML from InDesign.

Build the tags. The next step is to create, or load, a list of XML tags and then apply them to the document content. The ad file doesn't contain any XML tag names yet, so you need to create them. Tags can be created one by one manually (FIGURE 10.13) or loaded from an existing XML file, InDesign document, or Document Type Definition (DTD).

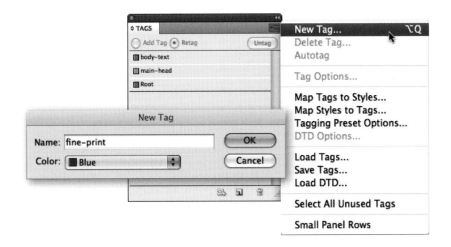

FIGURE 10.13 Use the Tags panel to create or load XML tags and assign them to the document content.

What should you name your tags? Almost anything you want, as long as it complies with XML syntax rules, which includes among other things being case-sensitive and using no spaces or special characters.

XML tags are equivalent to HTML code elements except they convey no styling information, only data identity. So, one school of thought suggests you name your tags for the type of data they identify, such as "productname," "size," "price," and so on.

On the other hand, tags can also be applied individually to characters, paragraphs, graphics, and can even be in nested configurations to help better organize and identify components of your content. Since this often mirrors how paragraph, character, table, and object styles are applied, another recommended method is naming XML tags to match the existing InDesign style names. This is especially valuable because InDesign offers a productivity enhancement that can automatically tag text based on how it's styled.

Apply the tags. Apply tags to each element you want to export. Free-standing frames and graphics that have no tags will not be exported. However, if a text frame contains even one tag, InDesign exports the tagged elements as you would expect but the remainder as untagged text. You can select each frame or range of characters and click on a tag name in the Tags panel to assign it manually. For text, it's most efficient to have the styles that are already applied to text match up to XML tags by mapping. Choose Map Styles to Tags from the Tags panel menu or the Structure panel menu. If the style and tag names match exactly, case-sensitive and letter for letter, you can save time by choosing the Map by Name option. The mapping feature can even apply tags to text formatted by character styles contained in nested- and GREP-based styling. If your tag and style names don't match perfectly choose tags manually from the drop-down menus (FIGURE 10.14). Multiple styles can be mapped to the same tag.

FIGURE 10.14 Correlate styles with tags by choosing matches manually from the drop-down menus, or select the Map by Name option.

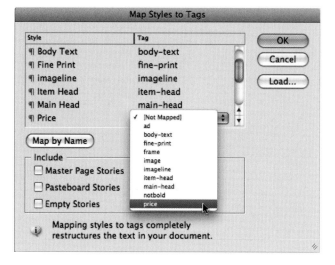

When tags are applied to content, there are visual indicators available in the layout. Choose View > Structure and select Show Tag Markers or Show Tagged Frames to see the color-coded overlays and brackets in Normal view mode (FIGURE 10.15).

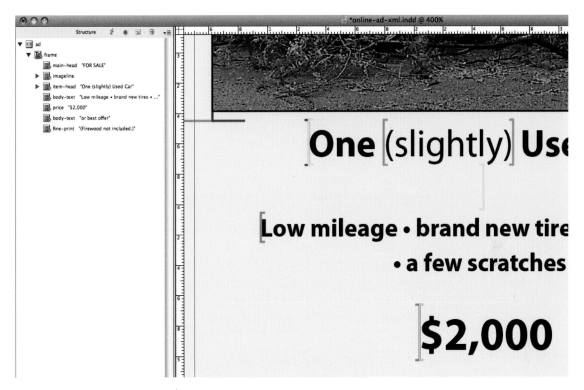

FIGURE 10.15 The layout displays visual cues to indicate tagged content.

Export as XML. The Structure pane displays and allows you to manipulate the XML structure within the document. You can drag and drop the elements within the Structure pane to reorganize and resequence as desired for export. Select the root or any of the child elements it contains to specify what will be exported (FIGURE 10.16).

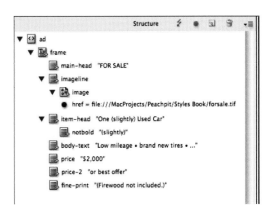

FIGURE 10.16 The Structure pane shows the XML components and structure of the document.

Now you're ready to export. You can activate the Export XML command in four ways: from the File menu, from the Structure pane menu, by right-clicking on the root or any of the child elements contained therein, or by pressing Command/ Ctrl-E. In the resulting dialog, choose XML from the drop-down menu and name the file. When you click Save, the XML Export Options dialog appears (FIGURE 10.17), allowing you to specify what will be included in the XML output. XML export options are similar to those offered by the XHTML filter with a few exceptions, like the ability to remap certain types of characters and to apply an XSLT transformation of the data during output (see the section "XSLT: Styles on Steroids").

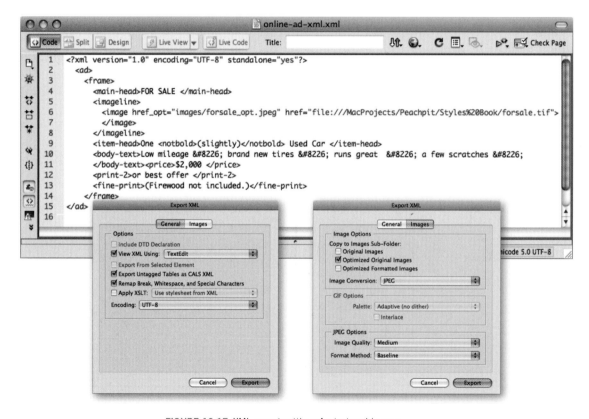

FIGURE 10.17 XML export settings for text and images.

Importing XML

When exporting XML from the flyer earlier, the process began with a file that had styles but no XML tags applied. The Map Styles to Tags dialog applied the XML tags to the content using the existing paragraph and character styles as markers. When *importing* XML, the XML file contains tags but no styles. FIGURE 10.18 shows a template with the boilerplate copy stripped out but with the tagged text frames left behind. It will clearly demonstrate what kind of magic is possible in an XML workflow. With a few clicks of the mouse, the pretagged frames will be populated with text, images, and price information. Then with a few more clicks, the layout will be completely formatted. It doesn't get much easier than that.

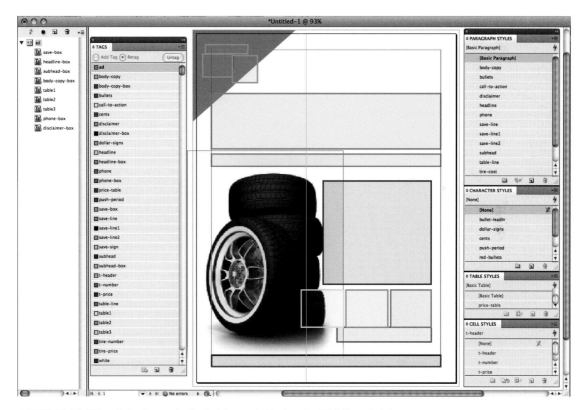

FIGURE 10.18 Although they're empty, the text frames in the layout exhibit the colorful evidence of XML tagging.

In FIGURE 10.19 you can see side by side the results of the import process:

1. From the File menu or the Structure panel menu, choose Import XML.

2. Browse to the XML file and click Open.

3. For this type of workflow, deselect all check boxes in the XML Import Options dialog and then click OK.

The data flows into the pretagged areas of the layout. One of the amazing properties of importing XML is that a piece of data will only enter a frame properly tagged for it.

4. Choose Map Tags to Styles from the Tags panel menu or Structure panel menu.

5. Choose matches manually from the drop-down menus, or click the Map by Name option.

This matches the incoming XML information with the character and paragraph styles already existing in the template, and styling is instantly applied.

The neat thing is that this process works the same way whether it's a one-page flyer like this or a thousand-page book. Although this capability is great as is, another feature would be the ability to automatically map object styles, too.

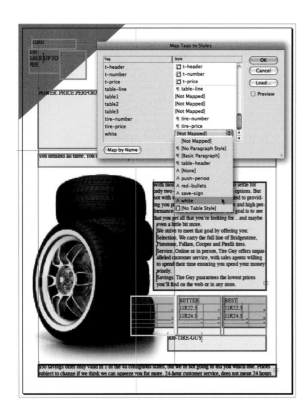

FIGURE 10.19 Unformatted XML content imported into an InDesign template (left) becomes instantly formatted by mapping tags to styles (right).

XSLT: Styles on Steroids

As noted already, XML doesn't contain, or support, any styling information. Formatting must be applied by another program or by an XML application. One of these applications was created specifically for XML. It's called Extensible Style Sheet Language Transformation (XSLT), and it not only enables you to format text within an XML file, but also to create and format structural elements. XSLT can apply CSS styling and convert the XML file into something completely different, such as a Web page, a text file, a completely different XML file, or even a PDF!

Adobe added an XSLT feature in InDesign CS3. You can apply XSLTs on both import and export. The feature is so powerful that you'll be limited more by your imagination (and your ability to write XSLTs) than by the technology.

You can use XSLT to reorganize or sort the content of an XML file by various criteria, such as price, title, and author name. And on export, you can use XSLT to generate instant Web pages (FIGURE 10.20).

FIGURE 10.20 An XSLT can be applied while importing and exporting XML. Here the content of the flyer is exported, and a Web page is generated with a few clicks of the mouse.

This chapter has only scratched the surface of all you can do with XML in InDesign. For a complete hands-on guide to the features and capabilities, check out *A Designer's Guide to Adobe InDesign and XML* by James J. Maivald and Cathy Palmer (Adobe Press, 2008).

CHAPTER 11

Style Management

INDESIGN HAS A POWERHOUSE combination of styles and style-related features. As you start to make styles an integral part of your projects, you'll find that you have more and more styles to manage. Unfortunately, for all that InDesign has in abundance for style capabilities, it lacks any dedicated method for managing, organizing, unifying, or reporting on the styles in a document or across multiple documents.

However, there are some workarounds and organizational options you can use to compensate a bit for this limitation, as well as some document housekeeping you can do to keep your styles from getting out of control. All these methods apply to character, paragraph, cell, table, and object styles, even if the specific examples described and illustrated in this chapter do not.

Style Organization Basics

When it comes to organizing the styles in your workspace some up-front planning can go a long way. Not that you must take all these steps from the very beginning of a project, or for *every* project, but most projects that seem simple at first grow complex faster than you realize. When that happens, step back and do a little style housecleaning.

Name styles meaningfully. The main priority is to name your styles in a way that makes sense. A style named "sec-drop-intro-alt" may make sense to you today, but by the end of the project, when you're burning the midnight oil to meet a deadline, will you remember what that style is? More important, when you pass the file on to co-workers will *they* have a clue what that style is? A logically named style like "Section Intro+Drop Cap (Alternate)," while lengthy, leaves little room for doubt about what the style is and where it should be applied.

Naming conventions. If you have a number of paragraph, character, object, and table styles that all apply to the sidebars in your project, a naming convention like "SIDEBAR-*MoreSpecificStyleInfo*" makes clear what part of your document's structure the style pertains to. It also makes the style names easier to find, especially as your panels fill with more and more styles. As you switch from the Paragraph Styles panel to the Object Styles panel, you'll eliminate any head-scratching about which styles apply to which page elements.

FIGURE 11.1 Edit style names directly in their respective panels.

Editing style names. Style names are editable directly from any style panel. There's no need to open the Style Options dialog just to rename a style. Simply click the style name, wait a second, and then click it again to make the style name editable (FIGURE 11.1). A fast double-click opens the Style Options dialog, so be patient. Be aware that when you click a style name to edit it this way, the first click on the style name will *apply* that style to any selected text or object. So, be sure to Deselect All (Shift-Command/Ctrl-A) before you start renaming styles. Selecting the style name with everything deselected also makes that style the default for any frames you create from that point forward. After you've re-named the style, it's a good idea to click back to something like Basic Paragraph or your most-used style to return to a more practical default.

Organizing style names. Each style panel menu offers the option to Sort by Name into alphabetical order. Style names can also be dragged to any location in the panel, so similar styles can be kept near one another in the list to reduce the amount of time spent mousing around to the next needed style. If you use styles that occur in a specific sequence (Headline, Deck, Byline, Intro, Body), you can arrange them in that order. Also, choosing Small Panel Rows from any style panel menu reduces the font size of the style names and the space between each, but the result is a panel so tight it's not much easier to work with.

> ## Unreliable Style Managers: Copy and Paste, Object Libraries, and Snippets
>
> Copying styles of any kind from one document to another adds those styles to the destination document if they don't already exist. If, however, any style of the same name *does* exist in the destination document, the styles of the incoming text or objects will conform to the appearance of the same-named styles in the destination document. This is default InDesign behavior: The destination document always wins. When you consider how many common style names people use (caption, body copy, category, company name, etc.), the potential for style clashes like this is pretty likely.
>
> Object libraries and InDesign snippets (which are essentially library items not organized in a library but stored as separate .inds files) can be used as style "receptacles," in a way. Any snippet created from a styled object includes the style information with it, as does any styled object added to a library. However, the same rule for copy and paste applies when dragging a snippet file into or placing a library item in a new document. New styles will be added to the document from the snippet or library item, but existing styles in the destination document will reformat any same-named styles applied to the incoming objects.

Style Groups

Once you start to amass a long list of styles and scrolling through your panels becomes an ordeal, consider organizing your styles into style groups. Style groups are folders into which you can organize related styles, similar to the folder-based method of organizing layers in Adobe Photoshop.

To create a style group, select New Style Group from any style's panel menu (or click the Create New Style Group icon at the bottom of the panel), name the group, and drag the styles you want to include over the style group folder that is added to the panel.

To speed things up a bit, first select the styles you want to add to a group, and then choose New Group from Styles from the panel menu (FIGURE 11.2). Name the style in the New Style Group dialog and click OK. The group is created with all selected styles moved into it (FIGURE 11.3).

FIGURE 11.2 Creating a style group from selected styles.

FIGURE 11.3 A style group (expanded to show its contents) in the Paragraph Styles panel.

Sorting styles into groups can reduce a long, disorganized style panel into a tidier, more manageable workspace (FIGURE 11.4). However, there's a potential downside—style duplication—and some behavior related to exporting grouped styles you should be aware of.

FIGURE 11.4 A project's worth of loose paragraph styles (left) and the same styles organized into logical groups (right).

STYLE DUPLICATION

Once a style is within a group, it has two separate identifiers: its name and its location (the style group where it resides). The location is indicated under the style's name in its Style Options dialog or anywhere the style can be called on, such as a style menu within the Cell Styles or Object Styles dialogs (FIGURE 11.5), where the group name appears in parentheses after the style name.

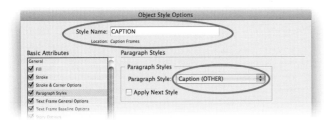

FIGURE 11.5 Style group indicators for an object style and the grouped paragraph style built into it.

This makes it possible to have two identically named styles in the same document. There could be a "Body Copy" paragraph style in the panel and a "Body Copy" paragraph style within an "Articles" style group in the same panel. If you load styles from or to a document in which styles are not grouped consistently, InDesign can't detect matching styles that may exist within groups. Instead, ungrouped duplicates of the grouped styles will be added to the document. This can create confusion and potential inconsistencies if it's not immediately corrected or, preferably, avoided.

If duplicate styles find their way into your document outside of their desired group, simply drag the style over the group folder. A dialog will alert you to the style name conflict and offer the option to overwrite (replace) the style in the group with the incoming style or rename the incoming style (FIGURE 11.6).

TIP

Duplicate styles should definitely be avoided. Yet InDesign almost *encourages* duplicate styles with the Copy Style to Group option available in each style panel's menu. Pretend this isn't an option and forget it's there. Instead, *move* your styles into any groups you've created. You'll save yourself a lot of potential style grief that way.

FIGURE 11.6 Moving same-named styles into a style group triggers a conflict warning.

EXPORTING GROUPED STYLES

How grouped styles behave in InDesign is only one consideration. Since style groups create a distinct hierarchy for the styles within them, what happens when those styles are exported from InDesign?

RTF export

When text to which styles in a group are applied is exported to the RTF format, those styles appear in the resulting file with the group name appended in parentheses at the end of the style name. When the RTF file is opened in Microsoft Word, you'll see this group name everywhere styles are accessed in that application (FIGURE 11.7). If that RTF document is later reimported into the InDesign document, the styles will be recognized as conflicts in the RTF Import Options dialog when Import Styles Automatically is chosen, but their location within the group is ignored. The styles are imported as duplicates *outside* of the group (FIGURE 11.8). Only Style Mapping each incoming style to the appropriate grouped style will properly organize incoming styles into groups. See Chapter 4, "Auto-styling Imported Word and Excel Files" for more about Style Mapping.

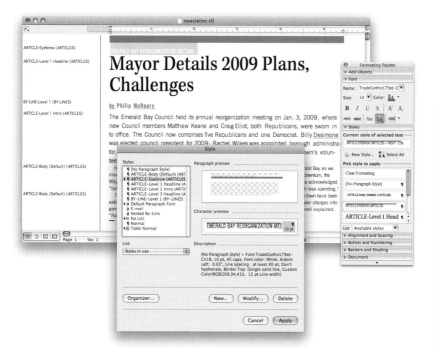

FIGURE 11.7 Grouped styles have their group name appended on export.

FIGURE 11.8 Imported RTF file styles duplicated outside of a style group.

HTML export

When styles are exported as HTML via the Export to Dreamweaver feature (see Chapter 10, "Styles, CSS, and XML"), the paragraph style "ARTICLE-Body (Default)" generates a tag of `<p class="article-body-default-">`. But if that style is in a group called ARTICLES, the group name is appended at the *beginning* of the style's tag, making the generated tag `<p class="articles-article-body-default-">`.

Quick Apply

If you opt to sacrifice the organizational benefits of style groups for fear of its potential pitfalls, there's another method for avoiding long scrolling panels or even switching between the paragraph, character, object, table, and cell style panels: Quick Apply.

The Quick Apply feature is a favorite among keyboard shortcut junkies who never want to lift their hands from the keys to move the mouse. Every panel menu includes a Quick Apply icon ⚡, or you can access the feature by choosing Edit > Quick Apply. But since it's intended to keep your hands on the keyboard, just type Command-Return/Ctrl-Enter to open the Quick Apply window.

Every style and variable in the active document—as well as every InDesign menu option, panel menu option, script, or item to which a keyboard shortcut can be assigned—can be accessed and applied to any selected object or text, or at any text insertion point using Quick Apply without ever touching the mouse.

With Quick Apply open, type any small portion of the style name you need in the field at the top and all potential matches instantly populate the list below it (FIGURE 11.9). Pressing Return/Enter applies the style to the selection and closes Quick Apply. A number of other key combinations are available that apply a style *without* closing Quick Apply or allow you to edit the style rather than apply it. TABLE 11.1 lists these key combinations.

FIGURE 11.9 A Quick Apply search for "cap" finds object, paragraph, and character styles related to captions along with miscellaneous menu items containing "cap."

TABLE 11.1 **Keyboard Guide to Quick Apply**

Keyboard Shortcut	Action
Command-Return/Ctrl-Enter	Opens Quick Apply
Return/Enter	Applies the selected style, menu command, or variable, and closes the Quick Apply window.
Option-Return/Alt-Enter	Applies a paragraph style and removes overrides
Option-Shift-Return/Alt-Shift-Enter	Applies a paragraph style and removes overrides and character styles
Command-Return/Ctrl-Enter	Opens the appropriate dialog for editing the selected style
Shift-Return/Shift-Enter	Applies an item without closing Quick Apply
Esc	Closes Quick Apply without applying anything

By default, Quick Apply runs a very broad search that includes everything but scripts and hidden menu commands in the results. You can change what Quick Apply searches for by default from the options menu (FIGURE 11.10) by deselecting any item to exclude it.

FIGURE 11.10 Quick Apply search options.

If you don't want to change the default but know that you're looking for one style type in particular, precede your search with a modifier, such as "p:" for paragraph styles or "o:" for object styles. TABLE 11.2 lists all Quick Apply modifiers and what they narrow the search to.

TABLE 11.2 **Quick Apply Search Modifiers**

Modifier	Limits Search To
p:	Paragraph styles
c:	Character styles
o:	Object styles
m:	Menu commands (including panel menus)
s:	Scripts
t:	Table styles
v:	Text variables
e:	Cell styles
ct:	Conditions

Managing Styles Across Documents

Suppose you were working on several collateral pieces for a client—a pocket folder, capabilities brochure, product spec sheets, order forms, and so on—that all use common styles but need to be in different InDesign files for organizational reasons or because each piece requires different page sizes. For consistency's sake, you make all components of the project use consistent styles for body copy, headlines, and table formatting—just to name a few. But the more you work in each file, redefining styles to suit your purposes, the less consistent each piece becomes. The longer this goes on, the harder it is to bring consistency back to all documents. Synchronizing the project's styles with InDesign's Book panel can prevent this "style drift" from occurring.

THE BOOK PANEL AS STYLE MANAGER

InDesign's Book feature and the Book panel that manages it were created so that long projects, like books, could be broken up into smaller documents but still be recognized as components of a greater whole. Documents associated with a book can be numbered consecutively from the last page of one document to the first page of the next, be printed or exported in one step rather than individually, and have all their styles synchronized to the settings in a single document, which is known as the synchronization source. It's this last capability that can be co-opted, in a sense, to make the Book panel act as a style manager, whether or not the files in that book are part of one continuous, long document project.

FIGURE 11.11 The Book panel.

FIGURE 11.12 Multiple InDesign documents associated with a book.

FIGURE 11.13 Accessing book-wide numbering options.

Creating a book

To create an InDesign book, choose File > New > Book, and give the book the name of your choice. The book file that's created will have an .indb extension. Instead of a new document, InDesign opens a new panel (FIGURE 11.11) to which the documents in your project will be added.

Adding documents to a book

Documents are added to a book by choosing Add Documents from the Book panel menu, clicking the Add Documents icon at the bottom of the panel ![icon], or by simply dragging InDesign documents into the panel from either the Finder or Windows Explorer (FIGURE 11.12).

Files are listed in the order in which they were added to the book. If multiple documents are added at the same time, they're listed alphabetically. You can change the order of any document in the list by simply dragging it above or below any other document. Since *this* use of the Book panel is to synchronize styles, not paginate the documents, the order of the files doesn't matter.

Disabling auto numbering

After adding your documents, you'll then want to disable the automatic numbering feature that's on by default for a book. Click in the blank area of the panel below the last document in the list. From the panel menu, choose Book Page Numbering Options (FIGURE 11.13). In the resulting dialog, deselect Automatically Update Page & Section Numbers (FIGURE 11.14), and then click OK. With auto numbering disabled, each document will follow its own internal page numbering starting on page 1 unless otherwise specified.

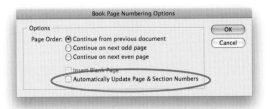

FIGURE 11.14 Turn off automatic numbering when using the Book panel only for style synchronization.

Selecting a style source

By default, the first document added to the Book panel is designated as the style source, meaning the document to which the styles of all other documents will be synchronized. The style source of a book is indicated by the Style Source icon before its name. Any document in the book can be designated as the style source by just clicking the blank square before its name.

If the style source does not contain styles that other documents in the book *do*, those unique styles will not be deleted from the other documents in the book when the styles get synchronized. They are left as is.

Choosing synchronization options

With your style source established, choose Synchronize Options from the panel menu. In the resulting dialog (FIGURE 11.15), select the styles you want to synchronize. Since the goal here is to use these features as a style manager, there are a number of choices in this dialog that do not apply and *should* be turned off. Master Pages, which is off by default, should definitely stay off when your book uses files with different page sizes.

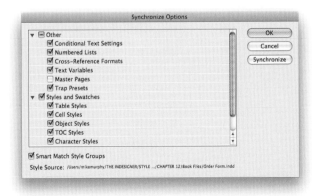

FIGURE 11.15 Synchronization options for documents in a book.

TIP

Remember that a paragraph style with nested or GREP styles will always include at least one character style, table styles can include cell styles, and object and cell styles can contain paragraph styles. So be sure to select *all* involved styles when synchronizing with the Book panel to avoid broken style definitions after the sync is complete.

The options under Styles and Swatches, which are all selected by default, are the options you want to concentrate on. Either leave all selected or deselect unnecessary style types (TOC Styles, for example).

CS4 added an option at the bottom of the Synchronize Options dialog called Smart Match Style Groups that can help you avoid style duplication in documents that use style groups (see "Style Groups" earlier in this chapter). When synchronizing styles across documents where grouping may not have been employed consistently, Smart Match Style Groups will synchronize ungrouped styles to same-named styles that are part of a style group. However, if any duplicate styles already exist in *any* of the documents being synchronized, the Smart Match Style Groups feature is ignored, even if it's selected.

Synchronizing the book

After your options are set, click Synchronize, then click OK. When you make additional changes to your style source, either choose Synchronize Book from the panel menu or click the Synchronize icon at the bottom of the Book panel to resynchronize all documents to the source.

You can reassign the style source to any other document at any time. If you've designated the client's newsletter as the style source but make significant style changes in the brochure, change the style source from the Newsletter.indd file to the Brochure.indd file before synchronizing again to pass the more current file's style along to all other documents in the book.

Until some future version of InDesign ships with a dedicated style management feature, this is as good as it gets.

Index